Farming, Fighting and Family

The literary talent has been handed down from grandfather to mother and then to daughter. This is a delightful account of country life in bygone days that will stir the heart of any Englishman.

Michael Dobbs, author and politician

This gentle, informative memoir draws the reader in by its telling of a superficially simple story which mirrors and throws light on the period in which it is set. It is a portrait of a country way of life which has gone forever, thrown into sharp silhouette by the life-changing backdrop of a world war.

The Second World War was an accumulation of un-numbered individual human stories like these and the book will attract both the general reader and those who collect and read everything about the war.

Michele Brown, author and publisher

Farming, Fighting and Family provides an invaluable personal insight into the crucially important contribution role which the farming community played in saving Britain from starvation in the second world. It will be essential reading for not only those interested in the conflict but also rural society in the countryside.

John Martin, Professor in Agrarian History,
De Montfort University, Leicester

Farming, Fighting and Family

A MEMOIR OF THE SECOND WORLD WAR

MIRANDA McCORMICK

FOREWORD BY MAX HASTINGS

First published 2015

The History Press
The Mill, Brimscombe Port
Stroud, Gloucestershire, GL5 2QG
www.thehistorypress.co.uk

British Library Cataloguing in Publication Data.
A catalogue record for this book is available from the British Library.

ISBN 978 0 7509 6183 7

Typesetting and origination by The History Press
Printed and bound in Malta by Melita Press

For Rupert, the next generation

I have … made as much use as possible of old letters and diaries, because it seemed to me that the contemporary opinions, however crude and ingenuous, of youth in the period under review were at least as important a part of its testament as retrospective reflections heavy with knowledge.

From the foreword to Vera Brittain's *Testament of Youth*

… if any had told me I'd be doing this [VAD nursing], I'd never have believed it. This generation's a terribly young one somehow … doing things because it's just happened to us & it won't be till afterwards that we'll realize what we did.

Extract from Pamela Street's diary entry for 12 October 1940

Contents

Foreword

Miranda McCormick comes from a most interesting family, with which my own had a close connection. Her grandfather Arthur Street was a Wiltshire farmer who became well known as a country writer and broadcaster between the 1930s and 1950s. In 1951, with my own father Macdonald Hastings, he created and for seven years co-edited a delightful magazine entitled *Country Fair*, to which both men also contributed many articles. Street's robust, wise and witty approach to life won him many admirers on such programmes as the BBC's *Any Questions?* and as a boy I myself knew him as a delightful companion. His daughter Pamela kept a diary of her own life, especially during the wartime years, and the correspondence of both her and her future husband's families through the 1939–45 era makes fascinating reading – I have quoted from it in my own book, *All Hell Let Loose*. Now granddaughter Miranda has brought together all the strands in a narrative of the Second World War experience, which paints a vivid picture of how the conflict impacted on an English family. It should find a wide readership among those who want to know what 'ordinary life' was like, in uniform and out of it, in those tumultuous years.

Max Hastings
September 2013

Author's Note

For the benefit of the modern reader, a note of warning needs to be given before the main text begins. In today's multicultural society, some of the descriptions and language used in the family papers from which I have quoted might appear offensive; words such as 'native' or 'darkie' do, occasionally, crop up. However this did not imply any deliberate racism on the part of the writers. It was quite simply the natural way of speaking among people of my parents' generation, for whom encounters with people of different ethnic groups were comparatively rare. Regrettable – and indeed reprehensible – as it may now seem, these children of the British Empire grew up with an innate feeling of superiority over 'Johnny foreigner', which revealed itself in their everyday language and attitude. In the decades after the war, however, such attitudes changed, even for the generation concerned. For example when, in his latter years, my father was asked which individual he had most admired during the course of his lifetime, one might have expected him to reply, 'Winston Churchill'; his answer was in fact, 'Nelson Mandela'. I have not attempted to edit out these politically incorrect expressions, because in my view they add to the authenticity and period flavour of the events described. I trust readers will understand their context.

Similarly I have only corrected the most glaring grammatical or spelling mistakes in quotations from the letters, diaries and journals, as in my view such minor mistakes again reflect the spontaneity with which the quoted material was written, and add to its authenticity.

Introduction:
When the Music Stopped

My parents met at a dance at the White Hart Hotel, Salisbury, on 31 August 1940. At the time my mother, Pamela Street, was working as a VAD nurse at the nearby Emergency Military Hospital, Tower House. My father, David McCormick, had been posted for officer training to Larkhill Camp on Salisbury Plain. To entertain such officer cadets during their off-duty hours, dances were arranged by well-meaning older ladies in the neighbourhood to introduce them to suitable local girls.

My father readily confessed to having cheated at the dance at which he met my mother. It was during a 'Paul Jones', the ballroom dancing equivalent of today's speed dating. Men would assemble in a circle facing inwards, whilst women would assemble in an inner circle facing outwards. The music would begin, with equal numbers of men and women in their respective circles joining hands and rotating in opposite directions. When the music stopped, the man and woman immediately in front of one another would enjoy a quick twosome until the music paused again, the circles would reassemble, and the whole process would repeat itself. My father was so captivated by the tall girl with the shy smile and long, dark, fashionably permed hair in front of him that he jostled his companions more than once to make sure he was opposite her again when the music stopped. The rest, as they say, is history.

★ ★ ★

The outbreak of the Second World War in September 1939 affected the lives of every man, woman and child living in the British Isles. For some – initially at least – the disruption was comparatively slight, but for the majority it would soon become profound. No generation was spared. Children were evacuated from areas deemed to be most at risk, such as London and the southern coastal towns, to be taken in by complete strangers the length and breadth of the country. Men of serviceable age were called up for active duty. Their womenfolk – sweethearts, fiancées, sisters, wives and mothers – had to cope not just with the emotional trauma of the departure of their loved ones, but were required to step into their shoes in the workplace or undertake specific war work in, for example, munitions factories. Younger women enlisted for the women's services or wartime occupations such as nursing or driving military personnel. Older men volunteered for the Local Defence Volunteers (LDV), soon to become known as the Home Guard. Everybody had to cope with the all-pervading fear and uncertainty. This fear abated temporarily during the first months of the war, a period quickly to be dubbed the 'Phoney War', but then in the spring of 1940 the Germans resumed their sweep through Europe and the battle for national survival began in earnest.

Today, though British people face deadly threats of a different kind, it is difficult to imagine what living through such extraordinary, life-changing events must have felt like, and for which group of citizens to feel the most compassion. I have a particular sympathy for my parents' generation – young people who had just completed their formal education and might have expected a comparatively carefree year or two before settling down to a lifetime of adult responsibilities. Instead, duty called, and all personal desires and ambitions had to be set aside. The survival of the British nation was at stake, and they were integral to the war effort.

Although the pages that follow concentrate mainly on my parents' very differing wartime experiences, in a sense the linchpin of this memoir is my maternal grandfather, the farmer/author/broadcaster A.G. Street, who at the beginning of the Second World War was already a household name. An ordinary Wiltshire tenant farmer, he became one of the leading voices of British agriculture during the Second World War, explaining to the nation the importance of farming as the fourth line of defence. Whilst still having his own farm to run, my grandfather Street's contribution to the war effort was enormous. By then a seasoned broadcaster, he was sent all over the country to report on various aspects of agriculture in particular areas. He lectured to the troops stationed on Salisbury Plain. He took part in early live local versions of *The Brains Trust*, the precursor to the long-running radio programme *Any Questions?* on which, after the war, he became a regular panellist. He was the first in his area to sign up as a volunteer in the LDV (Home Guard), and was frequently on night duty. Yet despite all this, the war years did little to lessen his prodigious literary output, much of which was written for reasons of propaganda. No fewer than seven of his titles were published during the war years; in particular *Wessex Wins* (1941), *Hitler's Whistle* (1943) and *From Dusk till Dawn* (1943) provide valuable insights into daily life during the Second World War from the point of view of the countryman.

Yet the real inspiration for this volume was my mother's five-year diary, spanning the years 1937 to 1941, which I discovered whilst going through her effects shortly after her death. It proved riveting reading. My mother was 18 when war broke out, but had already started the diary two years earlier. In this volume, roughly the dimensions of an average paperback, each page is divided into five small sections in which the diarist could make a brief note of events on the same date each consecutive year. Therefore, for example, turning to the page for 3 March, my mother's birthday, one can see how she spent it in 1937, 1938, 1939 and so forth. Her diary reveals how a naïve, somewhat indulged, yet well-meaning teenager gradually became aware of the imminence of hostilities. It goes on to describe the immediate impact the declaration of war had on her family; various types of war work in which she became involved; and last – but by no means least – how her relationship with her future husband began, and her reactions when, having received his commission in the RA, he was posted overseas in the spring of 1941.

Much later in life, at a time when she had already become a prolific novelist, my mother wrote of her entries for 1940 in this five-year diary as follows:

> I had not long left school and was – as I see it now – incredibly young for my age. I took scarcely any interest in politics or international affairs. Economics might have been another language. I was entirely egocentric. Riding and hunting – in which I gave no thought to the fox, one way or another – had now been super-seded by the importance of growing my hair into a page-boy bob, boyfriends and making do on what seemed the princely sum of £24 a year dress allowance. And then a little German with a black paint-brush moustache turned my world upside down. The entries in my diary, naïve, comic, tragic as they are, seem to portray 1940 far better than anything I could write today.

My mother went on to become a life-long diarist. I subsequently unearthed her diary for 1941 and another for the beginning of 1942. There was then a break until the spring of 1945, but this hiatus was more than compensated for by the wealth of other family papers she had kept.

One important source for this volume was her unpublished autobiography, *Time on My Side*, which contained valuable chapters about her wartime experi-ences. Another was a couple of semi-autobiographical novels she had written decades apart. In *Many Waters*, the heroine and her best friend become, respectively, a VAD nurse in a local military hospital and an officer in the ATS. The later novel, *Hindsight*, was about the reunion of an elderly English woman and her wartime American admirer.

Although my mother's literary career only started in earnest in her later years, she had ambitions to become a writer – no doubt heavily influenced and encour-aged by her father's unexpected literary success – from an early age. She first began writing poems whilst still at the Godolphin School, Salisbury, several of which appeared in school magazines. After leaving school she spent much of her time composing poems which were occasionally accepted and published in magazines such as *Everywoman*, *The Field*, *Farmer's Weekly* and later even in *Punch*. Several were composed during the war years, and add another, more lyrical dimension to her descriptions of the period.

Besides my mother's diaries and other writings, by far the most valuable source material for this volume was the hoard of family letters, written during or shortly after the war period, that I discovered my mother had kept. My mother wrote to her parents assiduously during the period of her ATS officer training and from her various postings once she had received her commission; her parents replied equally assiduously, often with exhortations on how to put up with the unaccustomed conditions in which their daughter now found herself living. My mother did not have a 'good' war in terms of derring-do behind enemy lines or suchlike. On the contrary: being of a highly-strung, anxious disposition – though conscientious to a fault – she was temperamentally totally unsuited to war work. She clearly tried her best at a number of wartime occupations, but they finally became too much for her and towards the end of the war she was invalided out of the ATS. This was also partly due to affairs of the heart, as the following pages will reveal.

Especially poignant are the many letters my mother both sent and received, sometimes after long intervals, to and from my father, David McCormick, the unofficial fiancé whom she was later to marry. Whilst reading them, a sudden thought occurred to me: several years earlier my father had bequeathed to me a piece of furniture in which I vaguely remembered seeing some of his own family's wartime material. I went to investigate, and rummaging through the drawers I struck gold in the form of two typed fragments from a memoir he evidently wrote shortly after the war. The first describes the period he spent at Dover Barracks in the spring of 1940, and includes a vivid, grim account of the part he played in clearing the boats returning from Dunkirk of bodies and body parts before they set off across the Channel again to collect more survivors or corpses. The second, longer fragment, describes in detail his time spent in the North African desert preparing for, and taking part in 'Operation Crusader'. I also found a cache of letters written between my father and his parents at various stages of the war. Amongst these was a batch of letters written to my father by his parents during the winter of 1941–42 once 'Operation Crusader' was under way, including several returned unread in their original envelopes many months later. These reveal his parents' – and in particular his mother's – intense anxiety that deepened each day that passed with no news of him.

In the pages that follow I have tried, as far as possible, to allow the voices of my parents, grandparents and other family members and friends to speak through unhindered; in a sense I am the editor rather than author of this volume. However to put the quotations into context, I needed to include some explanatory text of my own. One immediate difficulty I encountered in so doing was how much knowledge of the Second World War I could assume that potential readers already had.

For example, for British-born people of my generation or older, the very name 'Dunkirk' automatically conjures up vivid pictures of the evacuation across the English Channel of the British Expeditionary Force in late May–early June 1940. The reason for 'Operation Dynamo', as it was code-named, having to be launched was in reality an appalling military disaster; however for reasons of propaganda at the time and national pride thereafter, it was hailed as a feat of considerable hero-ism, even giving rise to the phrase 'the Dunkirk spirit'. My generation and older ones hardly need to read yet another account of this episode in British history. Yet speaking to younger people, in particular those born abroad but now living here, made me wonder; some really knew very little about it, and I am writing as much as anything for future generations. 'Dunkirk' apart, I myself had only a hazy knowledge of certain episodes and campaigns of the Second World War. Faced with this dilemma, in the end I decided that my yardstick should be my own ignorance. Therefore whenever I came across any reference to aspects of the Second World War that I did not fully understand, I made it my business to find out about them, and wrote the explanatory text accordingly.

★ ★ ★

One passage from my mother's unpublished autobiography seems a fitting way to end this Introduction:

> The miracle of the Battle of Britain was only truly brought home to the nation after Winston Churchill's speech in the House of Commons. I have often thought that if there was one 'intangible' which helped us to win the Second World War it was the voice of the Prime Minister: 'Never in the field of human conflict was so much owed by so many to so few.'
>
> Young modern historians denigrate him. But they weren't *there*. At that moment. There was something infinitely inspiring, infinitely reassuring about the man at the top during the war years. He may have had his faults – who hasn't – but he was surely the right man at the right time. He had the kind of charisma which spurred you on to greater effort.

Leaving aside the validity or otherwise of my mother's opinion of Churchill, for me the key phrase in the above quotation is 'they weren't *there*', which brings me back to the whole point of this volume. My generation wasn't *there*; neither was my son's generation nor those to follow. This is why it seems imperative to record the first-hand accounts of members of my family who were indeed *there*, during the Second World War, before they are lost forever.

One

Before the War:
The Streets

rthur George Street was, in his own words, 'just a humble tenant farmer' when his daughter, Pamela, was born. Few could have foreseen how her formative years would be affected by her father's unexpected success in occupational pastures new.

Some three years after the end of the First World War, the country was enjoying a period of peace and relative prosperity. This is how, in a later memoir, Pamela described her home town, and her father's status within it:

> The West Country town of Wilton, near Salisbury, was a small peaceful place when I was born on its outskirts in 1921. Nevertheless, it could boast two thriving industries: a carpet factory and a felt mills [sic]; while the surrounding country-side – until the depression – supported a third: thousands of acres of productive rented farmland belonging to the lord of the manor, the Earl of Pembroke at Wilton House.
>
> My father was one such farmer on this estate. Having, to his great regret, been rejected by the army in the First World War, owing to crippled feet, he had taken over Ditchampton Farm on the death of his own father in 1917.

Arthur's father, Henry Street, started his working life as a grocer's apprentice, and by the time of his marriage to his wife Sarah, was running a grocery shop in Wilton. He evidently made a sufficient success of it to enable him to take on the tenancy of Ditchampton Farm – 300 acres close to the town – and to become an equally successful farmer. As Pamela put it: 'The Streets, as it were, had moved up a peg.' Henry Street was a charismatic, somewhat domineering individual, nick-named 'the organiser', and it was perhaps inevitable that as a young man Arthur Street – himself a forceful personality – would one day come to blows with him. The second youngest of six siblings, Arthur was born with his feet pointing in the wrong direction. He spent his early years in irons to correct the condition; his consequent immobility obliged him to yell to attract his family's attention, which in turn went on to influence his adult character.

Pamela went on to describe her street forebears as 'solid, honest and hard-working. All were exponents of self-help, perhaps none more so than my father, who had to overcome physical disability.' Her maternal family, however, were something of a contrast:

> My mother's forebears were very different. They were the Foyles from the Felt Mills. They might have had the same work ethic as the Streets, but they were mercurial, quixotic, good-looking, proud, compassionate, generous and poor. In my youth I was given to understand that Grandfather Foyle – who died in 1918 – had been the Manager of the Mills; but I came to realise he must have been more of a foreman.
>
> Granny Foyle was the daughter of a well-to-do clothier from Trowbridge. She was doted on as a child and had silk stockings specially made for her. Perhaps it wasn't surprising that her father did not think that Francis Foyle … was good enough for her. But she was a fine-looking spirited young woman and married him, nevertheless.
>
> They had seven children, two boys and five girls, and lived in what the family referred to as The Mill House. But I suspect the fact that it was little more than a hovel was the reason why the owners of the Mill allowed my grandmother to go on living there after her husband's death.

In 1911 Arthur Street quarrelled bitterly with his father Henry, and to assert his independence sailed to Canada, where he worked as a farm hand – a period to which he later referred in his first, best-selling, book *Farmer's Glory*, as 'A Canadian Interlude'. The explanation he gave for the row was as follows:

> I can see now that it was inevitable that we should come to serious argument as time went on. I was most certainly an insufferable young pup in many ways, as, I think, are most of us at eighteen or thereabouts. Anyway, some two years after I left school we came to the parting of the ways. My idea was that I had become a sort of errand boy between my father and the foreman, and that this was hardly good enough for a man of my qualifications. My father's idea seemed to be that he was blessed with a half-wit for a son … I said that I was tired of being an errand boy, and wanted a job of my own with some responsibility … My father said … that if I knew of a better job, why not take it? Youth's pride being mortally injured, I said that I damn well would, and was rebuked for swearing in addition to my other crimes.

This was not the whole truth of the matter. Evidence came to light many decades later that one of his other 'crimes' was to have got a maid working in the Street household in the family way. Legal and financial arrangements were made between Henry Street and the girl's father for her confinement and the maintenance till the age of 14 of the resulting child, on condition that the maid's family should have no further contact with the Streets. It was hardly surprising, therefore, that the young Arthur Street needed to be removed from the scene with all possible haste.

In early 1914, having proved that he could indeed stand on his own feet, Arthur returned home. Despite the hard work, he had enjoyed his time in Canada to the extent that he hoped his father might lend him sufficient funds to purchase some land of his own in the 'new' country. Henry Street refused, and Arthur returned to Canada empty-handed. However one beneficial outcome of Arthur's visit home was his meeting with Vera Foyle and their subsequent courtship. Pamela wrote thus about the Foyle family's reaction: 'When my father started taking an interest in the youngest daughter, Vera, the family was both surprised and flattered; for the Streets had become members of a higher social stratum, however much they might once have been in a lower one …'

After Arthur's return to Canada the pair continued to correspond. At the beginning of the First World War Arthur tried to enlist in the Canadian army, but was rejected because of his crippled feet. Consequently he made arrangements to sail home and attempt to enlist in the British army. On 18 October 1914 he wrote to Vera:

> I can't get into the Canadian contingent owing to my feet and I suppose it'll be the same when I get to England. I'm almost afraid to come home. All the other fellows around Wilton will have gone … Up till this I've always been able to hold my own with other fellows in spite of my feet at all outdoor sports and this is getting on my mind … I suppose I ought to be jolly thankful I can do what I can considering they never expected I should be able to walk when I was a baby.

Arthur sailed home a couple of months later. Shortly before his departure he wrote to Vera about the perils of crossing the Atlantic in wartime: 'I'm not worrying a bit about sailing. You see when one is born to be hanged you can't be drowned and the Prodigal Son is sure to turn up alright like a bad penny. I'm sailing on Dec 2 on the *Lusitania* from N. York … I'm a bit excited with coming home.'

On returning home, Arthur's worst fears were realised; once again he was rejected for active service on account of his deformed feet. However, with so many members of Ditchampton Farm's workforce called up and his father in failing health, there was more than enough to keep Arthur busy on the land. Yet he was still in no position to support a wife, and a lengthy engagement ensued until the death of his father in 1917 changed his circumstances; Arthur finally took over the tenancy of Ditchampton Farm and married the long-suffering Vera Foyle.

The young couple prospered; in the first years that followed the Great War, farming experienced something of a boom time. The Corn Production Act of 1917 guaranteed farmers a minimum price for their grain, and returning servicemen and townsfolk flocked to buy or rent farming land. This is how Arthur Street described the period in *Farmer's Glory*:

> As all the world knows, the war ended in November, and it was as if a heavy weight had been lifted from the whole country. The reaction to this was that the whole population went pleasure mad. All classes indulged in a feverish orgy of all those sports and pastimes which had been impossible for four long weary years.
>
> And I was as bad, or as daft, or, possibly more truthfully, as criminally extravagant as any one. I kept two hunters, one for myself and one for my wife; and glorious days we had together with the local pack. I went shooting at least two days a week during the winter. We went to tennis parties nearly every fine afternoon in the summer, and in our turn, entertained up to as many as twenty guests on our own tennis-court, and usually to supper afterwards.

He then went on to describe the difference the advent of the motor car made in enabling farmers to seek pleasures further afield, such as taking seaside holidays, and how he took up golf in 1919:

> and in 1921 I was the proud possessor of a handicap of eight, which statement tells only too plainly the amount of time I must have spent at the game ...
>
> My world went very well then. I was newly married, and my wife was an ideal playmate. The war was over, for ever and ever, and farming had returned to its old splendour. Farmer's Glory was then a glory of great brilliance. How were farmers to know that it was but the last dazzling flicker before the fusing?

Pamela Street's birth in 1921 coincided with the repeal of the Corn Production Act. Ironically, cheap wheat from those self-same Canadian prairies that Arthur Street had been breaking a decade earlier was now beginning to flood the market. By the early 1930s farming's steady decline had turned into a full-blown depression. As a consequence, in the Street household the hunters had to go; shooting, tennis and other parties were things of the past, and Arthur Street was working hard to stave off bankruptcy. His solution was to terminate the tenancy of one of his two farms and to put all his arable fields to pasture, concentrating entirely on dairy farming. Not only did he become a milk producer, but also a retailer. Pamela writes of this period of her childhood:

> The first time I was made dimly aware of the situation was the Christmas of 1928. I was seven years old then and my father gave me a very cheap edition of *Hans Andersen's Fairy Tales*. Wretch that I was, I remember being disappointed with it

because it contained no really good coloured pictures and the print was so small. He had always been generous with presents and I think this one puzzled me, even at an early age.

Then later on, we did not own a car like the parents of the other children I knew in the little town of Wilton … instead, we had a large van with A.G. STREET, OPEN-AIR MILK written on its sides. In order to save us from complete bankruptcy, my father had changed his whole system of farming, and now, besides getting up at four thirty a.m. seven days a week to milk seventy cows in an open-air milking outfit, with only the help of one pupil, he also started a milk round in Salisbury, putting on a white coat and doing the delivering himself straight after the morning's milking.

How my father was able to manage all this I simply do not know, except that he always had the most enormous capacity for hard work. He worked all day and every day non-stop, and on Saturdays he would sit at his desk and work far into the night, totting up figures in the milk-books; he would then stump up to bed for a few hours' sleep, before the Sunday morning round-up of the cows started the week rolling all over again

Financial hardship was not the only serious problem confronting the Street household during this period. When Pamela was 6, Vera Street fell ill with what was eventually diagnosed as a duodenal ulcer, and following two operations she very nearly died. There followed a long period of convalescence, but Pamela felt that her mother never fully recovered. Into the breach at this point stepped Pamela's cousin Vivi. Violet Boon was the daughter of one of Vera's impoverished sisters, and had joined the Street household shortly after Pamela's birth to help out with the new baby. Having already taken on considerably more domestic responsibilities, she now became indispensable, assuming the role of cook, housekeeper and nurse. During the critical phase of her mother's illness Pamela was sent to stay with her grandmother and aunts; being unaware of the severity of her mother's condition, she greatly enjoyed this period.

Arthur Street struggled on stoically despite all these vicissitudes until one day in November 1929 something occurred which was to change the course of his life, and his family's fortunes, forever. Whilst recovering indoors from a bad bout of flu, an already frustrated Arthur read an article about farming in the *Daily Mail*, the inaccuracies of which caused his temper to reach boiling point. Vera Street, almost equally exasperated by a husband who had been behaving like a caged lion, threw down the gauntlet, suggesting that if the article were that bad, why didn't Arthur try to write something better? Pamela later described how he rose to the challenge:

She could hardly have made a more sensible suggestion. Using the stub of a pencil and one of my old exercise books, he scribbled out a thousand word counterblast.

He then gave it to my mother to read who told him that if he took out all the 'damns' and 'blasts' and 'bloodies' she thought it wasn't too bad. Quietly, he acted on her advice …

I suppose my father must have got it typed somewhere, because in those days a typewriter was an unheard-of thing in our house. It was then posted off to the *Daily Mail*. By return came an acceptance and the offer of three guineas. I think he thought that to earn that amount of money in so short a time, without any outlay of capital or physical energy, was not only a miracle but somehow immoral.

The article in question was entitled 'Handicaps on Agriculture' and began in Arthur Street's typically forthright style:

Most of those who are writing about the present depression are suggesting that somebody or other should do something for agriculture, never that agriculture should do something for itself. A generation of farmers must arise who can get a living as farmers in spite of any Government, rather than with the aid of any Government's intervention …

Pamela went on to explain what happened next:

So, having tasted blood, having, as it were, tapped another source of income, he 'played his luck'. He was no gambler but he certainly believed in luck. He went on. He bombarded Fleet Street with articles, as well as local papers. He received many a rejection slip but, gradually, his pieces on farming and the countryside saw print, until the editor of the *Salisbury Times* asked him to write a weekly column, for which he paid my father seven shillings and sixpence, rising to seventeen and six as time went by.

Arthur's literary luck was to continue. One day a piece of his in the *Salisbury Times* on ploughing caught the eye of a well-known local novelist, Edith Olivier, whom Arthur would later refer to as his 'literary fairy godmother'. The daughter of the former Canon Olivier of Wilton, Edith was evidently something of a force to be reckoned with. Amongst the local residents she had acquired a somewhat 'fast' reputation. Between the wars she became a familiar figure in London literary and artistic circles, befriending such 'bright young things' as Rex Whistler, Stephen Tennant and Cecil Beaton. When not in London she constantly entertained such friends at her home, the Daye House, in the grounds of Wilton Park. Arthur Street described her as 'a rather volatile lady who seemed to dance as she walked'. One day Edith 'danced' unexpectedly into the Street household, waving a cutting of Arthur's article in her hand: 'This is charming, Arthur. You must write a book. I insist.' Completely taken aback, Arthur asked with what subject any book of his might deal. He described the way she answered thus: 'Edith waved her cigarette airily – even when she is sitting down her hands talk expressivley in the language of Editian swoops … "With the one thing you know something about, of course, farming".'

The seed was sown: Arthur began writing *Farmer's Glory* that very same evening. When, some weeks later, Edith telephoned for a progress report, Arthur had already written the first three or four chapters. Edith asked if she could borrow them for the weekend as she would be having a publisher friend to stay, to whom she wanted to show Arthur's work. Somewhat reluctantly – Arthur being ashamed of the messy state of his typescript – he took round what he had written so far and beat a hasty retreat. The result was that later that weekend Richard de la Mare of Faber & Faber called on Arthur to say how much he had enjoyed the early chapters, and made an offer to publish *Farmer's Glory* once it was completed. Though flattered and tempted, Arthur refused to sign a contract then and there, on the basis that he was not prepared to sell something he did not yet have, and would prefer to wait until he could hand in the finished product. But the offer was all the encouragement he needed to carry the project to fruition, and *Farmer's Glory* was duly published by Faber & Faber in January 1932. Soon afterwards a complimentary review appeared in *The Times Literary Supplement*, quickly to be followed by any number of favourable reviews in both the local and national press; A.G. Street had become something of a celebrity. He would not allow success to go to his head, however, and carried on with his daily milking and milk rounds, frequently being brought down to earth by the good-natured ribbing of his local farming friends.

The publication of *Farmer's Glory* made little impression at the time on his daughter Pamela. She was now attending the Godolphin School in Salisbury to which, despite financial hardship, her parents had somehow managed to send her. The significance of her father's success only dawned on Pamela when a school friend made a comment about it on the bus to school one morning. She later recalled: 'I was surprised to hear our doctor's eldest daughter saying my father would now be famous. The thought had never occurred to me, but I could see that interesting developments might possibly take place.'

Following the publication of *Farmer's Glory*, Arthur Street found himself deluged with requests for articles from editors of newspapers and magazines both local and national. Shortly afterwards he was asked to start writing a weekly column in a new farming magazine, *Farmer's Weekly*, a task he kept up for the remainder of his life. His publishers signed him up for a couple more books, and in March 1932 he received a letter from the BBC proposing that he deliver a series of talks on country matters. In a later autobiographical book, *Wessex Wins*, he describes with modesty and humour how, with the aid of his BBC producers, he mastered the art of broadcasting, and thus embarked on the third strand of his threefold career as farmer/author/broadcaster.

It was perhaps inevitable that before long Arthur found himself wooed by politicians of all hues. He was invited to speak at the Bonar Law College, Ashridge, at the time very definitely a Tory – though, as he found, generously open-minded – debating forum. He described this as an intimidating experience; that his efforts were well received, however, can be judged by the many times he was asked to return. Nonetheless, some of his views on agriculture were unpopular even amongst his fellow farmers – in particular his reasoning that in times of peace and competition from cheap corn imported from overseas, British farmers should grass down their arable fields and go in for livestock farming. Thus in a time of war there would be a wealth of fertile soil for when the same pastures required ploughing up again and Britain could become self-sufficient in corn production – a major contribution to any war effort. That Arthur Street was correct became more and more obvious as the international situation deteriorated towards the end of the 1930s.

In the summer of 1937 Arthur was invited by Douglas Marshall, the then Canadian Minister for Agriculture, to address a series of farmers' meetings at agricultural colleges in the Canadian and American Midwest, a part of the world in which agriculture was experiencing a financial crisis following several successive years of drought. A shocked Arthur returned home to record his impressions of the 'dustbowl'. His views were met with both praise and criticism, but as always he put the interests of the land ahead of any political vested interests.

Arthur Street was now a seasoned and respected broadcaster, and needing a London base, he was encouraged by his publishers to join the Savage Club, subsequently befriending fellow members in all branches of the arts. In the early days of television it was only a question of time until the BBC invited him to take to the screen. On his first attempt, in the summer of 1938 – a ten-minute performance in a series entitled *Speaking Personally* – a fierce thunderstorm was raging; lightning struck the building, causing one of the studio cameras, inches from Arthur's face, to explode. He won many plaudits for the unflappable way in which he continued with his talk, so that despite the lack of picture, the sound carried on uninterrupted. Arthur went on to make several more television appearances before the war put a temporary halt to that form of broadcasting.

★ ★ ★

What was happening back at Ditchampton Farm whilst the 'Guvner' was immersed in his new occupations? One consequence was a marked improvement in the Street family finances, to the extent that Arthur Street was soon able to employ a foreman, thus liberating himself from much of the day-to-day running of the farm. He also arranged for Peggy Boon, Vivi's sister, to help with typing his manuscripts and dealing with the farm paperwork and wages. In 1935 he was able to give up milk retailing altogether. Farming pupils – another source of income in the lean years – were no longer needed. Vera Street, with the help of the indispensable Vivi, frequently found herself playing hostess when Arthur's new friends in the literary and broadcasting worlds came to visit. Despite her comparatively modest background, Vera Street was a keen homemaker with innate good taste, and now that the financial situation had improved she was allowed – and indeed encouraged – to indulge her passion for antique collecting.

In her early teens Pamela was diagnosed with progressively poor eyesight and advised to spend time away from school in order to rest her eyes. To keep her occupied, her parents gave her a pony called Toby, with whom she instantly became besotted, spending all her daytime hours either riding or grooming him, only returning reluctantly to the farmhouse when summoned at mealtimes or bedtime. As her riding skills swiftly progressed, it became clear to Arthur Street that she would need to spread her wings beyond the boundaries of the home field, so he bought himself a horse in order to accompany Pamela further afield. Father and daughter grew particularly close as a result of their joint riding activities. By 1937 the Streets had acquired no less than five horses, and had taken on a groom-gardener. Before long, Arthur took up hunting once again, with his now proficient daughter in tow. Pamela later wrote of the magical early mornings when the pair would depart en route to a local meet:

> Early in the season we would sometimes set off in pitch darkness, clattering down the silent streets of Wilton. We went single file, although at that time and in those days we never met any traffic. I can see the sparks from Peter's [her father's hunter] hooves now as they struck the tarmac in front of me. Not a soul was about; just occasionally there was a light in an upstairs window, where, perhaps, someone was sitting up with a sick child or an elderly parent …

One aspect of hunting that both father and daughter appreciated was that it was by no means the province of the privileged few, as Pamela emphasised when writing about her hunting experiences many decades later:

> At the appointed place, sometimes high above the little village of Broad Chalke, there we would meet the Master, Colonel Llewellyn Palmer, the handsome amateur whipper-in, a sporting parson, the Reverend Mr. Keating Clay, George Spiller, the dealer who sold us Toby, with his granddaughter Mavis, on a leading rein, a girl from the Godolphin, Sybil Edmunds, who was to become my best and lifelong friend, the devastatingly glamorous young woman who ran the Pony Club, the son of our local blacksmith and so forth …

It is somewhat ironic that many decades later Pamela became virtually 'anti' bloodsports, and was clearly ashamed of her youthful enthusiasm for hunting – rather a harsh judgement on herself considering the milieu in which she grew up, when hunting was an unquestioned normal country pursuit.

★ ★ ★

Pamela started keeping a five-year diary in January 1937, when she was nearly 16. Reading the entries for 1937 and 1938, it seems that her day-to-day concerns were those of a typical teenage girl of any era. Although riding comes across as ·something of an obsession in the early part of the diary, it also records details of her school days, visits to and from family and friends, anxieties about teenage acne, and a burgeoning interest in the opposite sex. They contain virtually no evidence of teenage rebellion; hardly surprising, perhaps, since there was precious little against which to rebel. For example, no eyebrows appear to have been raised when she spent whole or large parts of days in bed, recovering from a previous evening's function. On the other hand Pamela held her parents in deep and automatic respect, particularly her father. Depending on circumstances beyond his control, such as poor harvesting weather, Arthur Street was liable to descend into morose, angry moods, causing the rest of the household to tiptoe round the home, speaking in hushed whispers. If her father laid down the law, Pamela would obey unquestioningly. Despite this, there is no doubt that theirs was an exceptionally affectionate and loving family. Writing many years later about her father's lecture tour of the American and Canadian Midwest in 1937, when the whole family were driven down to Southampton docks by the groom-gardener to wave Arthur goodbye and then again to greet him on his return, Pamela wrote: 'I suppose we must always have been an emotional and rather tender-hearted family.'

To demonstrate the point, Pamela goes on to relate how on his return, Arthur had been so keen to see his family and get back home that he pulled strings to be allowed to leave the boat on the evening of its arrival rather than the following morning as the rest of the passengers were obliged to do:

> Although it was the summer of 1937, there were obviously some far-sighted people acutely aware of the political situation, because Southampton was having a mock black-out that evening. Hibberd, a conscientious but rather nervous man, had the greatest difficulty in finding the correct dock. In the all-pervading gloom, I remember my father, all alone, bolting down the gangplank, like a large hunter desperately anxious to get out of its horse-box.

The year 1937 was Pamela's last at the Godolphin School, during which she worked – with increasing apprehension – towards her School Certificate. It was not until 30 August, whilst on holiday with a cousin in Jersey, that she received the longed-for news, recorded thus in her diary: 'I have PASSED School Cert!!!! Never been so surprised!' It seems that the Street parents held out hopes for Pamela to gain a place at Oxford, so when she returned to the Godolphin for the autumn term, the school started taking the necessary measures. Pamela clearly had somewhat ambivalent feelings about this decision, as she reveals: 'Mumsie and Daddy have horrible idea of my taking some exam for Oxford so am in the most frightful muddle about forms and everything.' One of the prerequisites of Oxford entrance was a knowledge of Greek, which Pamela had never previously studied. It seems she was not a natural pupil: 'Have to do Greek for responsions! So had first lesson – absolute double dutch.' It quickly became apparent to the school that Pamela's heart was not in the academic life; on 18 October she writes: 'Apparently aren't OK enough to go on with Oxford unless really want to …' Pamela's real ambition was to go on to art school, eventually in London. To their credit, instead of showing their disappointment at her choice, Arthur and Vera Street supported Pamela in her application to the Salisbury College of Art, which she began attending for two days a week in January 1938.

Pamela's first entry for 1938 marks the beginning of this new phase of her life: 'Started own dress allowance!! £26. So as have left school feel very grown up.' Pamela's parents had evidently decided that since their daughter was not destined for an academic career and would be unlikely to be able to support herself, efforts must be made to increase her social life in the hopes that she would eventually make a suitable match. In October 1937 she started ballroom dancing lessons at Miss Pinniger's school in Salisbury, an institution which taught several generations of young Wiltshire men and women. Pamela's diary records the various dances she attended during the 1937–38 winter season. On 7 January 1938 she wrote: 'Am now allowed to wear a little (and only a little) lipstick.' However stamina was never one of Pamela's strong suits, and as much as she enjoyed social events such as pony club or hunt balls, these took their toll. There are several references in the diaries to Pamela spending whole days in bed recovering from a previous night out. On 13 January, following two evening engagements in a row, she wrote: 'I really don't think that the gay life is suited for me. Feel awful.' This lack of stamina was later to prove a considerable handicap when it came to war work.

Two other recurrent health problems during this period were teenage acne and eczema in her ears, which caused them to run, and which sometimes prevented her from taking part in outdoor activities. One rather self-pitying entry for 2 April 1938, reads: 'My ears are just frightful … Oh drat everything … I am a poor fish what with eczema in the ears, one of them a bit deaf, eyes, one worse than the other, spots etc etc oh my hat …' Just what a sympathetic and indulgent father Arthur was can be judged from the birthday present he devised for Pamela's 17th birthday on 3 March 1938. Unable to be with her at Ditchampton Farm owing to a broadcasting engagement, he instead wrote her a letter to be opened on the day, enclosing the following spoof legal document:

THIS is an AGREEMENT made on the third day of March in the year 1938, between ARTHUR GEORGE STREET of Ditchampton Farm, Wilton, in the county of Wilts, hereinafter called the PARENT, and PAMELA STREET of the same address, hereinafter called the DAUGHTER, which shall be implemented by the said PARENT, when and how the said DAUGHTER shall direct, as follows:-

THE PARENT AGREES:-

1. On or before March 3, 1938, to instruct William Vincent Moore of the Garage, Ditchampton, Wilton, to begin on March 3, 1938, teaching the said DAUGHTER adequately to drive a motor car, to provide the necessary L placards, and to continue such teaching until the said DAUGHTER shall have passed her driving test to the satisfaction of the authorities responsible, and to pay the said William Vincent Moore the customary fees for such services and tuition, the first lesson to take place on March 3, 1938.

2. To pay for a complete permanent wave of the said DAUGHTER'S head of hair, as when and how and where the said DAUGHTER shall prefer.

3. As and when and where the said DAUGHTER shall desire (always providing that the said DAUGHTER first obtains permission from the person familiarly known as the ARSENAL* and that such permission is advised by Dr Watson of Salisbury, or some other local medical man in good repute amongst his fellows in the profession) to pay for a consultation with a London skin specialist of high standing and also for his advised treatment, such advice and treatment being designed to remove from the countenance and ears of the said DAUGHTER the spots and blemishes which for some time have been blighting the said DAUGHTER'S young life ...

It is hereby suggested that in return for the PARENT'S compliance with the terms of this agreement the said DAUGHTER shall, to be best of her power and goodwill, refrain from casting a gloom over the household of Ditchampton Farm, particularly with regard to the effect of such gloom upon the aforesaid person familiarly know as the ARSENAL.

GIVEN under my hand and seal this third day of March in the year of our Lord, 1938

SIGNED, Arthur George Street

That this present was received with suitable gratitude is clear from Pamela's consequent rapturous diary entry: 'Pop (Mummy too) gave me my birthday present!!!! So marvellous. 1) Driving lessons. 2) Perm!! 3) Skin-man. Oh *lovely*!!! Pop Mummy are quite [*sic*].'

Besides being the possessors of five horses, the Streets were by now a 'two-car' family; Arthur drove a large Humber Snipe, and a Baby Austin had earlier been

---

*   Arthur and Pamela's nickname for Vera Street.

purchased in which Pamela could learn to drive. Pamela's diary records that she passed her driving test on 25 April 1938. She later wrote of her father's reaction:

> My father was always very keen that I should do things in the same way and at the same time as other girls with whom I had been brought up, but I understand that the first day I took AXY (as we called the car) out by myself after passing my test, aged him considerably.

Pamela's diary entries for the remainder of 1938 read in much the same way as those for 1937, but now include references to art school, at which she once professed she made scant effort. This remark was probably made more out of modesty than truth. One successful result of Pamela's art school training was the family Christmas card that she subsequently composed that year, a copy of which survives to this day. Pamela's diary records much praise for her card from such disparate friends of her parents as Lady Radnor, the cartoonist and her father's fellow Savage Club member Leonard Raven-Hill, and Mrs Holtby, mother of Winifred Holtby, the author of *South Riding*.

At the end of 1938 and beginning of 1939 Pamela was due to attend a number of dances, and a constant preoccupation was that of finding suitable partners to accompany her. Two young men had by now taken her fancy: one, Ian Benson, was the handsome young whipper-in of the Wilton Hunt; the other, Robin Sayer, was a pupil on a neighbouring farm. It appears that although both were on friendly terms with the Street family (Ian sometimes borrowed Street horses for hunting or riding at local point-to-points) and frequently visited Ditchampton Farm, Pamela's feelings remained unreciprocated. On 7 December 1938 she writes: 'Awful down in the dumps. Lost Ian and Robin and nobody to partner for all the forthcoming dances …' On one occasion her parents' solution was to import a partner for Pamela from the agricultural college at Cirencester. The result was evidently a success; Pamela's entry after the event records: '<u>Oh marvellous time</u>. Frank was awfully nice. Robin danced twice. All OK … And best of all Ian and I got on awfully well although I kept cutting his dances by mistake etc but he was really very sweet about it and everything is just lovely.'

By now Pamela had begun to follow her father's broadcasting career with genuine interest. On Sunday 2 October 1938 she writes: 'Daddy's Harvest Home Broadcast last night was huge.' Then on 19 December she writes: 'Caught 2.30 to London to meet Pop and went to Alexandra Palace for television to watch Pop. Marvellous.' The following day she continues: 'Met Freddie Grisewood, R. Arkell, Mr. Middleton, S.A.B. Mair all last night.'

As the 1930s progressed, Arthur Street would have been as aware as any of his contemporaries – indeed probably more than most – of the increasingly serious international situation, but he evidently shielded his daughter from his concerns. Pamela later wrote of this period:

By that time I was far more preoccupied with riding and hunting than anything else. Wars took place in other countries, the kind we learned about for School Certificate. And anyway, had not my parents said that the 1914–18 war was a war to end all wars … As far as I was concerned, my own country was the best place on earth and I was thoroughly enjoying the 1930s.

By the spring of 1938, it was beginning to dawn on even the sheltered Pamela that this so far idyllic period of her life might not last. The first reference in her diary to the possibility of war comes on 15 March 1938: 'I'm afraid this diary is frightfully narrow because there's an awful lot happening abroad etc. Hitler has marched into Austria and got it!'

Contingency planning for war was by now gaining momentum. On 24 April 1938, Pamela's diary records that the Air Ministry had requisitioned a poultry farm owned by one of her uncles, a flat acreage of land on Salisbury Plain suitable for an air-craft landing strip and outbuildings. Further entries for the year showed Pamela's increasing awareness of the threat from abroad. On 16 September she wrote: 'Being me forgot to put down there is a frightful international situation. Chamberlain to Hitler etc etc. I don't know much.' Then on 21 September she wrote: 'Still ter-rible Europe pot-boil.' And on 26 September: 'The war situation is getting worse and worse …' The following day her entry becomes more personal: 'Saw Ian. He was terribly sweet … and I said if there was a war he was to come and wish us goodbye!!!! … War situation is still awful.' On 28 September Pamela reports: 'War situation still bad and everyone digging trenches for air raids.'

During 1938 Pamela made several references to attending a first aid training course, presumably by way of preparation for future hostilities. After taking the final exam on 2 December, she was clearly worried about the outcome: 'First Aid exam by Dr. Taylor Young. Lot did quite wrong forearm bandage just like me.' Despite such doubts, two days later she records that she passed successfully.

One incident during the hunting season of 1938 made an enduring impression on Pamela:

It was just after Mr. Chamberlain had returned from Munich with his *Peace with Honour* slogan. It was a golden morning, the kind one sometimes gets in early autumn, when all the colours of the countryside seem so much more vivid than at any other time of the year. We were on top of the downs waiting at a cover. The sunlight was just beginning to disperse the mist in the valley below, so that we watched it come into view, rather as if someone was turning a spotlight on a stage.

A rather happy-go-lucky gentleman said to my father, 'Don't you think it's mornings such as this that ought to make us feel grateful to Mr. Chamberlain?'

I fear my father's reply was more or less unprintable. So far as he was con-cerned, we may have got peace, but there was no honour attached to it.

Two

Wilton at War
(1939)

The year 1939 started for the Street household in much the same manner as the previous one, with the usual riding activities and local dances. Despite the possibility of military conflict which, as far as Arthur Street was concerned, Chamberlain's visit to Munich had done little to dispel, plans were soon under way for a radical makeover of Ditchampton Farmhouse. This took place later that summer, during which time Vera and Pamela Street were packed off to the seaside to be out of the way. Pamela later wrote about the reasons for the alterations:

Although both the farm and house were rented, my father decided it was worth having quite extensive alterations done. He wanted a study tucked away somewhere, instead of his present one at the front of the house, where he said he was in full view of anyone arriving at the front door and therefore much too easily 'got at', as he put it. He also wanted the staircase moved, as it annoyed him that it was the first thing one saw on entering the hall and was far from beautiful; and my mother and father wanted a larger drawing-room where they could entertain and where I, too, might have small parties if they put down a suitable floor for dancing.

The extra space thus obtained was very soon to prove invaluable, though hardly in the way the occupants of Ditchampton Farm had originally intended.

At various stages in Pamela's diaries she recorded the books she was currently reading, amongst which were *Tess of the d'Urbervilles*, *Gone with the Wind*, *Testament of Youth* and *South Riding*. The last two deserve a particular mention in terms of the intellectual development of the young Pamela. She started reading Vera Brittain's *Testament of Youth* in 1937, shortly after she began keeping a diary, and a rather self-conscious entry in October that year reads: 'Am reading *Testament of Youth*. My diary isn't anything like a diary should be apparently.'

Vera Brittain's great friend, Winifred Holtby, wrote *South Riding* just before her untimely death (indeed it is mooted that Vera Brittain may have completed the final sections for her posthumously). Mrs Holtby, Winifred's mother – herself from Yorkshire farming stock – was an admirer of Arthur Street's work and had managed to befriend him. When the latter was due to speak at a luncheon club in Yorkshire in February 1939, she offered the entire Street family hospitality at her home in Harrogate for a few days afterwards. Pamela's feelings about this experience were decidedly mixed:

> It was just after Winifred Holtby died, and Mrs. Holtby laid great emphasis on the fact that I was to occupy her daughter's one-time bedroom. Being a somewhat imaginative young girl, I did not care for the idea at all. I was more than a little afraid of Mrs. Holtby, who was a very imposing old lady and reminded me of my Grandmother Street. After dinner on the first night of our visit, she wound up some long story she was telling us by suddenly directing her gaze towards the corner where I was sitting, stifling a yawn and saying, 'And now, my dear, you *may* go to bed.' I obeyed immediately, although secretly hoped to have been ignored until we could all go upstairs together.

By now Pamela's artistic aspirations had been matched or even superseded by a determination to follow in her father's footsteps as a writer. Throughout the year her diary is punctuated by references to poems or articles being posted off to various publications and almost invariably being returned with the customary rejection slip. Occasionally, however, Pamela succeeded. Her first literary effort to see print was a humorous poem composed earlier that year, 'Wessex Wins', a title Arthur Street liked so much that he subsequently borrowed it for a forthcoming collection of essays and broadcasts published in 1941. In a talk to a local historical society many years later, Pamela remarked that it was 'rather a cruel poem'; what she meant – as her diary reveals – is that the poem was based on Robin Sayer, the pupil on a neighbouring farm whose affections Pamela had tried in vain to win, and this was her way of hitting back. Cruel or otherwise, the poem shows Pamela's natural talent for rhyme and rhythm, together with a somewhat precocious aware-ness of social nuances. It was published in a magazine called *Everywoman* later that year, accompanied by her own cartoon illustrations:

Wessex Wins

The parents of Claude Shillito in justified alarm,
Sent their wanton son from Chelsea down to work upon a farm,
Hoping fallow field and fences,
Might restore him to his senses,
Whilst a little wholesome pig-sty wouldn't do him any harm.

So in condescending manner this too precious high-brow boy
Descended on South Wiltshire quite complete in corduroy,
Thought old Giles a priceless fellow
With a rather raucous bellow,
And his farm of ten score acres an amusing sort of toy.

Then the anxious local mothers begged him fervently to call,
Would he partner dear Belinda at the Wire and Poultry Ball?
At the village entertainment
Would he don a shepherd's raiment?
And Claude said, most obligingly, he'd love to do it all.

But although they tried their level best this gigolo to spoil,
Claude began to take an interest in his unaccustomed toil,
Found the finest thing to rake on
Was his bread and cheese and bacon,
Which he ate as only those can eat who work upon the soil.

So he settled in Mudhampton, and the life of Cheyne Walk
Seemed to fade into the background as he learnt the native talk,
Whilst the mysteries of sowing
And the art of turnip-hoeing,
Made the country rather grow on him, as charlock grows on chalk.

And when Ma and Pa, relenting, went to visit him one day,
They both returned to Chelsea filled with horrified dismay,
For on seeing how he'd stuck it
They informed him he might chuck it,
Claude said simply but quite firmly that he'd much prefer to stay.

Pamela's financial reward for this effort arrived on 28 July, as she records: 'My cheque came from Everywoman's, and they've paid me five whole and untarnished guineas!!!' But elsewhere in her diary she writes of her frustration at her lack of progress: 'At present I am just drifting. I do wish I could get at something definite, like Pop's new book … I'm never going to earn any money.'

There are one or two references early in the year to Pamela's plans to 'go away', by which she meant to attend an art school in London, and how to achieve this without upsetting her parents, or more particularly her mother; it seems that Arthur Street was more accommodating towards his daughter's wishes because on 1 August she records: 'Caught 9.30 to London to meet Pop. Looked round the Chelsea Art School which we liked and the London Central …'

All too soon, however, any thoughts of a serious artistic or writing career would become irrelevant.

In an age of constantly updated news bulletins beamed to us via satellite from every corner of the globe, it is easy to forget how comparatively difficult accurate news would have been to come by in 1939. In those days the voice of authority was the British Home Service (the precursor to today's Radio 4), and it was commonplace to find whole families huddled round the wireless to listen to the nine o'clock evening news which, in any case, was censored. Reports of the alarming unfolding events in Europe could not have been easy for an average 18-year-old to grasp. Despite this, Pamela's diary makes it clear that she was trying to keep herself well informed.

On 15 and 16 March 1939, the Nazis – having already annexed unopposed, in May of the previous year, the Sudetenland part of Czechoslovakia, and emboldened by the appeasement policy of other Western European nations at the Munich Conference the following September – occupied the rest of Czechoslovakia. During this period Pamela's diary records: '*March 6th* … the world is in an awful mess and I am very ignorant of the whole situation … *March 18th* … Another European bust-up … *March 19th* … Hitler gone back on Munich.' By now the threat of war on English soil was becoming very real, and further measures were being taken to protect the civilian population. On 6 April Pamela states: 'We had our gas masks fitted … Oh dear no end to Hitler's doings. Awful mess abroad.'

Despite the current uncertainties, it appears that life in the Street household continued as normally as possible, and that there were a number of bright interludes. Arthur Street was more in demand than ever as a broadcaster, and Pamela's diary records that on 7 May he took her mother and her to a Ladies' Night at the Savage Club, which Pamela much appreciated: 'Never enjoyed myself more – it was marvellous. Table with Mr Purvis and Mr Hogan etc etc etc. Lovely show. Enjoyed Hugh E. Wright and Billie Bennet & the Western Brothers. Dorothy Sayers in the Chair & everything topping …'

Pamela's diary goes on to mention a Polo Club Ball, flag-selling outside Barclays Bank when one of her boyfriends sought her out and gave her a whole shilling (which she considered very generous), and then on 17 June a darts match at the Black Horse Inn at Teffont, where Arthur Street was commentating for a live broadcast. Work was now well under way on the renovations at Ditchampton Farm, during which she and her mother were dispatched to the seaside, where they stayed at various lodgings or small hotels near Studland Bay for much of the summer. At one point that July, Pamela records: 'Mummy and I both agree it's been one of the most lovely holidays we've ever spent – went from start to finish without a hitch.'

However, on their return mother and daughter found that Ditchampton farmhouse was still far from habitable, and for several weeks they lodged at the Black Horse Inn in nearby Teffont. But eventually, with all members of the family exercising considerable elbow grease, the farmhouse was ready to be lived in once again, and plans were made to make use of the newly extended drawing room. Much in vogue at the time were 'sherry parties' for young people, and on 18 August Pamela states: 'Wrote out 40 girls 26 boys invitations to Sherry Party which will be on the 16th Sept, lovely I hope …'

Sadly for Pamela, events abroad soon conspired to prevent the eagerly awaited party from taking place. On 23 August the Germans signed a non-aggression pact with the Soviets (with secret provisions for the division of Eastern Europe, including the joint occupation of Poland); on 25 August Britain – acknowledging the futility of its former appeasement policy – signed a pact of alliance with Poland. War now seemed almost inevitable. After a few days' delay during which time Hitler tried, unsuccessfully, to secure the neutrality of England and France, on 1 September the Nazis advanced into Poland. The British government immediately declared the mobilisation of the British Armed Forces, and put in train the mass evacuation of children from London and the southern coastal ports. On 2 September Britain and France issued a joint ultimatum to Germany to withdraw from Polish territory, which would expire at 11 a.m. the following morning; having received no response within the time limit, at 11.15 a.m. on 3 September Prime Minister Neville Chamberlain made the formal announcement that Britain was now at war. Pamela records this period as follows:

August 23rd The international situation has got a lot worse.

August 24th Terrible situation – war peril imminent.

August 28th The first cubbing meet. Fifield Bavant. Lovely and misty. Daddy and I got up and went in the car. Ian was whipping in as usual and Tim [the Wilton Huntsman] said if there was a war he'd hunt on a bicycle.

August 29th The crisis continues … it seems very unreal somehow.

September 1st The war seems to have started. Germany has invaded Poland … Daddy and I fetched the children [evacuees] from the bus from Portsmouth. It was just terrible. Why, why, why.

September 2nd We have three little girls – all 7. Rosemary Weston, Marian Helyer, Joan King. They are awfully sweet and very good considering the terrible time they must have had. We haven't actually declared war and this waiting is just terrible.

September 3rd War, nothing else except that there's war. It's just too terrible to think about and everything suddenly seems nothing at all – just a frightful blank as though you might wake up any minute and find it wasn't … Mrs Helyer [mother of one of the 7-year-old girls] and a baby have come.

September 4th Sent off all the cancellations to my party ... Went to a gas lecture by Mr. Ayres.

September 5th troops are all over Wilton and the officers want to billet here ... It just seems unbelievable that we are at war ...

Owing to its proximity to the military bases on Salisbury Plain, the little town of Wilton did indeed suddenly find itself catering for more than its fair share of military personnel. In the summer of 1940, Wilton House became the head-quarters of Southern Command, while Wilton's main hotel/public house, the Pembroke Arms, was requisitioned as an Officers' Mess. Pamela later wrote about how the news of war was received at Ditchampton Farm, and what the immediate consequences were:

On 3rd September, 1939, my mother, father, Vivi and I sat in the drawing-room at Ditchampton Farm and listened in silence as Mr. Chamberlain's voice came over the air, telling us we were at war with Germany. In keeping with countless other families all over Britain, there was a sudden and dramatic change in our way of life.

Charlie Noble, our foreman, being a reservist, disappeared virtually over-night; our farmhouse became filled with evacuees from Portsmouth; my father's income looked liked immediately being reduced to half or even a quarter of its usual amount, as it seemed that most of his broadcasting work would cease. For this reason, by mutual agreement, his secretary [Vivi's sister Peggy] left to take a job elsewhere, and I became a glorified untrained land-girl cum secretary in her place ...

Despite these consequences, Arthur's writings during the period testify to his sense of relief and regained pride that Britain was finally fulfilling its international obliga-tions and would no longer be appeasing the Nazis. His views were clearly shared by many other Wiltshire farming folk, as illustrated by the following remark made to him by an elderly farm labourer, whom Arthur met a few days later 'toddling down the road with his gas mask slung on his shoulders': 'I niver thought to come to thease caper, maister,' he said. 'But 'tis better so. We cain't goo on like we bin gwaine on the last year or two. Wold 'Itler's comb maun be cut.'

From Pamela's point of view, the evacuees clearly presented the first prob-lem. Her new bedroom, which she was now obliged to relinquish, had just been repainted in colours of her own choosing for the following reasons:

As I had been passing through a rather melancholy stage owing to unrequited love, I had chosen mauve walls and grey paintwork, and the whole effect was slightly macabre, but it suited my frame of mind.

But at the beginning of September 1939 I had to stop being the tragedy queen and give over my boudoir to three little girls from Portsmouth until another bedroom could be made ready for them. They were enchanting children, but they had never seen running water in a bedroom before. Quick as a flash, the leader of the gang filled up the basin and splashed gigantic wet murals all over one wall. The next thing we knew was that the mother of one of them arrived at the back door carrying a baby. We were already full up, but my mother and Vivi had not the heart to send her elsewhere, so she lived with us for quite a long time and was very useful helping to look after the other children.

In the weeks that followed, the Street household was required to take in not only the aforementioned evacuees, but also two young officers on training duties on Salisbury Plain, and also an official from the Ministry of Mines, which had been temporarily evacuated to the Wilton Felt Mills. Arthur Street wrote, in early November, the following paragraph in his wartime memoir *Hitler's Whistle* (a collection of articles published in *Farmer's Weekly* and other country magazines during the period):

The amount of war-time accommodation that the countryside is providing for war-enforced visitors is amazing. Today in addition to its native population the rural scene is filled with soldiers, airmen, evacuated women and children, and government servants galore. For instance, at the moment my own house has somehow found room for a mother and three little children, two billeted officers, and also a government official. The last mentioned now occupies my study, drat him, but his conversation in the evenings almost makes up for this.

However inconvenient the evacuee programme may have been for country-dwellers, at times the legendary British sense of humour still prevailed, as Arthur Street goes on to illustrate:

Just now evacuee stories are legion, but this is probably the shortest and best of them all. It conerns a maiden lady who lived in a small house in the country with one maid. One morning the bell rang. The maid admitted the visitor, and then rushed upstairs.

'Please mum,' she blurted out breathlessly, 'you've got to have two babies, and the man's downstairs!!!'

Another immediate consequence of the outbreak of war was the reduction in Ditchampton Farm's workforce. To compensate for this, Pamela learnt how to drive a tractor and help out generally on the farm, as her entry for 6 September reports: 'Drove the tractor to help Pop with the oats. The *Farmer's Weekly* wrote because they no longer want Daddy – it's terrible. There's nothing for him to do except farm and it means we're more or less — [sic]. Nothing will ever be the same now.' The next day's entry was somewhat more optimistic. With the resilience of youth, Pamela wrote: 'Better day altogether. After all there is something in just having to do things when everybody's in the same boat ... Helped again with the oats.'

Arthur Street begins his entry for 20 September in *Hitler's Whistle* as follows: 'Now that I do a minimum of sixty hours weekly as a farm hand I find that writing takes a very back seat.' He describes his workforce at one point during this period as consisting of 'two old-age pensioners, myself, and my daughter driving the tractor'. They were now occupied with silage-making. Arthur goes on to comment on Pamela's unladylike language whilst engaged in this hard and unpopular task: 'My daughter, realizing her limitations, confines hers to uncomplimentary remarks about the tractor in moments of stress ...' Undoubtedly at this time, Pamela, as a novice tractor-driver, had much to learn, as an anecdote she later recounted illustrates:

> I remember once my father leaving me chain-harrowing in a field on top of the downs ... for some reason I found it incredibly difficult to ... keep a straight line. Nothing one does in the countryside can ever be secret; one's work is exposed to full view for miles around; sooner or later a farmer on the opposite slope noticed the rather wavering stop-go, stop-go efforts on our side of the valley. It so happened that he had to go into Wilton, met my father and remarked that he must have engaged a new tractor-driver. My father had not left me long, but he was back in that field within minutes. I rather expected a ticking off, but he roared with laughter and proceeded to get up on the tractor and give me a few more hints on how to deal with the situation.

Pamela also took charge of the weekly wages, a task she found equally daunting, as her entry for 8 September makes clear: 'Peggy has got a job at the Post Office so handed over the wages to me and it's like a nightmare with all the wretched insurances etc.'

On 9 September Pamela was back again behind the wheel of the tractor, musing about the war situation: 'Drove the tractor most of the day — cultivating. It also cultivated me ... It just seems ridiculous to think we're at war — there seems no news and Poland's gradually getting beaten up — it's awful ... hunting seems very far away now.'

Two days later, Pamela indignantly recorded her views on people who still felt entitled to hunt now that war had been declared and the Street household had other priorities: 'Phillips [the Master of the Wilton Hunt] wants to keep on the hunt. I think it's dirty. Things don't make any difference to some people.'

Ditchampton Farm's workforce was soon to be augmented by another, this time four-legged, helper. Once war had been declared, as the last diary entry testifies, all thoughts of hunting were banished from the Street household. Arthur Street sent his hunter, Jorrocks, away to be trained for the harness, a specialised procedure that by no means guaranteed success. Many horses, accustomed to being ridden in the conventional way, did not take kindly to this new form of treatment. Therefore when Arthur Street was telephoned with the news that Jorrocks had graduated with top marks and was ready to be collected, it was with his heart in his mouth that he and their groom-gardener were driven by Pamela the 8 miles to where Jorrocks was waiting, hitched up to their float. Despite the fact that he had not driven a horse in this fashion for over twenty years, Arthur was able to guide Jorrocks home, as he later described in *Hitler's Whistle*:

> He then trotted home like a gentleman, and since that day he has hauled the milk, pulled the broadcast during wheat sowing, and done ploughing and all sorts of jobs with no mishap … What he thinks about it I don't know. He has no notion of what it is that trundles and rattles over behind him, and the position of his ears shows that he is somewhat worried about it. But as we have never let him down before, he reckons that we are not doing it now, and so does his war work like the gentleman he is.

This reference to ploughing deserves particular mention. For reasons already described, during the agricultural depression Arthur Street put his arable fields to pasture and concentrated on livestock (in his case dairy-farming), urging fellow farmers to do the same. As war approached, this decision was credited with admirable foresight, since the result was a wealth of fertile pasture that could now be ploughed up again for arable use. War Agricultural Committees the length and breadth of the country were soon set up to supervise farms in their respective districts, and given powers to force farmers to plough up their pasture land, since the fourth line of defence for Britain was to become self-sufficient in home produce, in particular cereals that it had now become too dangerous to import from across the Atlantic. At one point in *Hitler's Whistle* Arthur Street commented that all over the countryside men on tractors or guiding horses could be seen hard at work ploughing up grassland. Pamela, wistfully remembering the previous hunting season and Jorrocks' role in particular, wrote the following poem about this phenomenon, which was published in *The Field* a year later:

Gone Away

It's a lifetime since that season and the cold sharp winter day,
When they ran from Poor Man's Gorse, through Holt and on …
And Jorrocks took those hurdles in the old sedately way,
And the field came jostling, thrusting, and were gone.

Gone away some time ago in hats of tin, not silk,
Leaving only Jorrocks, now in harness, hauling milk.

Poor's Gorse lies still this morning, and there comes no Tally Ho,
From the mist that hangs in patches on the down,
But something in Ten Acre moves already to and fro,
And the green field's melting slowly into brown.

The sun breaks through the grey sky and the strips of dark earth meet,
Jorrocks plods on steadily – ploughing up for wheat.

The day wears on to evening and some heavy drops of rain
Fall fast upon the newly turned-up ground,
Men and horses finish and start slowly down the lane,
By Holt and Barner's thicket, homeward bound.
Jorrocks in his blinkers scarcely sees them on ahead –
In front of him the carter's coat has changed to pink instead.

So when a fox next breaks behind the gorse – the usual way,
And hounds and huntsmen crash through Holt and on –
Jorrocks will be there, perhaps a little blown that day,
But he'll follow gamely after and be gone …

Gone away! They'll cry behind the clustered streaming pack,
But the echo of that 'Gone away' will mean they have come back.

The hunting expression, 'Gone away', held a particular poignancy for Pamela during this period of the war. Behind this poem lies the deep sense of loneliness she was by now experiencing, since the crowd of young people with whom she had up till then been mixing had recently dispersed – the young men to go into the armed forces and the young women either into the women's services or other types of war work. Highlights of this period were unexpected meetings with old friends back on leave visiting their families; as one of her diary entries put it, 'You seem to snatch at every friendly face.' On one occasion the oppposite was true. Ian Benson, the whipper-in of the Wilton Hunt, on whom Pamela had developed a lasting teenage crush, was one of the first young men in the district to be called up. Pamela's last glimpse of him was in a car passing in the opposite direction, about which she noted plaintively in her diary: 'It <u>was</u> wretched just making do with a wave …' Worse was to come in early October, however, when she was invited to the Benson household to find Ian on a period of leave, accompanied by an unoffical fiancée. In her diary she wrote: 'Without exception I think today has been the worst I've ever had to go through …'

Despite her early heartbreak and loneliness, Pamela continued dutifully with her new wartime occupations. Her diary includes entries such as: 'tractor all morning'; 'tractored all afternoon'; 'ploughed a bit'; 'typing & hectic work'; then on 28 October she announced with some pride:

Started the tractor & moved on the bail quite happily without Pop! Cecil Beaton wanted to take my photograph on the tractor but at the last minute couldn't find his camera (Ha!). So I went straight to bed simply streaming cold & stayed there.

This diary extract requires further explanation. The tractors used on Ditchampton Farm at the time were Fordson Ns. These were the most common workhorses in Britain during the Second World War. The Fordson N was by no means an easy machine to operate, needing to be started by manually cranking the engine with a starting handle. Its transmission system made it somewhat temperamental, and compared to certain rival models it lacked horsepower. Therefore it is to Pamela's credit that she managed to get the tractor going without help.

The 'bail' was Arthur Street's outdoor mobile milking unit, which he first began using when he put his arable land to pasture in the late 1920s. It was the brainchild of A.J. Hosier, a farmer in the north Wiltshire village of Wexcombe. Pamela later recalled the exciting day when, as a small child, her father took her to inspect this invention by the man they subsequently dubbed 'the Wizard of Wexcombe'.

The society photographer Cecil Beaton (whom the Street family would have known through their friendship with Edith Olivier and her set) had been commissioned at the beginning of the war, for propaganda reasons, to take photographs of attractive young men and women either in uniform or engaged in unaccustomed war work. A photograph of Pamela, on her tractor, would have fitted the bill perfectly.

Pamela's diary for the remainder of 1939 continues to be punctuated by references to events abroad, and records how, during those first few months of the war (later described as the 'phoney war' before its effects were fully felt on the mainland), life seemed to fall into a pattern:

September 28th Warsaw has fallen now so that's that & presumably we'll soon get it.

October 16th They've caught a spy at Salisbury taking flics of the Chilmark [ammunition] dump ...

October 30th It's odd that now we seem to have settled down to the war and the awfulness at the beginning wears off.

November 4th This war is queer. It's sort of stale-mate and nothing doing ...

November 9th the war continues in a vague and mysterious manner …

November 30th Russia has attacked Finland – oh it's all awful …

December 13th The war just goes on & on & Russia is fighting Finland & the world is going up in smoke …

Pamela's entry for 9 October shows that after a month of catering for the evacuees and the new billetee, life at Ditchampton Farm had evidently become strained: 'For no reason at all am awfully tired. Everyone is, & Mummy has got so fed up with the refugees and Mr Horton.' Happily for the Streets, however, the situation was soon to improve, for on 14 October Pamela's diary states, 'Mrs. Helyer, Marion & Rachel left'. There had been no bombing of Portsmouth or London at this stage and it was now considered safe for the evacuees to return home.

Moreover, Arthur Street's literary and broadcasting work would soon resume. As early as 11 September Pamela records: 'Pop has heard from the F.W. [*Farmer's Weekly*] who *do* want him. So had some typing to do.' Then on 10 November she writes: 'BBC rang up at 10 for Pop to go & broadcast so dashed him into the train practically straight from the plough!'

In the penultimate chapter of his book *Wessex Wins*, Arthur Street elaborates quite extensively on this incident. On the morning in question he was happily absorbed in his ploughing work which, as a result of his experiences in Canada some decades earlier, he had always regarded as the king of agricultural jobs:

God was in his Heaven, the aeroplanes were in the sky, the sun shone, the birds sang, and all was as right with my little world as war would let it be. Into this plough-man's paradise came a car, bearing Pamela with an urgent message from the B.B.C.

'The B.B.C.'s just rung up, Daddy. Someone's ill and let them down, and they want you to go to London at once to do an Armistice talk for overseas early tomorrow morning.'

One can understand the urgency, from the BBC's point of view, to find a replacement to give an armistice talk, commemorating the end of the First World War, in the very year that what would become the Second World War had just broken out; it needed to be given by an already seasoned and respected broadcaster such as A.G. Street. Nonetheless, Arthur's mind was focussed on – to him – more pressing matters. His account continues:

'Do they? Well, you can go home and tell the B.B.C. to chase its little self into the Thames. I've just got this plough to shine again, and I ain't stoppin' it for anybody.'

'Daddy! Don't be silly. The B.B.C. said it was important!'

'So's ploughing important, a damn sight more important than the B.B.C. Pam, you should show a better sense of values.'

'P'raps, but come along. You know you were moaning some weeks ago that all your broadcasting stopped owing to the war. Well, now there's a chance to do some, you want to go ploughing instead.'

The upshot of this exchange was that Arthur Street went back to Ditchampton Farmhouse, rang the BBC and haggled with them for a somewhat exorbitant fee which finally persuaded him to be dragged away from his wartime ploughing and give a wireless talk which, in his opinion, many others with no agricultural commitments were equally qualified to do. But now, possibly thanks to Pamela's urgings, at least he was firmly back in the broadcasting business.

Happily for Arthur Street, a week or so later on 22 November, Pamela's diary records that his foreman Charlie Noble came home, having been granted exemption from military service on the grounds that his civilian occupation was essential to the war effort. At a stroke Arthur Street was liberated from day-to-day farm work and could concentrate once again on writing and broadcasting.

Pamela also found herself freed from some of the practical farming side of her war work, although this in itself caused her to feel guilty. However her parents had evidently decided that during the Christmas period her earlier efforts should be in some small measure rewarded, and that she should be given, albeit it in a low-key way, the party that had been cancelled earlier that autumn. Evidently a sufficient number of Pamela's young friends had been granted time off war work for the Christmas period. The party went well, for on the evening of the day in question, Pamela records: 'the party was a huge success & I think everyone enjoyed themselves enormously.'

And so the tumultuous year of 1939 drew to a close, with Pamela still performing limited, largely secretarial, war work on the farm, and Arthur Street now firmly established as one of the leading voices of British agriculture. In an article later re-published in *Hitler's Whistle*, ever conscious of the importance of British farming as one of the main lines of national defence, Arthur Street signed off his final piece for the year as follows:

And so, although these are the last notes for 1939, I have decided to wish all my friends, neither a Happy nor a Prosperous New Year. Instead, I wish them a New Year during which, whether the war ends or continues, the townsfolk of Britain will realize and appreciate the enormous value of that stable godsend, the land of their own country.

Three

The 'Phoney War' and Descriptions of 'Dunkirk' (January–June 1940)

For British civilians – particularly those living in the countryside – the 'phoney war' continued well into May 1940. However, out at sea the conflict was already being waged in deadly earnest. No sooner had England declared war on Germany, than on 3 September 1939 the Nazis demonstrated their indiscriminate ruthlessness (in a horrible echo of the sinking of the *Lusitania* in the early months of the First World War) by sinking the passenger liner *Athenia* near the starting-point of her journey across the Atlantic. The German navy, and in particular their U-boats, would immediately become a lethal menace to Allied shipping, both military and civilian. Meanwhile Allied troops were massing near the Belgian border, where any immediate land offensive was expected.

Just how much of this news filtered through to the general British public is unclear; certainly there are no direct references to it in Pamela's diaries for the period. Instead she constantly emphasises the 'unreality' of the war. On 3 January 1940 Pamela records selling programmes for an amateur production of *Cinderella*, and then being taken skating by friends. Her diary entry continues: 'Strange as it may seem from this there is still a war.'

Pamela's first opportunity to engage in direct war work, albeit of a mundane nature, arose in early 1940 when she was taken on by the Food Office at the council offices in nearby Bourne Hill, issuing ration books and identity discs: '*January 5th* Had to go & see Mr Smart about a job in the F.O. and am starting tomorrow – terrific.* Wonder what I'll do and be like.'

---

* Some of the adjectives Pamela used in her diaries then had different meanings. By 'terrific' she meant 'terrifying'. By 'fantastic' she meant 'unbelievable'.

It appears that the following day, 6 January, was something of a red-letter day for more than one reason: 'Started my job. Wonderful muddle. ½ day … Ronnie came to dinner and we went to the White Hart dance and it was marvellous. I don't know whether it was 12th night but I have actually been kissed which seems extraordinary when you come to think about it.' A few days later Pamela was invited to a dance by another young man, after which she reports: 'Rex was very very nice & kissed me goodnight which was amazing'.

Pamela's love life may have been improving, but things were not destined to go so smoothly in the workplace. As early as 8 January she records:

My boj [sic]. Very hard day as heaps of people in and the start of rationing.

January 15th My boj still going on and I haven't got the sack yet.

January 23rd Still boj & boj. Wonder if I'll get very boj-like. It's a great pity I wasn't more appreciative of time before. Now there isn't any.

There follows a series of diary entries that show that Pamela was becoming increasingly exhausted and frequently obliged to take time off work. Finally on 2 March she reveals: 'Ma took me to the doctors & that is the end of my boj – well – well – well!!!'

Pamela was not the only member of the family to have suffered from ill-health during the early months of 1940. As she writes on 1 April, when her mother was in bed with a heavy cold: 'It's been a terrible winter & Ma & Pa have had continual colds every other week …' But on 7 April, Arthur Street's 48th birthday, the Street household was evidently in a happier mood: 'Pop's birthday … Planted a walnut tree with great celebration that I gave him …' In the final pages of his book *Wessex Wins*, Arthur Street expands on how this gift symbolised his faith in the eventual outcome of the war:

In the spring of 1940 I sought a more tangible way of expressing my faith in Britain's future than by mere protestations in words, either spoken or printed. So when Pamela enquired what I wanted for my forty-eighth birthday I informed her that I wished to plant a tree, a walnut-tree, for I had always deplored that Ditchampton Farm lacked this necessary feature. Wonderingly she procured one, and on the 7th April 1940 I planted it with my own hands.

At this age no man can plant a tree unless he has faith in the future of his country and of himself, and this the war has given me … I have planted my walnut-tree in the sure and certain faith that if I am spared to farm Ditchampton Farm when it first produces nuts I shall be living under a British flag and system of government that will permit me to offer those nuts to whomsoever I may please.

This was the kind of wartime propaganda material Arthur Street was encouraged to write. Whether or not he truly believed his own words, the events of the day after his birthday, however, must have caused him to question this faith, for his daughter recorded: '*April 8th* Germany has invaded Denmark & Norway – in complete control of the former and has landed at several places in latter. It's terrific. The spring offensive. What will happen?'

From now on the war comes much more into focus in Pamela's diary. On 17 April she recorded that the whole Street family went down to Southampton to wave goodbye to her cousin Philip, who had enlisted in the navy, commenting that 'the docks were absolutely alive'. On 27 April Pamela wrote: 'The war goes on like a great big weight which gets a bit heavier every day.' The ever-perceptive Arthur Street clearly recognised the impact the war was having on the womenfolk of his household and did his best to lighten this weight. On the following day, 28 April, Pamela records: 'Pop took Mummy and I out to the Haunch* to feed and drive through Downton. It is a very nice world when you can forget the war.' But there was no escaping the bleak news that by now was being broadcast daily, as the entries in Pamela's diary continue:

May 3rd The situation in Norway gets blacker every day.

May 4th We've retreated a lot in Norway. I think if Daddy doesn't want me I shall go & do something in the Infirmary, because I'm just useless at the moment

May 10th Hitler has invaded Holland and Belgium – Poland, Czech, Norway, Denmark and now this – it's awful …

Pamela was by no means as useless as her self-deprecating diary entry for 4 May suggests, for on 13 and 14 May her entries read respectively: 'Tractored all day – very burnt', and 'Tractored all the morning & got very brown'. Additionally during this entire period she was continuing to do typing and other office work for her father and drive him to and from Salisbury station when he was summoned to London to broadcast.

On 15 May Pamela wrote: 'Pop has joined the local Defence for Parachute troops. Holland has given in.' The moment when Arthur Street was finally able to enlist with the LDV** was of particular significance. Arthur had been deeply hurt by his rejection from active service, on account of his deformed feet, by the military

---

* The Haunch of Venison, at the time considered the best restaurant in Salisbury.

** Local Defence Volunteers, as they were known before they were renamed the Home Guard.

authorities both in Canada and England during the First World War. Therefore the opportunity to defend his country – albeit at the more mature age of 48 – would have been a source of great pride, and he subsequently took his duties very seriously. Pamela later wrote about the moment when the call for LDV volunteers went out:

> On Wednesday, May 15th, after Holland gave in, we all sat listening to the wireless as Anthony Eden broadcast a request for Local Defence Volunteers … It was a glorious late spring evening and, as soon as the broadcast ceased, my father left the room and I heard his car going down the drive. I wondered where he could possibly be going. Next day I discovered that he had been the first round at Wilton Police Station to put his name down. At last, in middle age, he found that his services were not rejected by those in charge of defending his country.

Possibly spurred on by her father's example, Pamela quickly volunteered to help out at Tower House, the local emergency military hospital, where a few months later she would become a qualified VAD* nurse. So on 18 May her diary entry reads: 'Went into T H for the first time … Didn't do really very much but liked being there.'

Pamela's entry for Friday 24 May touches both on domestic life and the catastrophic events that were now taking place on the other side of the English Channel: 'Started hay-making. Tom & Ian [the two billeted officers] went off v early this morning. Horrid feeling inside … The Germans have got Boulogne, Abbeville but they can't win because they mustn't. There's been heaps of internal arrests of fascists here.'

For the next couple of days Pamela continued working at Tower House, but then on 27 May her diary states: 'Mary Way rang up about some canteen work [at Salisbury station] for a rush tomorrow.' This would have been Pamela's first inkling that 'Operation Dynamo', the evacuation of British, French and Belgian troops from the beaches of Dunkirk in late May and early June 1940, was already under way. The Allied forces massing along the Franco-Belgian border – from which any German offensive was expected – had been taken completely by surprise by the Blitzkrieg tactics of a second, simultaneous, rapid offensive of Panzer divisions through the seemingly impenetrable natural barrier of the Ardennes region south of the French protective Maginot Line. The German tanks suddenly appeared at the Allies' rear, sweeping up towards the French coast, thus effectively cutting them off from any retreat westwards back into French territory. One by one the French towns near or on the coast – Abbeville, Boulogne, Calais – were taken by

---

* Voluntary Aid Detachment, an organisation providing amateur nursing services to British and Allied forces during the First and Second World Wars.

the Germans, and an emergency plan to evacuate the Allied troops from Dunkirk was implemented. In addition to Royal Naval vessels, an armada of smaller craft of all shapes and sizes crossed and re-crossed the English Channel to pick up the exhausted troops waiting on the Dunkirk beaches, both rescuers and those waiting to be rescued being continuously strafed and dive-bombed by the Luftwaffe or under fire from German positions inland. With hindsight it seems little short of a miracle that some 340,000 Allied troops made it back onto English soil in this ad hoc manner.

Pamela's diary for this crucial period of the war is a précis of the events she witnessed and the small part she played in them; however it shows how the enormity and gravity of the situation quickly became apparent. Her diary for late May and early June 1940 continues:

> *May 28th* … Cut up bread and butter at the canteen for B.E.F.* troops coming back from Belgium because Leopold has given in to Hitler and been a complete traitor to his country …

> *May 29th* On the station all day – our troops are pouring back – it's terrible – practically the whole of our army trapped and trying to get out. The navy have been marvellous but the troops keep saying about the incessant bombing and they're terribly done up.

> *May 30th* Station 2–6. Still coming back. The awful atrocities the Germans have committed are terrific. It's a help to feel you can do a little even if it's only giving a few something to drink. They're so grateful …

> *May 31st* An ambulance train went through either today or yesterday but it's such a rush it's difficult to remember. We gave them tea – it's more like a nightmare than anything else. Vi fetched me because the roads are blocked. Pop out all night.

> *June 1st* Spent the day resting as on night duty tonight … They're getting frightfully strict because of all this fifth column business and the roads are blocked.

> *June 2nd* From 10 last night till 10 this morning. Spent the night in a railway carriage … it's just fantastic – I don't think I'm me at all. Awful rush in the middle of the night – and French through this morning. But we've got to come through one day I'm certain …

---

* The British Expeditionary Force, first deployed along the Franco-Belgian borders with Germany after war was declared in September 1939. Hostilities began in May 1940 following the German invasion of France.

June 3rd Hay-making at home but still the station for me because the French troops are still coming through …

June 4th Station all the morning. Pop hay-making & I feel I should be there but this evacuation job will soon be over I think. Thank heaven they were able to get them out – it's a miracle but it gives you some hope. Mummy brought 4 invalid soldiers from Tower House to tea …

This wartime experience on Salisbury station made a lifelong impression on Pamela, and she later wrote or lectured about it in different formats. Perhaps the most vivid version was the fictional account she gave of it at the beginning of her novel *Many Waters*. The main characters here are based on two of her maternal aunts rather than her younger self, but there is no doubt that the events described are exactly as Pamela herself would have witnessed them:

The trains kept coming.

There had been over twenty of them passing through Westonbury [Pamela's fictitious name for Salisbury] station during the night – one roughly every half-hour. All their carriages and corridors were packed with soldiers in varying degrees of exhaustion. In the dimness of the black-out it had just been possible for volunteer helpers to discern their dishevelled bodies, some stretched out, dead to the world, lying half on top of each other on the floor; some without boots, their feet so swollen that they were incapable of struggling to the windows for the cups of hot sweet tea and sandwiches being handed to their more fortunate companions, who did their best to pass them back inside. Occasionally, an excited French voice could be heard above the deeper gruff chorus of 'Bless you lady', 'Thank you, ma'am.'

It was by now eight o'clock on the morning of Saturday, June 1st 1940. A bright summer sun was just beginning to break through the early morning mist covering the valleys of southern England. The survivors of the British Expeditionary Force were coming back from Dunkirk.

When fresh volunteers arrived at the station to relieve those who had been on night shift, Katy Mason and her sister, May Lodge, drove back to Netherford to snatch a few hours' sleep – although not before they had dealt with the various messages which had been thrust into their hands by men desperate to let their families know they were safe. Scrawled on the back of cigarette packets or odd scraps of paper, Katy and May had sent off quite a collection of these since they had offered their services at the beginning of the week. Where possible, they telephoned relatives. If not, they posted the missives, made all the more poignant by their brevity: 'I'm O.K. Mum', 'Be seeing you, Ginger.'

Like most of their friends and neighbours, the evacuation from Dunkirk had taken them completely by surprise. Even now, witnessing but an infinitesimal part of it with their own eyes and listening to snatches of servicemen's conversation, it was hard to take in that it was really happening. Official news was, of necessity, negligible. It did not seem possible that the British Army was withdrawing, defeated, from the continent, that some of the men to whom they ministered that morning had been ferried across the Straits of Dover by the Margate lifeboat – others, by a small Thameside tug. The situation was unthinkable, unprecedented, a nightmare from which they would awake …

The authorities – and indeed many civilians, including Pamela's parents – fully expected the Germans to launch an immediate invasion on the heels of the retreating troops. The reference in Pamela's diary entry for 31 May to her cousin Vi being sent to collect her from Salisbury station and the roads being blocked was a direct consequence of this belief. If the Germans were to invade, Pamela's parents wanted her with them at home. The fictional characters in *Many Waters* describe the efforts being made by the authorities to outwit any invaders:

> As Katy turned down the lane towards their home, the signpost saying NETHERFORD ¼ MILE had already disappeared and they could see anti-tank traps being erected a little further on towards Wilhampton [Pamela's fictitious name for Wilton]. Nazi invasion was feared imminent and both women knew that the Government had given orders that anything which gave an indication of the name, direction or distance to any place must be obliterated.

Thankfully the Germans did not press home their advantage. Pamela's diary for the remainder of the first week of June finds her back at work on the farm hay-making, but also intermittently helping out again on Salisbury station: '*June 7th* Station again in afternoon because the B.E.F. troops are all over the place & returning again and there is such a lot to do.' Accommodating a beaten army back in England was a monumental and hitherto unparalleled operation. Emergency military camps on Salisbury Plain would have catered for a fair number, but there was much to-ing and fro-ing of personnel, which kept the canteen volunteers at Salisbury station busy for several days after the evacuation had officially been completed. But finally Pamela's duties came to end, and she found herself back at Ditchampton Farm, brooding on how best to contribute to the war effort: '*June 11th* Hay-maked all day. I broke the sweep. Life is so busy just now there isn't time for anything. I am having a terrific toss-up with myself. Shall I join the Fannies or be a nurse. I'm late in the day, like England, but the war is just terrible and I'm desperate.'

More bad news continued to come from across the Channel, as Pamela carries on:

> *June 12th* The Germans are pressing on like a tidal wave but they'll have to wash back some day, I expect.

June 14th Paris has fallen. It's too bad to think about. Somehow life goes on ... but when you think of what they're doing out in France it makes anything short of a 12 hr day seem wrong.

Evidently this latest calamity forced Pamela to make up her mind about her immediate wartime role, for the very next day her entry reads simply: '*June 15th* I am going to try to be a V.A.D.'

★ ★ ★

The evacuation from Dunkirk was also being witnessed, at rather closer quarters, by a young man whom Pamela was shortly to meet. David McCormick, having enlisted in the Royal Artillery at the outbreak of the war, finally received instructions to report to the Fifth Field Training Regiment in Dover at the beginning of March 1940. Like Pamela, he later chronicled some of his wartime experiences, including his time spent at Dover Barracks before, during and after 'Operation Dynamo'. David's memoir begins with a description of his attitude towards the outbreak of the Second World War, evidently shared by many young people of his generation, including Pamela herself:

Before the war I was like Voltaire's Candide. I believed that all was for the best in the best of worlds. I have a profound faith in human nature and am one of those who seek to see the best in others, and overlook their worst qualities ... Also I am the possessor of one asset, which, if overindulged, becomes a weakness: that of seeing the other man's point of view. Consequently I could not believe that Germany really intended a war. I thought then that perhaps after all the Germans had been rather harshly treated at Versailles,* and I could understand why they wanted room to expand their increasing population. In the early stages of the Nazi aggression I thought perhaps all was just and for the best ...

When I allowed myself to look at the facts I was very worried but I refused to admit that after the calamity of the Great War that Europe could possibly allow such a horror to occur again. Consequently when war actually descended upon us I was not surprised, but rather permitted myself to be taken by surprise.

The Dunkirk evacuation rapidly disabused David of such a youthful, Panglossian attitude. In his memoir, having described his period of training, he goes on to give

---

*   This was the peace treaty signed at the Palace of Versailles in 1919 after the end of the First World War, which amongst other stipulations required Germany to cede much previously German-held territory to its neighbours France, Belgium, Denmark, Czechoslovakia and Poland.

a vivid account of how he and his companions heard about and experienced the unfolding events:

While we had been playing at soldiers at Dover events had taken place on the other side of the channel. The Germans had started their advance through Belgium, and soon we began to realise that all was not well. Then came the withdrawal of the B.E.F., and the gunfire, which we had heard occasionally when the wind was in the west, became gradually a continuous distant thunder. In the evenings the sky was lit up with a reddish glow. One evening volunteers were called for to go down to the docks. There we found our troops arriving from the other side, haggard, tired, and dirty. Some said 'the damn froggies' had let them down, others that our anti-tank rifles were no good. 'Our bullets just bounce off the tanks,' they said, 'the Germans rush down the roads in their tanks throwing out hand grenades as they pass. If we do hold them up for a few minutes, they just radio back for aeroplanes, and then we get bombed to blazes. We can't stop them and we never see the R.A.F.' Units were being continually cut off from the main body, and no one knew where anyone else was. They told us that some of the French were going to defend Paris, others just going. They had seen groups of French soldiers surrendering, being relieved of their arms and told to go, and then being shot in the back when they had gone a few yards away. Forty men who had been hiding from machine-gun fire under the pier at Calais arrived in a tug. They said they had been rescued just before shooting themselves. They had been watching the Germans herding refugees down to the water's edge, and then mowing them down with machine-guns. The *Maid of Orleans* came in covered with holes. Thirty had been killed and ninety wounded by shells and bombs while leaving the harbour. Somebody said the *Maid of Kent* had been sunk. On one destroyer all the officers on the bridge had been sniped whilst entering Calais. Everyone seemed to have seen deliberate bombing and machine-gunning of refugees. One soldier, who had tramped to the coast from Rheims, said 'You probably won't believe it but I saw a motor-cycle combination captured by the Germans, who shot one tommy and tied the other, who was wounded, into the side-car, then poured petrol over him and set the outfit on fire.'

David commented about this last-mentioned incident in a letter to his parents: 'If these fiends ever come to this country or we ever get to Germany I think we will know what to do with them.'

Three of David's letters to his parents from this period still survive. Despite the restrained style in which it was then customary for young men of David's background to write, it is clear that the events he witnessed affected him profoundly, as the following extracts reveal:

Thursday May 23rd Of course we have heard a lot of guns & bombing going on
& fairly frequent air raid warnings. Some people in our regiment are spending
all night stretcher-bearing down on Dover. I expect our turn will come soon …

For myself I feel that I am in a very dangerous place now, if the Germans
decide to attack England either in their flat-bottomed boats or by parachutes. I
feel that an air raid or two on Dover are only to be expected, but we are quite
a long way from the Harbour & should be quite safe. But if they decide on any
night parachuting on the days I am out I might just as well be in the B.E.F. [David
was frequently out much of the night on road-block duty] …

We are rigidly confined to Barracks. Two Sundays running I have spent on duty
all day & I am feeling quite depressed about everything …

Tuesday May 28th I don't think now that anyone could take anything but a very
pessimistic view of things. I have been down to Dover harbour lending a hand
& am very shocked at what I have seen & heard. I am also out every other night
on road duty, & the other night when we had three German planes over I had
no sleep for 25 hours & then only 1½ hours, then on again for 14 …

The air attack was a magnificent sight. As far as I know the Germans only
dropped a mine outside the harbour, which went off with a terrific bang. We saw
two shot down & splendid fireworks for about ten minutes. All the pompoms
all along the coast got going with lines of red bullets & there were several heavy
A.A. guns going off & the guns from the destroyers in the harbour.

Wednesday May 29th We are up practically all night on this something road guard,
which is a 24 hour affair lasting till 6 p.m., we then go to bed & are woken &
taken down to the docks at 1.45, where we undergo physical strain & mental
torture until 8.30 carrying corpses about & loose hands & brains are all in the days
work. I feel very upset & sometimes feel like crying when I am down there. It is
all so pointless & I hate the callousness with which it is treated by the majority
of our people who chiefly go down to see what they can pinch in the way of
cigarettes & money from the hit lying about in the dock …

It seems a miracle to me that Dover has been left by the Germans, as practically all the B.E.F. troops have been landed here. One night about a week ago
we were having a slack time down there & fell asleep on a whole lot of packing
cases, which we discovered when day broke were about 1000 land mines & crates
of hand grenades. One bomb on these would have just about finished Dover
harbour I should think …

I feel that our danger is over now. If the Germans were going to bomb us
they would have long ago. Now that they have missed their market they would
be very unwise to waste their planes on Dover. But I still feel slightly uncomfortable when sleeping in England's front line trenches, which incidentally are

extremely uncomfortable & make one into a white & chalky mess, & shall
be quite pleased if the rumours that we are going to be moved to Wales or
Gloucester materialise …

In the event, David and eleven of his companions, who had earlier been singled
out for officer training, had to wait a couple more months before being posted,
neither to Wales nor Gloucester, but to Larkhill Camp on Salisbury Plain, where
they soon found themselves being entertained, during their time off duty, by local
families such as the Streets.

Four

A Defiant Nation: Nursing, Officer Training and Romance (July–December 1940)

Although the anticipated invasion of England by the Germans following the evacuation from Dunkirk never materialised, British civilians were kept on tenterhooks all through the long, hot summer of 1940. Reconnaissance photographs revealed fleets of flat-bottomed barges waiting in ports across the Channel. However these craft were designed for river use rather than for potentially choppy open seas, and would have made an easy target for the RAF. Therefore the Germans' strategy was for the RAF to be annihilated before attempting the crossing (code-named 'Operation Sea-lion'), which needed to take place before the onset of the equinoctial tides and potential storms in September.

Events did not go as smoothly as the German High Command anticipated, however. This was the period about which Winston Churchill, who had taken over as prime minister in May following the resignation of Neville Chamberlain, famously declared, 'Never in the field of human conflict was so much owed by so many to so few.' During what became known as the Battle of Britain, young British airmen waged ceaseless battle against the numerically superior German air force in the skies of southern Britain. Both sides suffered severe losses, but the RAF proved so surprisingly skilful and resilient that by 17 September 'Operation Sea-lion' had to be postponed indefinitely.

During the course of the summer, however, while the outcome was still in doubt, British civilians could only watch and hope as vapour trails from aerial dogfights criss-crossed the skies of southern England. Most of the action took place in the South East, so for residents of Wilton and the surrounding district sightings of overhead skirmishes were rare. In her diaries during this period Pamela frequently comments – almost with feelings of guilt – on the sense of unreality that such monstrous events should be taking place only some 80 miles or so away from her place of comparative safety, or indeed only 30 miles away in the instance of the bombing of southern coastal ports, which had begun in earnest. Nevertheless air-raid sirens constantly interrupted the Street family's sleep, and they frequently spent nights in the cellar. As Pamela's diary attests, Arthur Street was out most nights on LDV duty, which he took very seriously.

In order to qualify to become a VAD, Pamela had to spend fifty hours working in an ordinary hospital. Consequently her diary entry for 17 June reads: 'Saw the Sister at the Infirmary & can start on Wednesday morning …' Her entry for later that day continues: 'France gave in at one o'clock. We are in splendid isolation.' The next day Pamela mentions 'seeing about uniform'; then on 19 June she writes: 'Started in the children's ward & fed babies … No settled armistice v France Germany yet …' On the following day her diary reads: 'Women's ward. Had an air-raid warning last night … Stayed in the back hall & Pop went out in uniform.'

This mention of uniform is significant. It took a long while for the Local Defence Volunteers to be adequately equipped with uniforms and weaponry, but uniforms were of psychological importance to the LDV members, enabling them to show that they were a serious force to be reckoned with. Going out 'in uniform' would have been a source of pride particularly for Arthur Street, after his experiences of rejection during the First World War.

Pamela's next entry reads: 'Men's ward – medical. Am petrified of the sisters – do everything wrong always …'

Given Pamela's highly developed conscience she was doubtless being far too hard on herself, but this was to be a continuing problem throughout her time both at the Salisbury Infirmary and again when she arrived at Tower House, the emergency military hospital. Feelings of guilt and low self-esteem clearly caused her to take all too seriously the hospital discipline meted out to her. Moreover the lack of physical stamina, from which she seems always to have suffered, ill-equipped her for the arduous hours, including night-duty, that nursing entailed. Her entries for the following few days bear further witness to this:

June 22nd Men's surgical. Saw some dressings – didn't mind all that. Get on very well with the mental defectives, otherwise feel a fool & my cap won't stay on …

June 23rd [a Sunday] Men's surgical again … I am a hopeless nurse – an old man yelled for a bedpan in the middle of a service & I forgot to use the screens …

June 25th Casualty. Awful sisters. Saw an op on baby. Didn't mind but felt a fool because of the sister. Came home – have finished. Air raid hooter last night – stayed in the cellar.

Pamela had now completed her fifty hours' nursing apprenticeship at the infirmary. In the interval between working there and starting at Tower House, she found herself once more caught up with the everyday life of the Street family. On 27 June she and her parents dined again at the Haunch of Venison to celebrate the publication of Arthur Street's latest book, his only detective novel, *A Crook in the Furrow*. In her diary Pamela comments about this, 'Ludicrous, isn't it?' This is one of the many references in her diary to the incongruity between the mundane domestic events that were still taking place despite the war, and the war itself. Another entry a few days later reinforces this feeling: '*June 30th* Some of the Southern Command are coming to Wilton House … The Peacocks [a theatrical agent and his wife, friends of her parents] came to tea *and* there's a war on!' By 3 July Pamela's recent period of inactivity during wartime was clearly troubling her conscience: 'Pop has to go to London tomorrow to the House of Commons to report on an agricultural debate. I'm ashamed of myself not having really done a thing. I do hope I'll soon get to Tower House.' She did not have much longer to wait, however, because on Sunday 7 July her diary reads: 'Went to the hospital & matron said she'd take me on but not my hair sort of thing – anyway I've got to put it back. Ha!' By this time Pamela had painstakingly grown her hair into the then fashionable 'page-boy bob', and was clearly disappointed at having to hide it under a nurse's cap. Presumably her hair passed muster on the following day, when she finally reported for duty at Tower House. But once again her diary reveals the continuing feelings of unreality and confusion that both she and others around her were experiencing: 'It's all a bit phoney, gosh what a war. Two new officers are billeted on us. People poked hither and thither & I don't believe anyone knows what they are doing – at least I know I don't.'

The diary entry for the next day includes a prescient remark by Arthur Street: 'Pa thinks the war'll go on for years. It's just too depressing to think about …' Evidently Arthur Street was not alone in this opinion, for on 15 July Pamela writes: 'The invasion hasn't happened yet and we're all on tenderhooks [*sic*]. Sort of bomb and bomb back and nothing else. Everyone says it will be a long war …' On a happier note, Pamela records on 6 August: 'Pa has just finished a bumper harvest. The wheat we rolled turned out marvellous.'

One thing that would have pleased Arthur Street, and his fellow farmers, was that during the summer of 1940 the weather seems to have been on their side. The results of this early harvest must have been a fitting reward for British farmers, who had been encouraged, and indeed in some cases compelled by local War Agricultural Committees, to plough up their pastures for cereal production.

Pamela's diary shows that she spent much of her time off duty in bed recuperating, often pondering on whether she had chosen the right wartime occupation. On 16 July she writes: 'Spent my second day in bed – Read 'I was Hitler's Maid' which was absolutely fantastic and almost unbelievable … I can't help it but I keep wishing I'd ATTED* if this war is going on. It's awful to recriminate like this but sometimes I hate nursing like poison.'

Unfortunately for Pamela, she soon had to buckle down to her nursing duties even more seriously. Instead of living with her parents in Wilton, some 3 miles away from the hospital, she was billeted on the Bishop of Sherborne in Crane Street, just outside the confines of the Cathedral Close in Salisbury. However terrified Pamela may have been of the Matron of Tower House, the Hon. Gertrude Best, the latter was evidently an astute and humane commander of her particular military team who took a personal interest in the staff under her command. On becoming aware of the sheltered upbringing of her latest recruit, she appears to have identified a particularly appropriate billet. Her choice was a sound one, because Pamela quickly became fond of her new hosts, describing Bishop Rodgers and his wife in her diary as 'frightfully sweet'. Her diary reveals that on 7 August she went to a party, 'and the Bishop waited up for me!' Later in life Pamela elaborated on this incident:

I had promised to be back by 10.30 and was there on the dot – he was too nice a man to let down and I knew how worried he and his wife were about the responsibility of a young nurse in their home. They usually locked up and went to bed at 9 p.m. As I returned to the fold, there he was standing in the hall wearing full regalia, including gaiters, beaming with pleasure at my safe and prompt return and proffering a tray on which there was a glass and a thermos of hot milk, explaining that his wife had already retired. Not the sort of thing the young of today would credit!

Pamela's stay with Bishop Rodgers and his wife proved relatively short-lived. On 19 August her diary reads: 'Matron said I was to go on night duty tonight. Had the morning off to part from the Rodgers with great reluctance. Horrid having to come up to the Home.' Many years later she expanded on this entry, explaining the reasons for her change of lodging:

Nurses on night duty all had to live in quarters within the hospital grounds, where a vigilant sister snooped round to see we were in bed by 11 a.m. each day. I found difficulty in sleeping. It was always light and the partitioned room had two cousins who made an awful racket and played *Just One of Those Things* on a gramophone.

Pamela's diary entries for the next couple of weeks are of necessity rather sketchy and scrappy given the change in her routine, but give a glimpse of how she was

---

* Gone into the ATS, the Auxiliary Territorial Service, forerunner of the British Women's Royal Army Corps.

feeling during her period of night duty: 'Sleep and work, work and sleep. Ack-acking* this morning along the road. Fantastic. Where are we? – what will happen? … Some day will everything come right? Will there be a future before it's too late?' A welcome relief came towards the end of August when Pamela was unexpectedly given a few days off duty. During this time Arthur Street took her to London for a meeting with a company interested in making a film of his second book, *Strawberry Roan*. Just how much this treat was appreciated can be judged from Pamela's enthusiastic entry for the day in question: '*August 30th* Went to London. Absolute heaven because I haven't been outside a 5 mile area for ages … Went to Blackheath to the film company people. Great fun. Had 3 air raid sirens – got home safely at 8. Gorgeous drive. Defences everywhere. All phoney.'

On the following day, a Saturday, another significant event in Pamela's life took place, though she could not have realised it at the time. Her diary records that she went to a dance at the very last minute. On the Sunday afterwards she states: 'Two people from Larkhill, David McCormick & Dick Bramley, came to supper. They were at the dance & rather fun. They say too that the army deprives you of all sort of confidence – same sort of feeling I have. Horrid.' This, then, was the weekend during which Pamela first met her future husband David, and it seems that they found they had things in common, even if – at least on Pamela's side – it was not exactly love at first sight. A passage in Pamela's later memoir explains the context in which she and David met:

At that time there were a number of well-meaning matrons in the district who felt that their particular contribution to the war effort was to entertain the troops by getting them introduced to suitable girls. They were known as 'mesdames', although I'm not sure I then knew the full meaning of the word. I met my future husband in a *Paul Jones* at the White Hart Hotel in Salisbury just after the Battle of Britain. I don't know who Paul Jones was, but he had a lot to answer for …

Any thoughts of romance on Pamela's part would have been almost immediately off the menu, however, as she had to return to work at the hospital the very next day. Evidently it was not an easy week. Her diary entry for Tuesday 7 September finds her letting off steam:

If S [one of the Sisters] has to suffer my cooking till the war is over she'd kill me. It's awful awful awful – everything I do is wrong. I feel put upon and a fool & everything else & I've lost all the self-respect I ever had … What a life! Oh!! Oh!! Oh!!

---

* Use of anti-aircraft guns.

At the end of the week a far greater worry was about to come. Outside Pamela's narrow world of the hospital, the Battle of Britain was nearing its climax. On Saturday 7 September Arthur Street drove up to stay in London in order to deliver a BBC broadcast the following morning. Pamela's diary for Sunday 8 September reads:

> London had the most frightful air raid last night. Came home [from the hospital] in the morning because I knew Mummy would be terribly worried. Daddy got through all right and arrived 11.30 thank goodness. It's awful to think about …

In his book about the Home Guard, *From Dusk Till Dawn*, Arthur gives a vivid account of this experience, which is worth quoting almost in its entirety:

> Without warning, during the first week-end of September 1940, came the threat of invasion. On that Saturday afternoon, evening and all night the Luftwaffe carried out its first real blitz on London. The enemy bombed that city almost continuously from 3 p.m. until about 3 a.m. Here I do not speak from hearsay, as I was sleeping at my club in order to keep a broadcasting engagement timed for 8.30 on Sunday morning.
>
> Not having enough military knowledge to know what was happening, I played bridge until the first 'All Clear' at about seven o'clock. Then, finding that a friend and fellow member, Commander Kenneth Edwards, R.N., agreed with me that September spelt oysters, we set out to find some. As we crossed Piccadilly the siren sounded again, but we both agreed that as this might well be our last chance of oysters, the thing to do was to walk on to Bentley's. There my companion found an old shipmate behind the bar who said that in spite of the Luftwaffe he would open oysters as long as we would pay for them, so we did our best, and a good best it was. We then went our several ways.
>
> Later on when I was back at the club the blitz began in earnest, and continued throughout that long summer night. We soon decided that a card-room three stories up was not the best place under the circumstances, and retired to the basement to continue the game. After a while bridge did not seem to be so interesting as usual, so every now and again some of us went outside to watch. We heard the crack of ack-ack guns and the heavy crump of enemy bombs. The attack seemed to be mainly along the river, and soon we were to see a glow in the sky as though the whole of the east of London was on fire. Somewhere about two o'clock there was a lull, and one or two of us crept along the street with an idea of getting some bacon and eggs at a Corner House. But before we had gone fifty yards a bomb dropped somewhere on the other side of the river, but close enough to make us hesitate; whereupon a constable advised us that bacon and eggs might be dearly bought. So we retired to the club basement, and gave both the Luftwaffe and the bridge-table best for a while.

All that may sound silly, callous and impossible, but I am telling it just as it happened. Also the time factor must be considered. At that date no one had experienced night bombing and therefore we did not realize what was happening. At that date one could motor up to London occasionally, and perhaps enjoy some oysters.

Anyway, that was my end of it, and I drove away from Langham Place at nine o'clock next morning in complete ignorance of what had happened in the countryside. Once out of London I was stopped by regular soldiers or Home Guards at every bend in the road until I arrived at Salisbury. This could not be merely a local exercise, so just west of Staines I enquired the reason from a regular sergeant. 'Don't rightly know,' he said. 'But there's one hell of a flap on, and we've been stood to all night. You'd best go careful.'

Arthus Street goes on to talk about church bells ringing out somewhere in southern England, which raised the alarm 'from London to Bristol and beyond'.* He himself was bitterly disappointed in having missed out on the action:

… And I, an enthusiastic Home Guard, had missed this first real job of work, simply because I had been broadcasting. Somehow that hurt.

London was at the time the prime target. Out of the immediate firing line, however, Wiltshire country-folk could still occasionally forget about the war, as Pamela's entry for the following day illustrates: 'Pop has sent me a cheque for £10 – lovely – very nice of him seeing that I have been actually paid £5 6s 11d. Home tomorrow!' Pamela eagerly awaited her spells of leave from the hospital, and her relief to be home at Ditchampton Farm is evident from the next day's entry: 'Home, sleep & food!!! Thank heaven. Lovely. Bought a frock and some shoes.'

Pamela had long since metamorphosed from a lanky teenager with acne into a striking, tall, slender young woman with fashionably coiffed dark hair and large hazel eyes set beneath winged eyebrows. Arthur Street's present to his daughter was clearly made to help her look her best for an event that was to take place the following day. By now Pamela and David McCormick were beginning to meet on occasions when both were off duty. Pamela's parents evidently encouraged the friendship, doing their best to provide hospitality for David and his fellow officer cadets back at Ditchampton Farm. In her later memoir Pamela wrote:

Throughout that winter, this particular Officer/Cadet and I saw quite a lot of each other whenever he could get down from Salisbury Plain. He would take me out to dinner or the pictures; while my parents, having enlarged Ditchampton Farm just

---

* The government had banned the normal use of church bells; instead they were only to be rung to warn British citizens of imminent invasion.

before the war and put down a parquet floor in the drawing-room and installed a radiogram, would give little tea-dances, a form of entertainment much in vogue at that time. I would bring half a dozen nurses from the hospital and my *Paul Jones* pick-up would bring half a dozen cadets, with whom he shared quarters near Larkhill.

The first of these occasions took place on 15 September, a Sunday, as Pamela records: '[various girl friends], David, Dick, Luke etc etc came to tea. We danced. Played foolish games. Went terribly well. Di & I went out to dinner with them. I was so tired I couldn't speak but great fun.' The following day, however, such light relief from war work was over, with Pamela returning to the hospital: 'Came back to school, school, school, depressed as the dickens, but I hope it will wear off. Somehow I can't think at all these days & I'm getting slower on the uptake than ever …'

On the next day, 17 September, Pamela was once more worrying about her father's safety: 'Pop may have to go to London again this week. They're still at it. Only 80 miles away and yet it seems thousands – so peaceful down here. Everyone seems to think invasion is coming but somehow I can't conceive it …' This last sentiment seems to have been shared by Pamela's nursing colleagues, as Pamela explained in her later memoir:

> Wrapped up as I was with … the day to day affairs of the Emergency Hospital on the outskirts of Salisbury … I never realised until afterwards the miracle that was taking place in the skies over the south-eastern corner of England and the seas which lapped its shores. I think we local VADs simply went about our duties, vaguely expecting Hitler to 'come on over'.

Pamela was by now finding her periods of night duty at the hospital increasingly arduous, as her diary entries for 19 and 21 September reveal. Sleep in the daytime was a near impossibility: 'Bed, bed, bed, but never any proper sleep. What a life … and it's going to be a long war … had my frightful paralysed fit again last night of not waking up.' This last rather curious entry is explained by a clearly autobiographical passage in Pamela's later novel *Many Waters*, in which the young heroine, Emily Mason, is also on night duty at a military hospital:

> She was feeling particularly weary that morning for, during the night, she had had another of her 'attacks'. They had been happening quite frequently lately and she had been given to understand that they were what was known as 'night nurses' paralysis'. They occurred at the end of the two hours' rest period, which all V.A.D.s were allowed to take, either between eleven p.m. and one a.m. or between one and three. At these times, owing to her lack of sleep during the day, she would disappear gratefully into some quiet part of the long makeshift hut – usually the linen cupboard – where she would fall into a kind of stupor.

When her allotted hours were up, one or other of the nurses would come along to wake her but, although she could hear a voice urging her into action, it took several minutes for her to regain full consciousness. Meanwhile she was aware of her limbs thrashing about frantically, waiting for her mind to get the upper hand over her body. It was a horrible experience and she had begun to dread it. Sometimes she wondered whether she was altogether cut out for nursing

By her own admission in her memoir written many decades later, Pamela was indeed probably not cut out for nursing. Explaining the reasons from a more mature perspective she wrote:

I was no good at it. I worried. Somewhere along the line I had absorbed worry … An over-active conscience is a terrible handicap. It shackles you. One is like a dog with a tin can tied to its tail … A conscience obliges you to do what you think is right and makes you miserable if you don't. Coupled with an over-active imagination, it is lethal. If you take up nursing, as I did, you go back to your billet tired out, wondering whether you gave Corporal Jones the right dose or whether Private Smith will have a relapse because you let him sneak an egg for breakfast when he was on M & B.*

There are numerous instances of this type of worry in Pamela's diary during her period of nursing. For example, on 19 October she wrote:

Kid's tonsils out. I just can't take responsibility. I'm hopeless – oh dear. I wonder if I'll ever be any good. A man with a hernia wanted lifting and I think I hurt him and I'm terrified he might have bust his stitches. It's awful being left alone. Sometimes I just want to go and bury my head somewhere and forget everything. I don't think I was ever the person who used to hunt and all that. Worrying's hell. The jerrys are over whilst writing this – you can hear the wretches but sister's got Jack Warner on the wireless. It's all so fantastic somehow. One long nightmare.

Pamela had already mentioned earlier in her diary how much the Sisters frightened her. One particular Sister was evidently her *bête noire*: 'I can't help it – I just can't work with Sister S … We just get on each other's nerves & she obviously hates me …' Decades later Pamela was to get her own back on this particular Sister, albeit in fictional form. In her novel *Many Waters*, the heroine Emily Mason, a young VAD nurse, has been asked to 'special' a certain Corporal Long, who was due to undergo a lumbar puncture. This meant that Emily had to put screens round his

---

* Sulphapyridine, an early type of antibiotic known as 'M&B' after the pharmaceutical company that produced it, May and Baker.

bed and give him one-to-one nursing care both before and after the surgical procedure. The incident that followed was almost certainly based on personal experience:

> Time hung heavily for both of them for, until there was a report on the spinal
> fluid which had been taken, she was still unable to join in the customary bustling
> activity of the ward. In one way Emily was relieved, as she was suffering from a
> particularly heavy period and would have liked nothing better than to sit down.
> Once, for a few moments, she perched on the end of Corporal Long's bed, doing
> her best to cheer him up with a little light-hearted conversation. Unfortunately,
> it was exactly at this juncture that Sister Matthews suddenly put her head over
> the top of the screen.
>
> Never before, could Emily recall having been the target for such wrath.
>
> '*Nurse Mason!*' Sister Matthews' voice seemed to reverberate round the entire
> ward. 'What *do* you think you're doing?'
>
> Emily was on her feet now, trembling. 'I ... I'm sorry, Sister.'
>
> 'Sorry is not enough for such a total breach of discipline. Come to my office
> at once.'
>
> There, Emily was subjected to a tirade which lasted twenty minutes. The
> woman seemed to be almost crazed with anger. Two splashes of heightened
> colour appeared on each cheek-bone. Her small dark eyes glittered. She charged
> Emily with having brought disgrace on the whole nursing profession, of being
> guilty of indecent behaviour, of deception and falling down on her trust.

Pamela's novel goes on to recount how this conversation was overheard by the
entire ward, staff and patients alike, and how afterwards when Emily returned,
fighting back tears, many a sympathetic glance was cast her way. The episode
concludes that: 'Middle-aged, unmarried and power-conscious, they [the Sisters]
one and all possessed the diabolical ability to terrify almost every young nurse who
came under their authority.'

Matters were coming to a head. It is no great surprise to read in Pamela's diary
for 18 October: 'Matron sent for me. Went to the doctors ... Something about rest.'
On 21 October, after the Matron at Tower House had received Pamela's medical
report from the doctor, she records: 'Miss Best rang up. She won't have me back
because of all this business until Dr A says I'm all right. It is a curse. I'm awfully
cross – there's nothing really the matter with me. Oh dear. It's exactly what they'd
expect of me ...'

Pamela was not to know how long she would remain on sick leave; in the event
she did not return to Tower House until the beginning of 1941. In the interim her
conscience gave her little peace; unable to pull her weight in the war effort, she also
felt guilty that she was living in a place of such comparative safety, as her entry for
23 October illustrates: 'Under orders stayed in bed nearly all the day ... Heather E

went to London yesterday and says it's awful … It's terribly sad but somehow one just doesn't realise it enough … Down here we just worry about how many silk stockings we've got …'

Being back at home rather than in the confines of the hospital enabled Pamela to keep a closer eye on the progress of the war. By now Hitler, having failed to defeat the RAF in time for the intended invasion of England, had instead turned his attention eastwards towards an increasingly belligerent Russia. The war was at this stage being fought on many fronts, including the North African desert – of vital strategic importance for the dominance of the Mediterranean. Snippets of war news are now regularly recorded in Pamela's diary:

October 29th … Greece has now been invaded by the Italians and the whole boiling over there … oh it's a funny world we're making history in …

October 30th … The Balkans are getting it now and all the Ozzies are over there …

November 2nd … Greece is fighting hard & we're helping them now. It'll be so awful if it turns out like all the rest …

This last diary entry continues with a rare flash of personal good news: 'The Field has accepted Gone Away [the poem Pamela had written almost a year earlier about the demise of hunting at the onset of the war]. Terrific after all this time.'

One beneficial result of Pamela's weeks of sick leave was that she was now free to meet David when he was able to get away from Larkhill. Pamela kept all of David's wartime letters, both those written before and after he was posted abroad. The early ones – dating from September 1940 – are short, formal notes about arrangements to meet, addressing her as 'Dear' or 'My dear Pamela' and ending 'yours ever', but they become increasingly affectionate in tone as the months go by. Because of the unpredictability of their respective periods of leave (Pamela's in particular were subject to alteration at the last moment), they were constantly frustrated in their attempts to get together. For example, as early as 24 September Pamela wrote:

They changed my day suddenly – just like that to tomorrow – I took my courage in both hands & asked Matron if I needn't. Then when I had it doesn't really matter about David and lunch and all those sort of things – not when the world's going up in smoke. Yesterday 83 children were drowned evacuating to America.* It's difficult to get things in proportion but you've got to go out I s'pose.

---

* This was the notorious sinking of the *City of Benares* (which actually took place on 17 September but was only reported on 23 September), which put an end to CORB (Children's Overseas Reception Board), a government-sponsored organisation for the evacuation of British children to the Dominions.

Whilst Pamela's period of sick leave made it easier for her to accommodate David's spells off duty, during the latter part of 1940 David was finding it increasingly difficult to take time off owing to pressure of work. His letters to his parents during his period of training at Larkhill provide many insights into the life he now found himself leading.

It appears that at the beginning, in late August–early September, the young officer cadets had a relatively easy time and made the most of their leisure hours. On 21 September David wrote to his parents: 'I have been to Salisbury nearly every day last week & am rather tired after a dance last night. If we don't have a reasonably good time here it is not our fault. We certainly try hard enough.' Matters were soon to change. The following week David told his parents: 'Now unfortunately the time of reckoning fast approaches, exams brew in the close future, & I find myself with hours of work to catch up. It is just as well as I have used up all September's petrol coupons & half October's [David had by then acquired a car, a small Morris].' In the same letter he complains that it was 'getting unpleasantly cold here' and in a postscript to his next letter, dated 30 September, he asks whether there might be an old eiderdown that they could spare. In due course the eiderdown arrived, and on 13 October he wrote: 'My eiderdown has got here … and makes a great difference. Everyone is very jealous of it but think me very bold to have it here.'

As regards his actual training, the following week's letter home paints this rather gloomy picture:

> We have a very depressing week ahead. We are platoon on duty which means that we have to get up at 5 every day & stand about for an hour or two for the next seven days. We also have to do this in the evening & are confined to barracks. Not only that, but we have our first gunnery exam at the end of the week & another exam … I spent most of the week swotting up the guts of cars for an exam we had on Friday. We seem to be always having exams …

David was the only member of his platoon to pass all his exams on first sitting, and wrote of his disappointment when his friends were put down a course or more and made to do the previous month's work again. Finally he told his parents that he would be 'passing out' around Christmas time, and had ordered his uniform, 'which is apt to lull one into a false sense of security'.

Despite the restrictions of David's training course (23 Course, 122 OCTR Larkhill), he and Pamela still managed to meet at some stage almost every week. On 26 October, by now on sick leave but evidently sufficiently rested, Pamela wrote:

> Went to Bath with David, John Ashlee, Simon Fleming. Great fun. We went to the flics and dinner & then met a party for dancing at the Assembly Rooms – it

was terrific and I <u>did</u> enjoy it only I wish I hadn't been the only girl except for the dance. Mummy was v. worried because of night driving.

However a month or so later Pamela's diary reveals that she was having some doubts about the burgeoning relationship: 'David & I went to the flics and there was a siren and a lot of bombs during the night. He is very nice but terribly spoilt – even more than Robin* was.' Similarly on 20 November she wrote: 'David came to dinner. There was an air-raid s[iren]. and we went to the flics. He is very spoilt – so am I. We don't get anywhere and he wastes money.'

Pamela's comment about David being 'spoilt' is perhaps not altogether surprising, since he came from a rather different background to her own. His parents lived in a large house in Weybridge. His father Edward – a scion of the wealthy American McCormick International Harvester family – had been sent over from Chicago, together with his two brothers, to be educated at Eton. Whilst there, he befriended Francis Samuelson, the son of a Yorkshire baronet, who invited him back to his family home, Breckenbrough Hall near Thirsk in Yorkshire, where evidently a romance between Edward and Francis's sister Phyllis was kindled. After her marriage, the strong-minded Phyllis had no intention of returning to the USA with her new husband, so, having lived for a while in London, she and Edward eventually set up home on St George's Hill, Weybridge. Quite apart from the obvious attractions of its thriving social life, centred round its tennis and golf clubs (Edward and Phyllis were keen players of both sports), this choice of location pandered to Edward's passion for early motorcars and aviation; the now legendary Brooklands motor-racing circuit and aerodrome were only a few miles away (and indeed this was where David had learnt to drive a few years earlier). A major centre of military aircraft production was also located nearby in the form of the Brooklands Vickers and Hawker factories; once the Blitz began, it became an obvious target. The McCormicks' home, Shaws, was therefore in the direct firing line, and did indeed sustain some minor bomb damage; this was why, at this stage of the war, Edward and Phyllis decided it would be prudent for them to decamp to the latter's family home in Yorkshire for the duration.

★ ★ ★

Whilst his daughter was absorbed by her problems with wartime work and her new admirer, Arthur Street was as occupied as ever with farming, writing and broadcasting. In addition he was heavily involved in his own war work, frequently being asked to lecture to the troops; he continued to take his Home Guard duties very

---

* Robin Sayer, re-named 'Claude Shillito', the 'wanton son from Chelsea', in Pamela's poem *Wessex Wins*, quoted in Chapter 2, pp. 30–1.

seriously, having now been promoted to platoon commander. His book *Hitler's Whistle*, published in 1943, consists largely of extracts from articles in *Farmers' Weekly*, *The Listener* and *Chamber's Magazine*. Together they form a chronological narrative of how the war was affecting the countryside. It appears that the morale of the Wiltshire country folk remained as upbeat as ever. On 20 October 1940 Arthur reported a conversation between two old farmhands – both members of the Home Guard – as follows:

> In between gathering mushrooms, snaring rabbits, listening to lectures on the art of war, and doing their regular observation duty at dusk and dawn, the rural members of the Home Guard keep their weather eyes open for Jerry during their farm work. At least the two in this story did.
>
> They were working in a field close to the hill buildings, with aeroplanes buzzing overhead every few minutes. Suddenly a different engine noise caused one of them to look up.
>
> 'Tom, look at 'ee. 'Ee doan' zim exactly,' he said to his companion.
>
> 'Thee bist right, Bill. Thic be a Jerry,' came the reply.
>
> 'Zo 'tis, Tom. Look at yer, thee bist the best zhot. Thee get the gun, I'll get me prong.'
>
> What chance has Hitler against a spirit like that?

A few pages on, Arthur describes the uneasy alliance between the farming community and the soldiery in the use of farmland for training exercises, advocating a policy of consideration and tolerance on both sides. The following paragraph illustrates the problem:

> Neither renting nor owning land gives a man full dominion over it during total war. As one old farmer put it to me the other day, 'You can't walk across your own fields without asking permission from the soldiers. When they first came, they asked for my identity card about three times a day. Now they know me, they don't bother, but call me Dad instead.' Which of course, is much more pleasant for everybody concerned.

Military imagery was beginning to creep into Arthur's prose. In the following example, he uses it both deliberately and lyrically:

> Over and around the ploughman's head wheel the November birds. Aircraft of all types, occasionally some which were made in Germany. Peewits by the hundreds, twisting and twirling in concerted formation against a watery sun. Black battalions of rooks, flying steadily and purposefully in search of newly-sown wheat fields. Platoons of white and grey seagulls alternately hovering and settling just in

front and just behind the plough. Whole armies of starlings marching drunkenly but importantly over the newly turned furrows in search of worms and grubs; and a few wary wood pigeons, that disappear swiftly, the moment the plough is stopped for some needed adjustment. All are typical November companions of the ploughman, save those alien mechanical birds from overseas.

By now cities other than London were also experiencing the full force of the Blitz, as Pamela recorded:

November 15th There's been a terribly bad raid on Coventry. Bombed all night.

November 24th All the Southampton people are here because of terrible air-raid. Unregisterable.

November 25th Couldn't go to Wales because Bristol has been bombed [Pamela had earlier received an invitation from a friend to stay at her home near Newport]. The world is rushing down the hill like the Gadarine [*sic*] swine and we're all going with it and no one can think straight … Mummy is very tired and everyone is on edge …

December 3rd Southampton from all reports is nearly flat. It's just awful and you can't realise it's so close and here we are just carrying on and thinking of going to dances …

Vera Street had always been a keen gardener. On 16 December the distaff side of the Street family evidently staged a minor rebellion against the wartime restrictions, albeit with pangs of conscience, as Pamela's diary reports: 'Mummy and I were awfully naughty. Took the car and went to Winchester because Mummy wanted some plants. It seemed a very unwarlike sort of thing to do and all very wrong.' The following day Pamela finally received the all clear to return to work, albeit on a part-time basis: 'Saw Matron and am going back for 3 days a week – something of nothing.'

Pamela did not return to the hospital immediately, however. Christmas was now approaching. Pamela's diary records that on 19 December David called with a present for the Streets. Pamela had evidently got over her previous misgivings about him, for her diary entry paints him in a far more favourable light:

David came. I have a most awful cold but he was terribly sweet and has got his commission and is going to Egypt … He brought us a bottle of sherry for being so kind to him which I think was frightfully nice of him. He has got ideas about things but I'm afraid he will become just a memory like the others …

A bottle of sherry might not sound particularly generous by modern standards, but at the time alcohol was in short supply – hence the fashion for tea-dances – and very expensive. War notwithstanding, in those days Christmas presents were much more modest than in today's consumer-driven society, and seldom purchased until a day or so beforehand. Pamela's diary for Christmas Eve 1940 illustrates how wartime privations made even such customary small luxuries extremely difficult to come by: 'Tried to do everything one should on Christmas Eve but shopping is terrible now and there are heaps of things you just can't get. Sweets and chocolates are a rarity.'

Pamela's diary for the remainder of the Christmas period chronicles a succession of family gatherings. On 29 December she records that 'Pop went into the Guildhall & entertained the troops'. Then on 29 December her diary finds her experiencing a conflict of loyalties:

> David rang from Yorkshire [he had gone to spend Christmas with his parents at his grandfather's home Breckenbrough Hall] – wanted me to go to London to the Grosvenor & celebrate New Year's Eve with him. Well. I couldn't. Mummy was quite decided. I suppose it was rather a tall order what with the Blitz and inappropriate etc., but oh Lord if it wasn't for a war …

To make matters worse, the following day she records collecting a certificate from the doctor enabling her to return to work. Her final diary entry for 1940 reveals her concerns at having to miss a potential landmark moment in her life – a last chance to meet David prior to his embarkation for Egypt, possibly receiving a proposal of marriage – because her conscience obliged her to report back for wartime duty:

> *December 31st* It's over – the year – I wonder where we'll all be next year this time. Gosh what a lot has happened in one sense. Somehow it seems to go on round you & it's all so extraordinary you don't take it in. Well I've sent my cert to Matron and David will come & I shan't be here when I might have been. I don't know what's the matter with me – in one way I'd give a lot to be and yet I just went and did it. I don't know. I think I'm going crackers but whenever anything nearly happens it doesn't – never. I've been terribly lucky but always just miss it – everything – well this time I had it in my own hands …

Whilst his daughter's final written record for 1940 was full of intensely personal concerns, Arthur Street's last published article for that year found him once again assuming his role as one of the main champions of rural Britain. At the end of this article, dated 30 December 1940 and reproduced in *Hitler's Whistle*, Arthur muses on how comparatively unchanged the countryside continued to be despite the war, and how successful it had been in fulfilling its wartime obligations:

Only those who really belong to the countryside know just how much of it has been on active service ever since the war began. Amongst a hundred-and-one things that the countryside was asked to provide were four main essentials – a safe refuge for women and children from bombed cities, greatly increased food production as a safeguard against famine, accommodation for a huge army in training, and a useful local defence force in every village. Being a farmer I naturally consider number two to be the most important; but, even so, I know that all four were necessary, and what is more that all four have been accomplished …

The whole world is mad, and so the whole countryside is at war. But when daybreak strips off the black eiderdown of night from the countryside the rural scene is the same as of old. The skylark sings on high, the dew is on the grass, the morning mists are hung out to dry, and only basin-like bomb craters here and there in the fields and the training aeroplanes above them show that the countryside is at war. The land remains, unaltered.

Another year had ended. But it was now clear to Arthur Street, and indeed most of the British population, that this was to be a long war.

Five

A Protracted Parting
(January–May 1941)

Once David was posted to Weston-super-Mare in early January 1941, Pamela had no idea whether or not she would see him again before he left for Egypt. This uncertainty should perhaps be put into context. By this stage of the war, the campaign in North Africa had assumed a vital strategic importance. In order to defend their interests and launch counter attacks on Axis-held territory in the Mediterranean, the British and Allied forces needed to establish a secure presence in North Africa, particularly along its coast. Since the fall of France, the pro-Axis Italian colonies of Libya, Eritrea and Abyssinia (now Ethiopia) were no longer threatened by the French colonies of Algeria and Tunisia to their left, and could instead turn all their military attention to their right towards Egypt. A former British protectorate, Egypt had a treaty with Britain whereby in the event of a threat to the Suez Canal (a vital link for Britain with India and its colonies in the Far East), it would allow British and Allied troops to be stationed on its soil. The Canal was now an essential lifeline for Allied troops and supply vessels, which to reach base depot could not risk sailing through the Nazi-infested waters of the Mediterranean, but instead had to sail the long way round the South African Cape, up the east coast of Africa to the Suez Canal. This was the voyage that David McCormick's regiment was preparing to undertake.

The military situation in northern Africa was constantly changing, however, and by early 1941, before Rommel and his forces arrived on the scene, the Allies had achieved some notable successes. Back in the summer of 1940, the Italian forces in North Africa under the command of Marshal Rodolfo Graziani had little appetite for conflict and were playing a waiting game, fully expecting Britain – like the rest of Western Europe – to fall to the Germans, in which case there would be no need for military action. But as the summer progressed and Britain held firm, Mussolini lost patience with Graziani and ordered him to invade Egypt. On 13 September – when the London Blitz was at its height – Graziani launched a cautious invasion with a few limited initial successes; but instead of pressing home their temporary advantage, the Italians contented themselves with building a series of forts into which they dug themselves for the duration. Despite being vastly outnumbered, the Allied forces launched 'Operation Compass', a highly successful counter-attack that by the end of January 1941 had not only routed the Italian forces, taking huge numbers of prisoners in the process, but had also taken the strategically important sea ports of Bardia and Tobruk and had even chased the Italians back over the border deep into Cyrenaica, the easternmost province of Libya. As a result of these successes, back in England the High Command must have been weighing up the pros and cons of sending yet more newly trained troops to the African desert, or whether to save them to spearhead a British offensive on the continent of Europe.

David's letters from Weston-super-Mare during this period both to Pamela and his parents reflect this uncertainty. On 7 January David wrote to his parents: 'I ... don't think I shall move again until we sail, which may be around the 18th though no one knows of course. Perhaps now Bardia has fallen we won't go at all ...' However in his next letter to his parents he wrote: 'I hear now that we aren't going until the middle of Feb & I am thinking that we probably won't go then either, or if we do it will be to invade France & Germany. It looks as if I am not going to miss much cold weather ...' Then on 25 January David wrote to Pamela: 'As you see I am not in Egypt yet – as a matter of fact I don't think I am going for a long time though we are still at 24 hours notice & we have got all our tropical kit – & you ought to see McCormick of the river in his shorts & topee; it is a fine sight ...'

★ ★ ★

Pamela's diaries and other writings leave no doubt that her and David's courtship was extremely chaste, as indeed were all her earlier youthful romantic relationships. Kissing was permitted, but nothing more. In her later unpublished autobiography Pamela explained, for the benefit of both current and future generations to whom such behaviour might seem incomprehensible, the sexual mores of the time:

There was no pill and the fear of pregnancy kept many a young woman on the straight and narrow, including myself. *Of course* there were illegitimate births in every stratum of society, girls who had 'fallen', or were described as 'having to get married'. *Of course* there was adultery and mistresses from royalty downwards; but there was never, in my little world, any overt reference to sex and I don't think I knew what homosexuality was. But I was aware that there *were* other sophisticated young women – mostly from the metropolis – who were probably clued up in more ways than one. They were deemed 'fast' and got away with it. We slower ignorant country types sometimes wondered 'fast at what?'

Being in the latter category, along with countless other contemporaries, we so-called 'good' girls simply dolled ourselves up hoping to look as attractive as possible to the hordes of servicemen who swarmed all over South Wiltshire. I don't think we thought much about sex, or even wanted it. In fact, one of my best friends said that she hoped her husband would leave *that* out, at least until after the honeymoon. It was love we were after, with a capital L. Marriage was the goal and though we regretted that so many nice young men didn't come across with the offer, we would no more have dreamt of providing them with what they probably really wanted, than we would have thought of giving the terrifying matron of the emergency hospital a piece of our mind.

In Pamela's case, her misgivings about the sexual act were probably even more extreme than usual. In her novel *Many Waters*, there is a passage in which the heroine Emily Mason is anticipating this side of her future marriage to her childhood sweetheart:

> But there was something else: something deeper, something which she found far more difficult to think about calmly and logically, a problem which was impossible to share with anyone … It was simply that she did not think she could face the physical side of marriage. The whole idea of it upset her. She was still unsure as to what exactly happened, but she had never forgotten the strange isolated incidents as a small child, when she had overheard those bewildering, frightening sounds coming from her parents' bedroom: the breathless energetic tussle which seemed to be going on, the creaking of bedsprings, the muffled laughter, her father's repeated whispers of 'darling', and then, finally, most horrendous of all, her mother's low moaning. It was something etched on her memory, vivid, indelible, which, however hard she tried, would not go away …

Despite this, by the turn of the year Pamela was still keen to continue her relationship with David McCormick. David had come back to Larkhill for one last course before being posted to Weston-super-Mare to await embarkation for Egypt, and Pamela was about to return to work at the emergency hospital. Her diary reveals her constant preoccupation with how they could co-ordinate their periods of leave. On 1 January 1941 Pamela wrote: 'Here starts the fifth year [of her five-year diary]. Waited for Matron & David to ring up. Still waiting. I don't think we will see each other somehow. Life is odd. Matron's got the M.B.E …' The following day's entry was rather more positive: 'Well Matron wrote & I'm probably going in on Sunday if not before. I rang David & he came and was frightfully sweet and all that and looked marvellous in his uniform …'

The pair managed to meet again on 4 January:

> Mummy sent in to say David had rung up and wants me out tonight. Went off in the afternoon after hectic rush. Convoy of 50 and 15 in our ward! Frightful time

meeting David because we missed each other. In the end met … he was really very sweet and loves me a little but probably just another fancy – anyway he'll soon be in Egypt.

David's letters to his parents and Pamela give a taste of what life was like with his new regiment, the 285/72nd Field Regiment RA. This was a north country regiment in the Tees & Tyneside division, and despite David's comment to his parents in his first letter from Weston-super-Mare that 'I am gradually getting used to my regiment', later letters show that his efforts to fit in with his new colleagues were met with a certain resistance. On 14 February he wrote:

There is a lot of ill feeling between the old officers & the new O.C.T.U. ones here. The old ones all come from Newcastle & knew each other before the war, & were in the French show together & naturally resent southerners & newcomers in their midst & with few exceptions do not extend the welcoming helping hand.

Elsewhere in the same letter, however, written when David was in bed recovering from a bout of flu (to pile on the nation's misery, there was a flu epidemic throughout Britain during this period), he commented: 'A lot of officers have been in to see me while in bed which is a good sign.'

To begin with David seems to have had comparatively little to do, as he and his new companions were expecting to leave at any moment, and were allowed generous spells off duty. In his first letter to his parents from Weston-super-Mare, David stated: 'There seems nothing for me to do except watch chaps cleaning guns …' Pamela would not have been amused by the following extract from David's next letter to his parents: 'I have been boozing in the pubs & picking up rather low type girls & rushing round with them. One was a girl who was professionally cut in half every evening by a wonderful wizard in the B.B.C.!'

Once it became clear that David's regiment would not be leaving imminently, training exercises and other duties became the order of the day. On 12 January David wrote to his parents:

I have got a section of 20 men to look after & am responsible for two gun tractors, two guns & four ammunition limbers. I do not know the men at all well yet as they are always away for some reason or other … My first lecture was on V.D. which was sprung on me ten minutes before I had to give it. It went down very well!

David also recounts this last episode in a letter to Pamela, but adds: 'I wouldn't mention it if you weren't a nurse. If you don't know what it is don't ask your parents for heaven's sake!!'

The winter of 1940–41 was an exceptionally cold one, adding to David's miseries on regimental training schemes. On 13 February he wrote to Pamela:

I have been doing an awful thing the last 3 weeks called a 'cadre' class. The word cadre always makes me think of dead bodies which is very suitable. The class is like to OCTU only very much worse. We spend the mornings marching, doing P.T. & gun drill, often standing in sorrowful circles on the beach looking balefully at some gun for several hours with snow falling on our gun and battledress till we look like the last picture of Scott's polar expedition.

I then have from 2 till 4 to look after my troop – a hundred & one jobs to be done. Very often I have to spend an hour or two inspecting some vehicle. I crawl underneath getting very dirty & say 'take that off' pointing at some mysterious part. The unfortunate driver takes it off and I then look at it from every angle & say 'oil it' or 'rusty' & the chap puts it back. All very droll, but quite the thing to do & as you can see all helps to win the war.

In another letter to his parents from the same period, David describes a different, even more arduous, training exercise:

Last night we went on a divisional scheme which involved leaving Weston at 11 a.m. All going off to a place near Bristol & spending the night there. No sleep & all night pulling guns out of bogs!! I spent 2 hours moving my guns from one field to another only half a mile away. We started at 2 a.m. to drive through the night till about 7 when we went into action. We spent the rest of the day standing about in the cold & occasionally moving to a new position, & at 6 p.m. it was announced that everyone except drivers were going to march home. So we walked home: a distance of 10 miles. Result being blisters on my heels, a headache & general depression – but supposed to be toughening. However I have been seriously putting the whisky cure into practice & am feeling much better …

In another letter to his parents David gave vent to his feelings of disappointment about the life he now found himself obliged to lead: 'I have been pretty depressed lately. Worked so hard & so long to become an officer & now I find the job is most uncongenial. Don't enjoy any part of it & I don't fancy being cooped up with this gang for years …'

★ ★ ★

Meanwhile, Pamela was finding being back at work at the emergency military hospital equally uncongenial. She reported for duty on 3 January, subsequently writing in her diary that it 'felt as if I'd never been away'. From then on her entries very much match those of the previous autumn; for example:

January 15th The most hectic day of days – one continual rush – man with haemorrage [*sic*]. Terribly short-staffed – absolute nightmare – oh lord. Washing bowls and bedpans and blood. Don't know when I'll get another day off … haven't heard a thing from David. What a war.

January 21st Awful. I've been changed. Put back to surgical. Oh lord it's so depressing … I can't stand Sister S – it's so difficult because she can't stand me either …

January 22nd The most frightful day without exception. Such a rush this evening that I thought it would never come to an end. Patients terribly ill – drip salines – it's like a nightmare – ghastly. I'm glad no one can see me now. I don't think I ever looked anything other than a shiny-nosed ugly skivvy – I'm quite frightened when I look in the glass …

January 24th Another frightful day. I'm certain she isn't human. XXX brought in a stretcher case at 6 and there was the usual rush round …

January 25th Thank heaven sister was off so the cat & mouse trick was too. However the case last night is pretty bad, hasn't come round & they think it might be compression. It's terrible the responsibility. Feeding him etc. This diary is terrible. Nothing but hospital but you seem to live in a world apart and the war news is second rate to the strain …

February 10th Well it's happened – the inevitable night duty – feel so depressed don't know what to do with myself …

February 13th Went to bed all day. Just go to bed, get up and go to bed again and all nights off have been stopped. It's a funny existence – sitting in the ward in a little cape and trying to keep awake …

Another, comparatively minor, source of irritation for Pamela during this period was the arrival of a different category of nurse. For the most part, Pamela got on well with her fellow nurses, who were mostly from the same locality and background. References to 'smarties', however, started creeping into Pamela's diary entries. These were girls from London and the Home Counties, viewed by Pamela and her contemporaries with some suspicion; for example on 8 February Pamela wrote: 'Got the most frightful girl on the ward … London smartie. Oh I am unkind but I've never struck anyone like her …'

To add to the Street family's domestic woes, rationing was by now beginning to make itself felt. Petrol rationing had begun in 1939, and from 1940 onwards the rationing of various foodstuffs was implemented in stages. By the start of 1941 all meat, butter, sugar, tea and margarine had been added to the list; jam, cheese and eggs were soon to follow suit. Clothes rationing would be introduced in June 1941, and already stockings were in short supply. In her diary entry for 5 January, Pamela writes of an altercation that she had had with her nursing room-mate over the loan of some stockings: 'she's terrible on stockings and the war – they're awfully difficult to get these days.'

On 10 January Pamela noted: 'Mummy is very worried about the rationing.' This was the period when people were being encouraged to 'dig for victory'. Vera Street was a lifelong keen gardener, and it must have been a considerable wrench – albeit in other ways a certain source of pride – for her to transform her carefully tended flower-beds into vegetable patches. Her mother's efforts were clearly the source of inspiration for another wartime poem of Pamela's, which was accepted for publication in late February by *St Martin's Review* for the 'princely' sum of 15 shillings – a rare piece of good news:

Lest We Forget*

Where the long herbaceous border
Grew beneath the garden wall,
Where the Pinks in sweet disorder
Tumbled like a waterfall,
Where the Roses blew so gaily,
White and yellow, pink and red,
Here with careful hoeing daily
Have I made an onion bed.

Here where now my Love-lies-bleeding
Jilted for a Carrot's sake,
Have I passed along unheeding
Armed with shovel, prong and rake,
Beans succeed my two Robinias,
Peas gave London Pride the poke,
And here's my bed of choicest Zinnias
Murdered by the artichoke.

---

*   The refrain from Rudyard Kipling's poem, 'Recessional'. Kipling was A.G. Street's favourite author, whose works he would have encouraged Pamela to read.

So now instead of merely showing
All my friends my latest buds,
I march them through the garden crowing
'Wait until you see my spuds'.
But was it thought or was it blindness
Next time Anne came round for tea,
With just her same well-meaning kindness
She brought a bunch of Rosemary?

★ ★ ★

This, therefore, was the inauspicious backdrop against which Pamela and David's courtship was being conducted. What, under normal circumstances, should have been a happy period of their lives, was marred by constant frustrations and even despair about when and how they might next be able to meet. Pamela's diary reveals that from the time of David's posting to Weston-super-Mare in early January 1941 till his embarkation in late April, the pair only saw each other on a handful of occasions. Despite the obstacles presented by their respective war work, David's letters and Pamela's diaries show an impressive degree of determination on both sides; for example on 10 February David, describing a new scheme for officers' weekends off duty, wrote to Pamela: 'We can't apply till the Wednesday before so how we are to get the same weekend off I don't know. They say that nothing that is easy is worth doing – so let's try anyway. People don't make things easy in this war.'

For her part, Pamela was constantly at odds with her conscience about asking for time off in order to see David. In particular matters came to a head in early March, when once again she was obliged to go on sick leave. Her diary reveals that she was suffering from a heavy cold, and on 3 March (her 20th birthday) came home to recuperate. It so happened that David had asked her down to Weston-super-Mare the following weekend, and Pamela's diary entries show how she agonised about how she would be perceived by the hospital authorities if she went ahead with the visit instead of returning to nursing duty:

March 1st David wired last night – next Friday & Saturday – told Matron and she said she'd do her best …

March 3rd [Pamela's birthday] … steaming headache & came home sick … probably next weekend is off …

March 4th Awful. Mummy rang Matron when Dr. Stratton had been and she thinks I've done it on purpose – mean old cat … I've mucked everything up completely & thoroughly. Probably shall lose job and David and everyone's in a flap …

March 6th Completely on tenderhooks [*sic*] about David and the weekend ... expect David will run off with a blonde ... I must see him soon or I shall bust ...

March 8th The doctor came and says I can go to Weston next week to get well – now won't the sparks fly ...

Evidently the family doctor's advice allowed Pamela to travel to Weston-super-Mare with a more or less clear conscience, and a few days later she describes the trip in enthusiastic terms:

March 13th <u>Went</u>!!! Just caught the connection at Bristol and David met me at Weston and kissed me on the platform and was very sweet. Terrified & stage-struck of Ma & Pa at first but they were really awfully nice. David & I went out with a whole lot of people to play darts at Bleadon and had bacon & eggs and didn't get in till 12 ...

March 14th ... they are very nice to me and David is sweet. How wonderful it is to have happened ...

March 15th ... went to the Imperial in the evening and danced ... Mrs M – I hope she approves of me – comes too now!

March 16th Going today. David's given me his photograph. Rode along the sands this afternoon – alternating between being violently happy and terribly depressed – he goes on a course tonight & Ma & Pa return tomorrow – we aren't engaged or anything like it yet to all intents and purposes behave as though we are ...

It is abundantly clear from Pamela's diaries and other writings that above all she was hoping for a proposal of marriage from David before he left. In a letter dated 13 February in which David suggested that Pamela should come to Weston-super-Mare and how she should persuade the hospital authorities to allow her the necessary time off, he added somewhat tantalisingly: 'If necessary you could say you were secretly engaged to me & I was going to Egypt. It would not be a bad idea at that!!'
Pamela's entry for 15 February records what took place after she received this letter:

David ... wants to come up next weekend and said I could say we were unofficially engaged if I got into difficulties. Well I tried but wasn't any good and I shall write and tell Hitler about it. It's awful. Here I am stuck here ... he won't want to come and probably go to Egypt before I see him. It's ghastly to think of because I'm half in love with him ...

Back in September 1940 Pamela's erratic nursing schedule had already frustrated David to such a degree that he took matters into his own hands, as her entry for 28 September reveals: 'David came to the hospital for me and sent everyone flying round including Matron …' Decades later Pamela used this incident in her novel *Many Waters*. The heroine, Emily Mason, recently engaged to her childhood sweetheart John William, is summoned to the Matron's office in the emergency hospital where she is now working. Expecting to be reprimanded for a previous misdemeanour reported by one of the sisters, Emily is amazed to discover John William rising from a chair in the corner, greeting her with a casual 'Hello darling'. The episode continues:

> 'You did not tell me, Nurse Mason,' Miss Butler remarked, while Emily looked first at one and then the other in total confusion, 'that you were *engaged*.' Her voice did not sound quite so threatening as usual. In fact, Emily reflected later, if she herself had not been in such a state of anxiety she might have noticed that it was quite pleasant, even benign.
>
> 'I … that is …' Helplessly, she turned back to John, standing there in his officer's uniform … She was astounded at his lack of embarrassment, at the way he seemed so utterly at ease in this terrifying sanctum … She noticed that there was a cup and saucer on a table by his chair. He must have been given *tea* …

Sadly for Pamela, however, David did not 'come up with the goods', albeit for totally honourable reasons, as her diary entry for 23 March – just after a rare visit by David to Wilton – explains:

> Heavenly day. Pop in Home Guard Parade etc. National day of prayer.* David and I went to Grovely [the wood overlooking Wilton] in the afternoon … Then we said goodbye because it's probably the last time we shall see each other now – he said he'd marry me if he wasn't going abroad …

Many decades later Pamela expanded on David's reluctance to become formally engaged:

> I suppose we had what was known as an 'understanding', not a particularly satisfactory liaison. But there were then many conscientious young men who, facing the prospect of death, did not feel it right to marry or tie a girl down by becoming officially engaged until hostilities were over.

---

* On 23 March 1941 a National Day of Prayer for victory was held at the request of the king.

Throughout this period David's embarkation for Egypt continued to be postponed, presumably because of encouraging reports from the area, to which occasional snippets in Pamela's diary refer; for example:

January 25th We're doing well in the east …

February 3rd We're smashing the Italians in Africa and the Greeks are going strong but <u>when</u> will it end?

February 7th The war goes on and on – sometimes when it's springlike you think it can't last and then you don't see how it can stop – there's marvellous news from the East …

The fortunes of the Allies were soon to change, however. Following their early successes in North Africa at the beginning of the year, the pendulum began to swing the other way. In mid February Hitler sent reinforcements to the North African desert, the notorious 'Afrika Korps', headed by the very able Lieutenant-General Erwin Rommel (later to be dubbed the 'Desert Fox', because of his unexpected lightning strikes behind Allied lines). Hitler was now concentrating on dominating the Balkan States (Romania, in particular, being important for its oil fields), and was obliged to come to the aid of its new ally Italy, which had recently launched an invasion of Greece, initially met by stiff opposition. In turn Britain came to the aid of the Greeks by sending a detachment of its North African forces to Greece in order to repel the invading Axis forces, thereby depleting Allied strength in the North African desert; the battlefield would shortly extend to the island of Crete. Moreover, as a Mediterranean base, it was essential to the Allied cause that the islands of Malta (then still part of the British Empire and situated halfway between the straits of Gibraltar and Alexandria on the Egyptian coast), which were currently experiencing heavy Axis bombardment, should remain in Allied hands.

More snippets about the progress of the war appear in Pamela's diary during this later period, for example:

April 5th We've lost Benghazi in Africa. Wonder what's happening …

April 7th Germany has attacked Greece and Yugoslavia …

April 8th Frightful news from the Balkans. Germans pressing in …

April 9th Bad news from Africa and Greece & Yugoslavia …

April 11th The Germans have got Salonika and pushing on in Africa and oh it's awful.

For these reasons it must have become apparent to the British High Command that by April 1941, regiments in waiting such as David McCormick's needed to be sent, after all, to the North African theatre of war.

Before David left, however, he and Pamela were able to meet a couple more times. Pamela's entry for 22 March reads:

> David came – we went to Salisbury and round by the kennels and it was lovely seeing him again and then we quite kicked over the traces and went to Jessie Sivewright's thing – it was nice to dance again and we didn't stay long. David was very sweet – he wants to pack me in his valise to take to Egypt or Libya …

David followed up this visit with a couple of affectionate letters. In the first, dated 23 March, he wrote:

> I got awfully lost on the way back here [signposts had earlier been removed in order to thwart German invaders]. In the end I had to disturb a loving couple in a car, as they were the only people awake in the neighbourhood. They were very nice and unclenched & led me onto the right road …
>
> Have put a kiss into the envelope so be careful opening it or it may escape!

David's next letter continued in the same vein; on 4 April he wrote:

> I am glad you caught the kiss! I will send you some more as they do not last! Their ultimate climax is to touch your lips & then they must flutter off & die. You cannot put a pin through them & shut them in a case!

★ ★ ★

During this period, Arthur Street was frequently commissioned by the BBC to deliver short propaganda talks from various venues around the British Isles. One such occasion occurred on 28 March, when he was due to visit a flax mill in Bridport on the Dorset coast. With Pamela on sick leave at the time, her father evidently thought it would take her mind off her problems if she were to accompany him. Her diary entry for the day in question reads simply: 'Went to Bridport with Mummy & Daddy. Quite like the old times except for barbed wire round the sea. Went over a flax mill …'

In *Hitler's Whistle*, Arthur Street elaborates on this visit. He explains that by the late 1930s, apart from the flax grown on King George V's estates at Sandringham and that of a handful of other producers, flax as a farming crop had all but died out in Great Britain, being readily obtainable from countries such as Russia and Belgium. By the early 1940s, however, flax was once again in demand for military usage such as canvas, tents and parachutes, and since it could no longer be imported from across the Channel, it needed to be home grown. Arthur Street – practising what he preached – was just about to plant his first crop of flax and made an analogy between military needs in 1941 and those in 1213, the latter exemplified in an edict from King John to the Sheriffs of Somerset and Dorset, quoted in the Bridport town guide, as follows:

> We command you that as you love us, yourselves, and your own bodies, you buy for our use all the oats you can lay your hands upon in the counties of Somerset and Dorset – also cause to be made at Bridport, night and day, as many ropes for ships, both large and small, and as many cable as you can, and twisted yarns for cordage for ballistae.

This was the peg on which Arthur Street was able to hang his broadcast, during which he repeatedly made his case for the importance of British agriculture to the current war effort:

> which is yet another case of history repeating itself. The sails of Nelson's *Victory* were made in the West Country from English-grown flax: and as past victories depended, so also will our coming victory in this war depend, largely on the produce grown on the land of our own country.

Although Arthur Street came across in his radio broadcasts and writings as the epitome of down-to-earth rural common sense, his public persona belied an altogether different side to his character. In the same diary entry in which Pamela referred to the Street family's visit to the flax mill, she continued: 'Afraid Daddy is one hell of a temper – quite inexplicable – nerves very bad and Mummy's getting worse under it …'

The reality was, in fact, all too explicable. Arthur Street was a worrier. Dotted here and there in Pamela's diaries are several other references to her father being in a bad mood about such things as lack of progress of the book on which he was currently working, or adverse weather during harvest or haymaking. Unfortunately at such times he was liable to vent his frustration on his nearest and dearest, which in turn affected the mental state of his delicate wife, Vera. Arthur Street was used to getting his own way, so his feelings of impotence as the war ground on inexorably must have been, for him, particularly galling.

★ ★ ★

Pamela managed one final visit to Weston-super-Mare before David's departure, this time accompanied by her mother. It is clear from family papers that both sets of parents approved of the potential match, and indeed on the Street side actively encouraged it, judging from all the hospitality given to David at Ditchampton Farm. After Pamela's meeting with David's parents at Weston-super-Mare she kept in regular touch with Phyllis McCormick by letter or telephone, and indeed continued to do so following David's departure. He evidently told his parents that he hoped to marry Pamela after the war, for in a letter written in late 1941, his mother gave him the following – albeit somewhat patronising – opinion:

> I have had a nice letter from Pamela giving what news she had of you. We wouldn't at all mind you marrying her; only we think it is a pity to get too much involved until you get back. However that is for you to decide. I can't think of anyone else for you and I like her much better than any of your previous 'girl-friends'!

Pamela and her mother travelled to Weston-super-Mare on 14 April, despite serious misgivings on Pamela's part, as explained in the following diary entry:

> We went. I was dreading it – I didn't know whether it was right or wasn't and it was because I think David was terribly pleased. He'd got rooms for us at the Grosvenor and had done everything and then he'd asked for a special dinner because it was an occasion and Ian and a girl came and there were carnations and Mummy was sweet & we went to the Imperial and danced and oh it was worth anything and David & I went into the air raid shelter for fun because it was all fun and because it was sad and there was a war …

The next day was evidently just as successful:

> Oh lovely day. David came to lunch and then tea and then we went and shopped and I bought him a camera and he gave me his badge and one of his handkerchiefs and we went out to Bleadon and got the landlady to take our photograph with it and then in the evening we went to the flics … and then it was goodbye – Please may it not be for very long …

The following morning Pamela and Vera Street returned home. This really had been David and Pamela's last meeting before his departure, and Pamela summed up her feelings in her diary as follows:

> Came home early – did not see David again. I don't think I could have borne it … I think we'd said everything there was to say and it was almost a relief to come back but thank you for the loveliest two days – Mummy, Daddy, David and everyone. I shan't forget – ever.

Judging from David's letter to Pamela following her visit, he had enjoyed it every bit as much; on 18 April he wrote:

> Pamela Darling, I have got your lovely letter & the photos. What a wonderful camera it is – it works! I have got a lot of films for taking away with me. I love the photo of you & me & you don't look cuckoo! Though slightly seaweedish! … It looks just what it was, a farewell outing for the soldier off to war …
>
> Darling, it was lovely seeing you & having you down here & wonderful of your mother to bring you. I did appreciate it so, & it made all the difference to my last days here …

On 20 April, a Sunday, David wrote another letter from a hotel in Cheddar, enclosing a couple of mementos for Pamela to keep:

> We have come over here for the day and had a lovely picnic … I wish you were here as you would love it. Have you ever been to the Gorge? There is a wonderful mill pool at the bottom surrounded by spring flowers & the gorge behind looks more like the Khyber than England & makes one sigh like high trees do. I am sending you one of the flowers full of meaning.*
>
> Do you have cuffs with your uniform? I am also sending you my links to wear for me till I get back.
>
> I wonder if you are back at work! I do hope they are all being nice to you, & are looking after you. I am not quite sure but I rather think that this is the last letter I can write before disappearing. It is very sad & I say to myself Oh to be in England now that April's here.
>
> I have fastened my horseshoe onto a silver chain I have bought for my identity disc & there is also a St Christopher given to me by Marjorie [a fellow officer's sister] on it. So I should be alright! …

The little horseshoe in question was given to Pamela in her early nursing days by a grateful patient, a survivor of 'Dunkirk'. In her diary for 13 July 1940, she wrote: 'Another man has given me a lucky horse-shoe which he brought back from France which is rather nice and very kind of him.' Whatever her superiors may have thought of her, Pamela was clearly popular with her patients from the word go.

On 22 April David wrote Pamela a final, brief, touching note:

> This is to say au revoir. I am afraid I can't say a great deal as there is an awful rush going on & I have much to do.
>
> You should get a letter saying that I have arrived safely in about 6 weeks time & a letter from me in about 3 months. What old news it will be!

---

*   A forget-me-not, now a little shrivelled dried sprig, still in the original envelope.

Everyone down here thought you were very sweet & much too good for me!
Goodbye Darling & thank you for coming into my life
David
P.S. Please stay in it!

David also wrote two final letters to his parents prior to embarkation; in the first he included some photographs of himself that Pamela had taken: 'I enclose some photos Pamela took of me & have asked her to send you a good one of us both which we got a bar woman to take of us.' Then in his letter dated 21 April, David wrote:

This is definitely <u>the</u> letter. There is not much to say except good-bye. Expect a letter forwarded by the Colonel's wife in about 6 weeks & a letter from me about 3 months from now …
I think I shall be sending my love to Aunt Alice* but of course one can't tell …

The letter to be forwarded by the colonel's wife did indeed eventually reach David's parents, and read as follows:

This is the letter which I am handing in to the Colonel's wife & if you get it at all it will mean that the question of death by drowning will be out.
So hurray we are at the other end on terra firma once more having had a perfectly ghastly trip I am sure. Cramped & bored I should think. I wonder where I am anyway not swimming.

On receipt of David's letter of 21 April, his father Edward McCormick wrote a very moving farewell letter in reply, which must have summed up the feelings of so many parents whose sons were leaving for active duty overseas:

23 April 1941

My dear David,
    I write in the hope that this letter may reach you before you actually embark; if not, it may take many weeks to reach you. Mummy and I have been very much affected by your leaving us and by your last two letters from Weston.
    To Mummy, in particular, the whole war centres round you and Anthony.** The chief motivating force in her life, ever since you were born, has been your health, happiness and safety. These are still her instinctive thoughts, and you don't need me to tell you therefore how devastating this parting with you both has been to her. I feel it too, and it appals me to think of the hardship, danger and

---

* This would have been code for one of the calling points *en route*.
** David's elder brother, at that time stationed in Ghana.

filth which will probably be your experience. There is no doubt whatever, in my mind, that this war had to come. A nazi victory can only mean the enjoyment of life by a very small number of chosen Germans and the souls of all people under them will be engulfed. You and Anthony are helping to rid the world of this plague, and, while personal feelings make me wish you were far away from it all, I am filled with pride at what you have already done and what I know you will achieve …

We have received your several little parcels, your watch, which Mummy likes to wear at times, your receipts etc …:

It was nice of Pamela to give you a little camera. We thought the snaps were excellent …

Mum and I send you our fondest love and blessing and pray for your well-being and safe return to us.

Dad

As his father feared, this letter failed to reach David before his departure, but when it did eventually catch up with him in Egypt it clearly touched him greatly. His letter of reply dated 15 July 1941 shows his appreciation, albeit expressed in similarly restrained emotional terms:

Darling Mummy and Dad,

I have had two more letters from you, Mummy, & one from you, Dad. They were the first ones you wrote & one was sent on the 24 of April, the day we sailed. They have taken a long time but that doesn't seem to matter; it is lovely to get letters & all the news seems new. Dad's letter is one that I shall keep with me …

The fact that this original hand-written letter exists today shows that David was true to his word. Edward McCormick's later letters to David were typed, and only the carbon copies still survive.

Six

Heartache, Hospital and High Seas (May–August 1941)

After the emotionally super-charged weeks leading up to David's departure, Pamela's initial reaction, as recorded in her diary entry for 4 May, is understandable; however this quickly transmuted into a continuous state of longing: 'Write to David every day. After the first shock of almost relief am beginning to miss him terribly and hopelessly …'

David's last two letters to Pamela arrived after he had set sail, and were eagerly received:

April 22nd David sent me another letter, a forget-me-not, and his links from Cheddar – oh & a wonderful letter too. Oh this awful war. When will it be over – when next people be able to love and get married in peace …

April 24th The last letter from David – so wonderful, and the slip.* Destination A wherever in the world that is … Wrote immediately but oh when will it reach him. He said I'd hear when he arrived but no letter from him till 3 months …

Pamela's conscience was bothering her once again about her current long spell of sick leave which, according to her diary, was largely due to the emotional upset prior to David's departure:

April 23rd I can't go back to the hosp 'cos Matron's away. I hope they'll still have me after all this time …

April 27th Hope I can start work again soon. Do hope Matron will be nice about it. Did I ought to tell her it was heartitis [*sic*] really?

---

* The 'slip' was a little square type-written form with a space in which departing troops could fill in their future addresses to which their loved ones could send letters.

During this period of waiting, Pamela had evidently recovered sufficiently to undertake a certain amount of farm work:

April 23rd Harrowed Wishford Arch. All day. Terribly cold but nice work …

April 24th Rolled Wishford Arch.

April 26th Rolled The Park …

April 28th Rolled again from 9 – 4. Top Down and Bottom Field …

In the late spring of 1941 the war news was becoming ever more serious, and Pamela's diary shows her following the unfolding events with a sinking heart:

April 22nd There is an awful situation in the Med. Germans pressing in on Greece – nearly over.

April 26th There is the most awful crisis. Greece war nearly over. They're trying for the whole Mediterranean and oh my goodness if they get Gib etc. Scare over Greenland. Nearly the whole world …

April 27th Listened to Churchill. He did a difficult job very well but oh my goodness the war …

April 28th On the news tonight we are evacuating Greece …

May 1st The war is perfectly awful. Evacuation of Greece nearly complete …

May 5th The situation in the east is almost as bad as it can be – and oh the war is a terrible thing … If only there was David …

May 8th The War just goes on hammer to teeth. Iraq. Egypt. The Atlantic. Have full support of the American Navy now …

May 22nd The Crete invasion …

May 24th Situation in Crete still continuing. Pop says it's a full dress rehearsal for us …

May 28th President Roosevelt declared a state of emergency in America. Crete is awfully serious – expect we shall lose it …

June 1st We took Pop fishing and came back to the news that we have evacuated Crete and Clothes Rationing has begun. When will it end – how can it and where is David?

The realities of war were by now being brought home, even to those living in the comparative safety of deepest Wiltshire, in the form of news of the disappearance or death of family friends and relatives. Pamela's diary entry for 23 May records a meeting in Salisbury with the father of a friend who had married her fiancé, Bob, shortly before the latter was posted abroad: 'Went down to the town and met Captain Richardson. Bobs is believed killed. Poor Barbara. It's terrible. Shall we get hardened to this I wonder …'

Even closer to home were the reactions of Pamela's prospective parents-in-law to their son's departure. In her entry for 28 April, only a few days after David had left, Pamela wrote: 'Mr. McCormick wrote a nice letter to Pop but I haven't heard from her. We gathered p'raps she's still too upset. Poor thing. It must be awful with 2 [sons].'

Meanwhile the Street household was coping as best it could with the wartime privations. Vera was kept busy tending her newly planted vegetable garden. To supplement meat rationing, civilians with appropriate facilities were allowed to rear one pig per family; on 29 April Pamela's diary records: 'Mummy & Daddy went to Motcombe to fetch the pig.'

Pamela's period of sick leave finally ended. On 29 April she reported to the matron at the emergency hospital with considerable trepidation: 'Went to see Matron – am going back tomorrow! Daddy said that I wasn't and couldn't say anything about David as it was ridiculous so I didn't.' Almost inevitably, Pamela's subsequent diary entries show her once again locked in the miserable existence that had already caused her such anguish. This time her conscience was to plague her still further; not only was she constantly agonising about her perceived professional failings, but she was also hideously embarrassed about receiving her nursing salary whilst on sick leave, and she went over and over again in her mind whether or not to confide to the matron, Miss Best, the cause of her most recent period off duty:

May 1st Came back and of course the bottom dropped out of everything …

May 2nd D. Hut. Sister Higgins … I hope I do everything right & and it's all all right. I'm an awful girl really. Trouble. They were good to bear with me. Should I have stayed on the land …

May 7th Feel so awful. I do wish I told Matron everything about David. It would have made it so much easier. I think I should have, as it is my conscience is getting heavier & heavier and if I don't look out I shall break down over that …

May 12th My stupid old conscience is again pricking me. I keep going over and over again the leave and David and wondering whether it wouldn't have been better to tell Matron or not – it is difficult. He was really at the bottom of all the trouble …

May 18th Sunday in [the hospital]. The awful depressed feeling & so worried about a little boy who got a wet pair of pyjamas on which was mostly my fault & I hope sister will change them. Oh dear he might get anything …

May 29th Night duty tonight. Sitting in bed in nn [night-nurses' accommodation] just thinking about all that's happened and everything that may. Oh will it, can it ever end. It's like one long dark tunnel with no one to switch the light on either. Feel so depressed I don't know what to do. Terribly home-sick & oh so missing David. I hope it's all going terribly well with him and I hope I manage to do what's right here but oh the waiting. Sometimes I think it's unbearable but so much worse for him.

May 30th I'm so silly oh why am I like this – I just feel so upset I don't know what to do. I must get better – I can't go on like this – it's like a nightmare & I still don't know what it's really about – David mostly & going sick & worrying about Matron. Oh it's all awful …

Whether or not her father would have approved, Pamela clearly realised that she was on the edge of a breakdown and there was only one possible course of action open to her. On 3 June her diary states:

Went to Matron this morning with all my troubles – all the whole jolly lot of them. She was terribly nice and I'm glad I've done it – I'm an awful fool but she was glad I came I think. Hope everything will be all right now – oh do make me a better girl or something. Mummy & Daddy have been so good & her really. It's me whose [*sic*] wrong …

Although her conscience had been eased temporarily, Pamela's diary entries for the rest of the summer of 1941 show just how much she continued to miss David, and how she longed to hear from him. The day of 9 May was a rare, red-letter one with good news, as her diary reveals: 'Had a letter from David from some secret destination – wasn't it wonderful! He hasn't gone yet or at any rate not then. Oh David David what an unsettling person you are but being David you can't mind.'

The letter to which Pamela referred was the first of several David wrote both to her and his parents during the course of his voyage, and which illustrate the conditions under which the servicemen travelled. The letters to Pamela are for the most part deliberately upbeat and frequently romantic in tone; those to his parents describe the practicalities of his new life in greater detail. It seems that before David and his regiment were properly under way, one more chance arose for the men to send letters home:

Pamela Darling,

This is the last letter I can write for some time and this is a quite unexpected opportunity as I thought I had gone.

I'm afraid I can't tell you anything about what I am up to except that it is all above board!

I am sharing an awful little room with Ian & Jim & 3 others. Fortunately we have also a bathroom which is the only place for our clothes. The bath is full of boots which is lamentable!

The food here is too good to be true. A grateful country is treating its sons nobly in advance. I hope its gratitude will be rewarded a hundredfold. The weather is lovely & sunbathing is in progress …

At the ship's first port of call David was able to post another letter to Pamela and his parents:

4 May 41
Pamela Darling,

We are halting on our way so I can send you a letter – specially arranged for the purpose! We are having a quite nice voyage & I have not been ill yet.

The weather is lovely & everyone is complaining of the heat except me – I love it …

I am not on very good form this evening because I was inoculated this morning and also I was officer of the watch last night which meant spending from 12 to 4 roaming about the ship … I sat underneath the funnel part of the time & was the only man in the strangest world. The moon was sitting on top of the mast & never moved, and looking up I thought I was lost on a stage set as we didn't seem to be moving and the funnel & ventilators were so large; then looking down I saw the still sea going by & felt like a Lilliputian on a toy ship. It was a magic moment & I wished you were there with me to share it … but there is much pain in the contemplation of such beauty.

Later in this letter David reminisces about his and Pamela's time together, and finishes with the admonishment: 'Please promise not to write to me if you don't want to. If you feel "I ought to write to David, I haven't written for ages", don't write as it will mean that I am a thing of the past for you.' Despite such noble sentiments, a postscript to this letter reveals David's true feelings: 'P.S. Longing to hear from you!'

In his letter to his parents written a day later, David repeats much of what he wrote to Pamela, but goes into greater detail about the conditions:

The food is almost like a peace time cruise with all the usual choice, 10 minutes to wait for things from the grill & so on; the only things which are bad are water, tea, coffee & milk, which are never too good anyhow on a ship & of course there is no cream. On the other hand I am in a tiny cabin with 5 others, with no room to put or hang anything & of course the window is locked up all night so you can imagine the fug. Also one or other of us is always on some duty or other involving getting up early or going to bed late or getting up in the night & waking everyone else up. I shall probably get my camp bed out of the hold and sleep out on deck soon …

Oddly enough I am being kept very busy what with lectures & lecturing, being a P.T. instructor every morning & censoring hundreds of letters. I can't say I am enjoying life much or looking forward to the immediate future. It is almost impossible to enjoy new experiences & places when they are all covered in khaki.

Although David had experienced Atlantic crossings in order to visit his American relatives, he had never previously sailed in warm waters. On 21 May he wrote again to Pamela and his parents, describing in both letters some of the novel sights he had witnessed: 'I have seen hundreds of flying fish – the best ones fly at least 200 yds – a shark, dolphins, & a large rectangular ray who tossed himself in the sunshine like a huge pancake.' When David's troop ship crossed the Equator, a quaint ceremony took place: 'When we crossed the Equator I was ducked at least 10 times in the best traditional manner & have been issued with a fine certificate of duckworthiness signed by the barber, King Neptune & 6 bears …'

In this letter to Pamela, David again describes how he was being kept busy:

Fortunately I do not have much time to reflect on my fate. I get up every day at 5.45. Your Dad would say 'Quite right too'. I have to take P.T. at 6. I make my troop do imaginary rowing exercises in the dark to the strain of the Volgar Boatmen. I then fight for the basin for a long time & eventually have breakfast at 8.30. Then follows a day of lectures. Much of my spare time is taken up preparing them. Apart from ordinary military subjects I am methodically reading a long book on the Campaigns in the Middle East in the last war with a view to lecturing on them. I am also learning Arabic & give my troop an hour's lesson a day, which is rather a joke as they don't yet know that I don't know it.

Despite the hard work, the men managed to find ways to amuse themselves. Further on in the same letter to Pamela, David records:

I have grown the most wonderful moustache. I don't know what you would
think of it. It is like a couple of stoat's tails, both in shape & colour. The officers
of the regiment had a moustache competition & although I was not able to enter
as I started a week late several people say I would have won if I had been in it. I
am quite proud of it.

Such light-hearted notes are rare, however. David's true state of mind during the
voyage comes through particularly in his letters to his parents, in which he reveals
his feelings of homesickness and isolation:

I find already now that distance separates one far more definitely than does time.
Do you feel the same? And surrounded as I am by friends of necessity rather than
of choice I find I am virtually alone. It is rather upsetting. I feel even now that
I am writing to a different world & one of the past. Life will be very different I
should imagine.

In his letters to both Pamela and his parents, David expressed his disappointment
and frustration about not being allowed ashore at the first opportunity:

I was very upset at not getting ashore at the place where I posted my last letter.
I was unlucky in the shore draw … It looked perfectly lovely & there were little
bathing bays à la best Tahiti tradition. The thing that struck me most about the
natives was the extraordinary variety of their headgear & the size of their feet &
the fact that they were pink underneath which made them quite indecent …

At the next port of call, however, David had better luck, and on 5 June wrote an
enthusiastic letter to Pamela, describing the people and places he visited. Strict
censorship meant that he was unable to tell her the name of the port in question
which was, in fact, Cape Town:

I have really got something to tell you for once, for we have been ashore. I can't
tell you how marvellous it was to get my feet on the ground again & to see a
female again after all these days at sea!! We ran into a terrible storm which we
ran before for a night & a day & then turned round and were pushed slowly
backwards. Eventually we got to port & tried all afternoon to get a pilot on board,
but could not and had to spend one more night at sea in the storm. All work had
to be stopped, all the food got spilled & masses of furniture & glass broken. I had
to go & watch 600 people eating pork, but survived!

We had five days on shore, & were allowed off from 2 to 2. I had five very good
parties & we have all spent all our money. The people were most hospitable &
terribly generous & kind. As soon as the news spread that we had arrived they

all flocked down to the docks in big American cars & whisked our men off to see the town & the country & gave them tea & baths & dinner & huge dances. They paid for masses of their drinks too. The officers were all invited to a lovely night club where they were wined & feasted & entertained & not allowed to stump up for a sausage. Down here, apart from losing their young men they are quite unaffected by the war. The town was a blaze of light at night & there was no rationing of any kind. The only war work they can do is to entertain passing troops & this they do with a wholehearted generosity & enjoyment. I have been censoring all the letters from the men in my troop to their homes & to the people who were kind to them in this port, & I was absolutely moved by their gratitude. Every letter was the same & the simple sincerity in the expression of their appreciation was really fine. One appreciates that sort of thing in the army & it reminds me, not that I am likely to forget, of all that you & your Mother & Father did for me when I was at Larkhill.

Many promising attachments & friendships were made here & one officer of about 40 married a girl he met during our brief visit. Ian & I were fortunate in meeting a couple of sisters who were very sweet & nice to us. We took them out to a night club some fifteen miles out where I was very impressed because at the end everyone stood up & sang 'There'll always be an England', looking at us, who were the only Britishers there … The country was quite beautiful & there were many flowers although it is late autumn here. The weather was like the sort of bad August day that one gets on holiday in England; everyone was wearing furs & overcoats & shivering. The foliage was all shrubs & trees which looked like small plane trees, but, as they were the only kind, had no name & were just trees. There were lots of huge mountains, some with snow on the top. They had no trees on their lower slopes as do the mountains in Europe, but rose out of the ground like huge stone teeth. I am told there are still leopards quite near the town & if the weather had been better I might have hunted baboons with a pair of Great Danes with some people I met.

The people all seem to belong to a rich & well-educated middle class & talk their own language among themselves, but when they talk in English their accent is most delightful & very attractive in the girls. The whole place seemed to have been very influenced by American ideas & I was surprised to find quite as many Europeans as natives, if not more, even in the country. No one seemed to do much work, but everyone was wealthy & looked well fed & happy. These two sisters were 18 & 19 & were earning £18 & £30 respectively as a secretary & a chemist …

Delighted though she undoubtedly would have been to receive such a long, detailed letter, the remarks it contained regarding the female inhabitants of South Africa must have given Pamela somewhat mixed feelings.

David had one more chance to go ashore before arriving at his destination, as he reported in another letter to Pamela dated 20 June, though this time it appears that the ship's reception was more muted:

Darling,

This is the third start I have made as the last two efforts got wiped out by perspiration & I was ashamed to send them to you. It really is quite hot. Last night I slept on the front end of the deck, where the breeze is greatest & in spite of that slept without even a sheet, & was forced to vacate my bed at 5 owing to the heat of the sun which was beating down on me. The official temperature at 6 was 96 in the shade & the temperature of the sea was 89; so little comfort can be obtained from a bath of sea water. I am told by the experts that it will get hotter every day too!

We had two days at another port a few days after the last one I mentioned; we did not receive quite the same reception from the townsfolk as we did at the other, as they have seen so many troops passing by, that it was like whipping a dead horse. On the other hand I was very moved by their send off, which is the first send off we have had. Hundreds of girls came down to the dock & everyone cheered & all the ships in the harbour hooted. I was quite moved & felt for the first time that I was really going to do something worthwhile. I made contact with some old friends the second night who were awfully nice to me & took me to a cocktail party, dinner & a night club. The first night we landed after dark & not knowing the town all got awfully boozed & I am rather hazy about the whole evening. All I do know is that we went into the country, driven by a madman who thought he was on Brooklands* & danced at a place which in the right company would have been very wonderful. You sat about with nothing but stars overhead, while Indians brought you long cool drinks & every now & then you danced on a floor which looked like a lake surrounded by fairy lights.

Well, Darling, we are expecting to get off this bark in a few days now, & about time too. We are all very tired of it, and although we all realise that wherever we go it will be far worse, we are looking forward to getting off & I am very happy to be where I am in the present circumstances, though I often reflect on the perversity of fate which necessitates all this unpleasantness for one who desires only a little place in God's sun in which to live in peace. Let us hope it will soon be over!

Strict censorship meant that David was unable, at the time of writing, to reveal the names of the ship's ports of call, or indeed the name of the ship itself. However the regimental diaries of the 72nd RA set the record straight. The regiment sailed from Liverpool on 24 April, on a hastily converted cruise-ship, the *Empress of Asia*, with

---

* Racing circuit.

2,410 officers and men on board. First they travelled north and stopped at the head of the Firth of Clyde, where they joined a convoy which then sailed westwards round the north coast of Ireland and out into the Atlantic before turning south. The first port of call was Freetown. Their next stop, where they received such a rapturous welcome, was Cape Town, and the last stop was at Durban. A confidential appendix to the regimental diary at this point reveals that the stopover at Durban was considerably lengthened by a semi-mutiny on the part of the ship's stokers, who having departed on shore leave, either returned too drunk to be capable of working, or else failed to return at all. In order to resume the journey, troops had to be 'volunteered' to take the stokers' places. In fact poor discipline amongst the stokers had already caused the ship to be considerably behind schedule, and it eventually reached its destination, Port Tewfik, Suez, on 24 July, ten days late. Whether David was ever aware of these difficulties remains a matter of conjecture; certainly they could not have been mentioned in letters home.

★ ★ ★

Back in Wiltshire Pamela was carrying on with her hospital duties, which she was finding ever more onerous. She lived for her off-duty periods back at Ditchampton Farm, for which her gratitude is recorded time and again in diary entries such as: '*June 11th* Home — sleep and food!!! … Wrote to David and it is lovely to be home.' To exacerbate matters, she was once again afflicted by daytime insomnia during night shifts:

June 5th Didn't sleep … What will happen to me? I must pull through. I can't be ill again through sheer worry of feeling guilty …

June 6th Didn't sleep again — it's awful but tonight Mummy & Daddy came in with a letter from David of all the wonderful things … He was somewhere on the way and his letter was oh so lovely. Just like him. What I've gone through for that boy at least I think I have …

June 7th Just too bad about this wretched sleep. Sister Edwards is doping me now thank heaven …

June 13th … am writing this now in the old night-nurses quarters — oh the waiting — one long wait for the dawn. Oh David I wonder where you are and what you're doing. Are you thinking about me I wonder? Sometimes I think you are because you seem so near … Somehow you went away when it was all just beginning and then sometimes I think it was right. If everything comes right in the end it will be worth the years of waiting …

At the beginning of July an incident occurred at the hospital that made matters even worse for Pamela:

> *July 3rd* The most awful thing that I have ever done happened last night. I couldn't connect Dr. Gubbin with the Surgical and it was a matter of life & death haemorrhage [*sic*]. Oh it was awful. I wasted masses of time getting through to him & everyone & in the end didn't do it. Completely lost my head. The man had another h at 1 today & foot off. Shan't ever forgive myself. If I'd been quicker he mightn't have …

> *July 4th* At last I've got something really to worry about. I shall never forgive myself not learning before. Oh the mistakes I make and the muddle and everything. His wife came last night to stay. I do pray he'll be all right …

> *July 5th* Telephoned & telephoned last night to learn but too late. The only time I could have been of real use & I failed. Full of reproaches – it's awful. Please may I soon do something all right & worth while to make up for the awful things I've done …

★ ★ ★

Around this time, other members of the Street household were preparing for a fête, which was to be held at Ditchampton Farm. In *Hitler's Whistle*, Arthur Street describes in some detail and brio the fête and its origins, modestly omitting, however, that the event took place in the grounds of Ditchampton Farmhouse. It appears that many decades previously a working party of local ladies had been set up to make knitwear for troops in South Africa, garments for slum children in Britain's cities, and more recently items for homeless evacuees and prisoners of war; this local organisation had now become integrated with the Red Cross, but was experiencing such lack of resources that its very existence was threatened. However a certain local maiden lady, who despite her gentle exterior evidently possessed a core of steel when it came to getting her way, prevailed upon the local residents to come up with what Arthur Street described as 'that age-old rural financial weapon, the garden fête'.

Despite wartime restrictions and rationing, the fête was evidently a big success. Wilton folk from all walks of life, together with locally billeted evacuees and members of the armed forces, flocked to enjoy a rare, nostalgic moment of relief amid the unremitting bleakness of the continuing war. An amateur orchestra was provided by the CO of the nearest regular troops; there was a bring-and-buy stall, a 'weigh all-comers' booth courtesy of a local farmer with his farm scales, a fortune-teller, an illegal raffle, clock golf and much more besides. At one point, in Arthur Street's words:

One Fannie, ably assisted by a local groom, took off her shoes and stockings and ran up and down with a white pony on the short green turf of a wide grass path, giving rides to small children by the score. The bring-and buy stall was thronged with people who both brought and bought. There was a twenty-yard queue outside the fortune-teller's tent. At every competition officers queued with privates, squires with farm labourers, keepers with poachers, and mistresses with servant maids.

The greatest success of all was the rummage stall, set up in an adjacent barn, scheduled to open later in the evening:

At seven o'clock the rummage sale was to open, and half-an-hour before that time a crowd of at least a hundred serious housewives, local and evacuee, were ready waiting. They looked so grim that the maiden lady called in her Major and some other officers to help control the rush when the barn doors were opened, and afterwards that same Major vowed that Dunkirk beach a year before had been a child's party by comparison ...

The partying and dancing continued until midnight; not only had the event been a great morale booster, but had also raised over a hundred pounds for its intended cause, enabling the ladies' working party to continue with its now vital wartime contribution. Pamela's diary entry for the day in question states quite simply: '*July 2nd* The Fête. It all went terribly well and masses of people. Mummy & Daddy did it very well and it was all wonderful.'

A few days earlier Pamela and Vera Street had made a rare trip to London so that the latter could look her best on the great day. In her diary Pamela comments on the war damage they witnessed:

June 26th Mummy & I went to London! Terrific event – hunting frock for Mummy – seemed pre-war somehow & all wrong. When you think how lucky we have been here & all they've been through ... It was knocked about – especially houses into Waterloo. Poor London ...

Despite such brief moments of light relief, all too soon Pamela found herself once again wrapped up in her bleak existence: '*July 14th* Just existence but you don't live somehow. I think half of me's gone out with David and I'm not certain where the other half is ...' During this dark period, thoughts of David did indeed seem to be almost the only thing that kept Pamela going, and the days she received letters from him were occasions for rejoicing, in particular 6 July, when she received the news of his safe arrival in Egypt: 'Mummy & Daddy fetched me and brought a letter from David and he's arrived safely. Isn't it wonderful.

It was written on the 16th of April & he gave it to the Colonel's wife to forward when she received the cable!'

More letters and telegrams now started trickling in from David. On 15 July Pamela received a letter written whilst he was still aboard the troop ship:

This morning Mummy came in with a letter from David … He'd gone ashore and everyone had been very kind. Poor thing cooped up on the ship. I think the reaction was terrific – please don't forget me David – somehow I hang on to a wonderful hope which is too wonderful to think might come true …

July 23rd This morning as I was doing the flowers in the sluice room Sister brought me a telegram. I thought it as just an ordinary one and then when I opened it, it was from David!!!!! Pop sent it on from home. His new address is R.A. Base Depot, Middle East & fondest love darling etc and it was just wonderful to get …

The gloom that pervaded Pamela's summer was not helped by the weather. Just as the previous year had been kind to British farmers and produced a bumper harvest, in 1941 the British weather displayed its typical fickleness, and from late July throughout almost the whole of August the rain hardly ceased. Pamela's diary entries reveal her concern for her father:

August 5th The rain is ruining the harvest. Poor Daddy.

August 7th Came home and helped a bit with the harvest … Everyone at home terribly busy and working like blacks – feel awful just being home like this and not really helping like everyone else …

August 15th Poor Pop with this dreadful weather. The harvest'll be ruined everywhere. Listened to Atlee [*sic*] telling us Churchill & Roosevelt had met at sea! Thinking of peace when it comes. Oh will it ever …

It was just as well for Arthur Street that some of his other occupations could raise his spirits. Pamela's diary records preparations for the filming of Home Guard activities near Ditchampton Farm, part of Arthur's war propaganda effort: '*July 25th* Came home for the evening … Saw the rehearsal of Daddy's home guard stunt which was very good indeed. All along the road from Arch to Bell Inn …'

Shortly after this Pamela also records a rare, and seemingly extravagant, family day out at the coast: '*July 28th* We all had a lovely day out in Bournemouth … I bought a 9½ guinea red coat which is very breath-taking and I don't know if it's awful to have done or not – also a blouse & uniform shoes. The sea was lovely but barricaded …'

Pamela had to wait several more weeks for further news from David:

August 18th Came home in the evening to two letters from David!!!!!! Just wonderful – he said such a lot – he'd had 'the disease' whatever that is but I hope better now. Poor David. Oh will it ever end. I was thankful to get a letter.

August 21st We all went to Bristol as Daddy had a broadcast. This-morning I had another cable from David!!!!!! His address is changed to F Battery 4th R.H.A. I wonder what it means.

Seven

Desert Life and a Difficult Decision (August–November 1941)

During the Second World War, the morale-boosting effect of letters from loved ones to servicemen overseas and vice versa, cannot be overstated. Once David's regiment had disembarked and made its way to its temporary headquarters, Camp Qassasin near Tel el Kebir, he found four letters from Pamela awaiting him. David's first letter to Pamela from Egypt, dated 1 July, illustrates their importance:

My Darling Pamela,
We landed on the 24th & drove all through the night in charabancs to a camp in the middle of the desert. Next day I was given four letters from you. Darling, they were so lovely & you said so many sweet things that I feel quite unworthy … The first one was written on the 28th just before you went to the hospital & has a lovely picture of you ploughing in it.* I can never really reconcile myself to the fact that you can do that sort of thing …

David then goes on to thank Pamela for her birthday wishes that had arrived just in time (his birthday was 3 July), and also for arranging to send him 'some sort of Christmas hamper':

It is terrible sweet of you, but you are very naughty to spend your money like that & you must promise never never to do it again. I have really plenty of good food here & it is most unlikely that a parcel will reach me …

---

* Pamela frequently illustrated her letters to David with little cartoons of her life back in Wilton.

Little did David realise how limited food would shortly become and how welcome such parcels would prove to be.

He then goes on to describe the camp, the tasks he was currently performing and his impressions of Egypt and its inhabitants in general:

Just now I am thirty miles from my regiment. I have been sent away to a workshop place where I am spending a week on my own, supervising the camouflaging of all our vehicles – 150 in all. I have to keep the right number coming and going & arrange meals for men & send all over the country for paint. They work all night & I am so busy that I had to steal an hour to write this. My hours of work so far have been from 5 a.m. to 1 a.m. every day. It is pretty grim but I like to feel that I am getting it done as quickly as possible …

There are so many things I should like to tell you about this country that I don't know where to begin. The desert is no longer a desert but a sea of sand with tents for whitecaps. There are miles of prisoners' camps. They look like chickens in chicken-runs with nothing but sand and sun around them. I felt very sorry for them until I found that we are all practically the same and it's not too bad at all. I can't cease to wonder at the enterprise of man who can turn all these hundreds of miles of sand into a town of huts & tents with waterpipes & sometimes electricity & showers & even cinemas …

The people are amazing. The young men & women are very beautiful but terribly dirty. In the towns the city slickers wear coats with very built-up shoulders & underneath a pair of pyjama trousers or a nightshirt. There was a group of natives digging near my paint shop this morning. A villainous-looking man with a huge black moustache, high boots with toes that turned up & with a white skull cap with a towel wrapped round underneath it was standing over them with a huge whip, which he used quite frequently. They are a lazy lot. In the workshops about fifteen will get round a Ford engine to lift it up all looking as if they are practically tearing their muscles off & singing odd chants to invoke Allah's help as well, lift it up a few inches & drop it on someone's foot. He then sits looking at you with wide eyes like a child & pointing at his foot. Any two British men could lift the same weight quite easily

I drove along a most picturesque canal coming here. There were a few hundred yards of the brightest green on either side – then desert. There were long thin bright green birds & men riding on donkeys & camels & wonderful barges …

One of the unfortunate consequences of the heat and general unhygienic conditions is illustrated in David's next letter to Pamela, written on 9 July:

I have got 'the disease' today and am lying in my tent on my camp bed in pink pyjamas surrounded by a wonderful mosquito net which I got while away. It hangs from a metal ring above my head & looks like the bed canopy in a Louis quinze bed chamber. Everyone calls me 'the bride', but I am feeling very sorry for myself & cannot laugh much. I don't know what 'the disease' is, but I am quite sure that it is caused by the officers' food being cooked by native cooks. It is nothing serious & everyone gets it; unfortunately I have to walk a quarter of a mile once every ten minutes & I haven't been able to hold food or water down for 36 hours …

[This country] is picturesque in parts, but so dreadfully dirty, & of course it is frightfully hot & dusty. There are sandstorms which sweep through the camp in great eddies every afternoon & plenty of mirages. I didn't think people saw them often, but they are quite plentiful …

David then reflects on the dangers of separation:

There is really an awful lot that I still do not know about you. All I do know is that there is no one else at all like you & that I have made an awful mistake in not smuggling you into my tin trunk & taking you here with me instead of leaving you like a ripe apple hanging over the top of the orchard wall to be stolen by the first naughty boy who comes down the road.

A day later, David was evidently on his feet again and even well enough for night guard duty. In answer to another letter just received from Pamela, he wrote:

It was a lovely letter and made me very excited getting it. I was up all night driving round the camp shooting Arabs & I stopped at about 12 o'clock to have a cup of tea & lay on my tummy in the desert & read your letter by moonlight. You said 'Goodnight Darling – I hope it's a nice night where you are' & it was the most lovely night with the biggest moon & hundreds of stars. Later there was an air-raid nearby & wonderful fireworks …

David's next letter to Pamela, written on 17 July, reveals how their relationship has influenced him:

You are a great inspiration to me & I think I am rather one to you too in a way. I feel that you would expect a very high standard of character & morals from me & I should set myself one when with you too. I should expect terrific things of you too which you would only have to fulfil by being your natural self. You have the three qualities which I think I value most in life, honesty, beauty & goodness …

It is not hard to imagine the impact of letters such as these on Pamela, even if several weeks passed before they reached their eagerly awaiting recipient, not always in chronological order. Whilst David's feelings for Pamela at this time were undoubtedly reciprocated, such letters would have subconsciously engendered in her a sense of obligation to their sender, which would come to be tested in the months – and indeed years – to come.

The last quoted letter from David also contained some important news about his changed circumstances, for which he explained the reasons in a typically self-deprecating manner:

As for me, I have left the 72nd. Although I always knew within me that I should never go into action with them, it came as a great blow to me & I hated saying goodbye to my section & the other officers I know so well now & to think that they would be going into action sometime without me. Although we left three officers behind in England the regiment was still four officers over strength & so four had to be sent to base as 1st line reinforcements. In a way it is rather a disgrace to be sent, as though the choice fell on me, all other considerations being equal, owing to the fact that I was the junior officer in my troop, at the same time if there is anything much to choose between officers naturally they always send off the least useful. But I have always thought myself pretty useless & I am surprised they did not discover it before … We may be here three days or three months, all depending on the intensity of the fighting in the Middle East.

As it turned out, David spent the best part of a month at Base Depot in Almaza, on the outskirts of Cairo, a period which appears to have been in many ways something of a holiday:

I have been into Cairo … It is so wonderful to walk about on carpets again in places like Shepheards [Hotel] & to have a bath & go to a proper toilet place after being in the desert, and it is wonderful to see shops & pretty girls. Of course it is pretty hot, the temperature in the shade is always over 100 during the day, but I rather like that. One is driven almost mad by all the street beggars & sellers of muck. People chase after you in hoards [sic] shoving matches & cigarettes & leather wallets & baby ducks & hardboiled eggs & fly swatters & dark glasses in your face, & whenever you stop people come & scratch about at your shoes & you have to kick them off & even then they crawl after you & give your shoes a brush every time they touch the ground when you are walking along … The evenings I spend going to night clubs & dance places or looking at cabarets, & drinking rather too much. Last night I saw one of these bellywobblers doing the most lecherous dance I have ever seen in my life.

There are two very amusing chaps with me from the regiment & we roar with laughter when we nearly get run over by runaway horsecabs or argue with blacks about money or get lost or swindled … I feel that leaving the 72nd is probably the best thing that ever happened to me, & the fact that fate is playing pingpong with me is exhilarating …

A letter to his parents written on 6 August, towards the end of David's period at Base Depot, confirms his enjoyment of all it had to offer:

Incidentally I am very glad to have left them [the 72nd] now as this has been a marvellous change for me & I have been having a good time here. I am afraid it won't be long before I am posted now & I am really rather looking forward to it as I have had enough of it. Just recently they have found a lot of work for me to do, but before that I had a fortnight of practically none at all. I joined a lovely club* where I went & bathed all day & am very brown now, nearly as brown as a real base officer, who can only be distinguished from a native by lifting up his shirt!

In the evenings I go either to open air cinemas or restaurants & dance. The cinemas are very wonderful & you sit under the stars & black girls come & bring you whiskys [sic] & sodas & sandwiches when you clap for them. The dancing places are great fun too & there are a lot of lovely girls. They speak all sorts of strange languages, but very seldom English & my three girlfriends so far have all spoken French to me, so you can imagine that intelligent conversation is 'out', especially as I have to try to talk French at the same time as trying to do a rhumba or carioca …

Around the same time David wrote a very similar letter to Pamela about these experiences, but added the reassuring paragraph:

I thought to myself this is where my love for Pamela will be tested, but it hasn't been at all. It has taken these dusky beauties to make me realise how completely I want & need you … Often I try to imagine that it is you I am dancing with, but I just can't. Darling the other day I went & looked at the Pyramids. I rode round them on a camel feeling very uncomfortable & rode back on a donkey. I was cornered by a holy man in the tomb of the Sphinx who insisted on telling me my fortune for 10 piastres. He told me that there was a girl in England who thought about me in the mornings. He said I would be back in England in 10 months, married to this extraordinary girl in 14 & back in Egypt with her in 6 years …

I enclose an enlargement of a photo taken by your camera of Stanley & I on our camels that day. It is a wonderful little camera & I will send you some more of its results …

---

* Most probably the Gezira Club.

David's period of comparative idleness came to an end on 12 August, when he and a new base officer friend, Mike Kershaw, were posted to the 4th RHA* as first reinforcements. Two months later, the 4th RHA would be reorganised into three eight-gun batteries, one of which – David's – was officially named DD Battery. The latter's informal name was the 'Jerboa', as the 'History of DD (Jerboa) Battery', printed in 1946, explains with some pride: 'The Battery was granted the great honour of the title "Jerboa" (Arabic for desert rat) by Brigadier Jock Campbell, commanding 7th Support Group, of which the Regiment formed the 25-pdr unit.'

Members of the 4th RHA already considered themselves 'Jerboas', as the beginning of David's later memoir about his desert war experiences illustrates. He was writing about the train journey that he and Mike Kershaw took from Base Depot to the temporary headquarters of the 4th RHA at Mersa Matruh, during which they happened to find themselves in a carriage with a fellow officer returning from leave in Cairo:

> 'You'll like the Fourth,' said the General, 'They're a jolly good crowd.' He wasn't a real general. In actual fact he was a Second Lieutenant, but his name happened to be Booth, so he was promptly nicknamed 'the General' after the Salvation Army leader. 'Of course we're a lot of rats, just desert rats', he went on; 'we live like rats, look like rats, and we will probably all be exterminated like rats', and he roared with laughter …

Up until mid November 1941, the 4th RHA spent the period on training exercises in the vast expanses of the North African desert, only occasionally encountering enemy forces, who were similarly engaged. Both sides were preparing for a major offensive, code-named – in the case of the Allies – 'Operation Crusader', the first objective of which was to relieve the strategically important port of Tobruk. In January 1941, in a significant victory, the Italian garrison at Tobruk had fallen to the Allies, and had been put under the command of Allied Australian divisions. Since the arrival of Rommel's forces later in the spring, Tobruk had become besieged; a couple of unsuccessful attempts to relieve Tobruk had been made during the summer by Wavell's forces. Wavell was replaced by General Claude Auchinleck, who went on to build up what would become known as the Eighth Army, of which the 4th RHA formed part. Rommel was determined to recapture Tobruk, whilst the Allies were equally determined to relieve Tobruk once and for all. The nearby German-controlled Benina airstrip at Sidi Rezegh was to become the scene of much heavy fighting, changing hands several times, and David would find himself in the midst of this chaotic engagement. This was yet to take place, however. Back in August 1941, David found the prospect of joining the 4th RHA

* Royal Horse Artillery.

more than a little intimidating: 'I had felt very nervous about being posted to an R.H.A regiment, as I had heard that they were exceedingly smart and everyone had at least six pairs of riding boots.'

Such fears proved groundless, for on reaching their destination, Rakam Bay – which David described as 'a beautiful little cove with a large white tent within ten yards of the sea' – he and Mike Kershaw were immediately made welcome, and called by their first names from the beginning. David was much relieved to note that his fellow officers' appearance was completely at odds with his preconceived ideas:

I thought these officers looked quite scruffy. They wore issue shirts, old cord trousers with little or no creases supported by wide faded blue canvas belts, and 'desert' suede bootees. The complete outfit was bleached by the sun to the colour of the desert, and they were all sadly in need of a haircut ...

Once inside the mess tent the officer in charge declared: 'You're guests tonight ... What are you going to have?' David's memoir goes on to describe the mess tent as follows:

The tent was furnished with a trestle table and a miscellaneous assortment of folding chairs, which were mostly on their last legs. In the corner was the bar, a small wooden table, on which were a few glasses, the cutlery such as it was, and the drink signing book. Around it were crates of Chinese beer, the only beer obtainable at that time, and some petrol cans full of water. Fly swatters lay around everywhere, and the sand underfoot was covered with dead flies. It was a local rule that you had to kill thirty flies every day before your first drink. There was an electric light wired to the battery of the mess truck. You could not see to read but it was all right for talking. We were plied with questions about England until bed-time. We had not liked to ask where we were to sleep, so we wandered out, groped our way to where our kit had landed when we threw it out of the truck, and made up our beds on the spot ...

The following afternoon, David and Mike Kershaw went to see the adjutant; the outcome of this visit proved to be significant in terms of David's survival during the ensuing fighting:

[The adjutant] told us one of us was to be posted to 'F' battery, the other to 'C', and asked if we had any preferences. I said I should like to go to 'F' as I liked the officers. At first Mike said he didn't mind, and then decided that he too would prefer 'F'. So the Adjutant tossed a coin and Mike lost. If the coin had fallen the other way I should almost certainly have been doing the job which poor Mike was doing when he was killed a few months later.

Before this tragic event, however, David's battery enjoyed a period which in his memoir he described as 'a pleasant simple life which many a town-dweller would have envied'. He and his fellow officers were awoken in the early morning, their heads and pillows still wet with dew, by a 'rat-tat-tat' from a Bren gun. Having dressed in the semi-darkness they would drive or walk to rejoin their troops for PT, after which they would repair to their quarters for a wash and shave from a mug of water from a petrol can and a swim in the sea before breakfast in the officers' mess. There then followed gun drill, vehicle inspections and such like, until midday, by which time work had to finish owing to the intense heat. David's memoir includes the following vignette describing a typical early afternoon for his troop:

> After lunch everyone had a siesta; it was too hot to do anything else. There was little shade as the sun was almost directly overhead but I used to choose a spot half in the shade of the outside of the mess tent, and spent till tea-time either snoozing or reading. Anyone passing through the troop area at this time of day would scarcely believe there was anyone alive. The troops were dispersed over a very wide area for safety from the air. Everyone had found himself some neat little cave or hollow, or else had slung a ground sheet across two neighbouring rocks to form a little shelter, and everyone would be on his back in his little home. A passer might stumble on what he would take to be a derelict lorry. Long ago the sun had sucked all colour from its paint, its mudguards would be all battered and it would have no windscreen or lamps, the sort of ancient crock one sometimes sees in roadside dumps in England. But if he took the trouble to lift the bonnet he would be surprised to see a spotless engine with all the working parts carefully cleaned and greased …

Later in the day David and his colleagues might have another swim or go over to one of the deserted Arab villages to gather fresh figs; at dusk they sometimes drove over to the cliffs to shoot rock pigeons returning to their roosts. David's memoir records that during their month at Rakam Bay they never saw a single German plane. His most nerve-racking experience occurred when, as Orderly Officer, he had to drive over to collect the battery's pay from the pay office at Bergush, on the other side of Matruh:

> On the return trip I ran into a sand storm. As I was feeling my way through the mine fields I suddenly became aware that pieces of paper were flying round my head and out of the window. The bundles of pound notes, which I had placed behind my seat, had somehow come loose. I jammed on the brakes and quickly trapped as many notes as I could with hands and feet. Then I walked back along the track and picked up a few more. I could see several fluttering away in the mine-fields. It was a sad sight but I could do nothing about it …

David's 'happy days' at Rakam Bay were soon to end. During the early summer, while the Allies had been occupied with Greece, the enemy had been import- ing considerable reinforcements, and a major military engagement was expected. Shortly before David and his battery left Rakam Bay their Commanding Officer, Jock Campbell, led them round the desert some 30 miles south to acquaint them with the defensive area to which they should move in case of emergencies. A few days later, there occurred what later became known as 'the September Scare'; David and his troop were ordered to move to the defensive area as quickly as possible:

> Although we were officially at three hours notice to move, we were away in forty minutes. Night was falling as we set off. We wound our way through the sand- dunes onto the open ground, then up the escarpment and joined the Sidi Barani – Matruh road. The gun-towers* looked very small but very business-like as they pulled the guns up the escarpment in the fading light. As I watched them from my position at the rear of the column I felt the thrill of anticipated adventure …

In the event the 'scare' turned out to be merely a German reconnaissance in strength. However David never returned to the camp at Rakam Bay, which was taken over by another RHA regiment. Instead he began a period of intense training in the desert, interspersed with a week's leave in the comparative luxury of Cairo, which in letters home he claimed to be quite undeserved, since he had only been with the regiment some seven weeks. On his return, his regiment received a visit from the Commander-in-Chief, General Cunningham, who gave a little talk about how to deal with tanks:

> 'Wait till you see the whites of their eyes', he said, and suggested as one method of putting them out of action that we should all lie down round the guns pre- tending we were dead, and that then when the inquisitive Germans came along to take a look at us, we should all jump up and put a round through their tank at point-blank range …

On 22 October a new commander, Major Terence O'Brien Butler, arrived to take charge of David's battery. David's first impressions of him were misleading in the extreme:

> He was a fat comfortable-looking young man, immaculately dressed in rather original clothes, who spoke with a slight Oxford drawl. He gave the impression of one who liked to live quietly and well, and I thought that with him in command of the battery we would lead an idle comfortable life. But his appearance belied

---

* A type of tractor used to haul the guns into position.

him. He proved to be an athlete of unbounded energy, and not only worked harder than anyone I had yet met in the army, but also saw to it that everyone else did too. The day started at half past five with the dispersal from leaguer.* We would spend all day rushing over the desert, practising coming into and out of action and sometimes firing at imaginary enemy, and often I would find myself still at work with the major in his tent poring over battery accounts well after midnight. No one was allowed to be in the officers' mess tent except for meals unless he was engaged in work of a military nature …

Up until the beginning of hostilities in mid November David tried his best to write a weekly letter both to his parents and to Pamela, though as training intensified this became increasingly difficult. Whilst his later memoir concentrates primarily on his military experiences and tends to gloss over the discomforts and privations of life in the desert, David's letters home convey a rather different picture. Owing to censorship he was unable to reveal much about his whereabouts or the military manoeuvres in which he was engaged, but instead he described his living conditions in some detail and, to his parents in particular, some of the ensuing health problems from which he was suffering, along with his general state of mind.

On 22 September, a week or two after the 4th had left their temporary camp at Rakam Bay, David wrote to his parents:

It is some time now since I was by the sea & I am very dirty. I washed my neck & feet in a pint of water today for the first time for about ten days …

We wander about like ships in the desert & you never quite know where you are. I am always terrified of getting a whole lot of guns lost! It is very easy to go round in a circle & end up where you started, particularly on a dark night. In the desert small points assume huge proportions, & men will die to capture a thing which looks like a large molehill & is quite useless, just because there is nothing else to fight for …

What a ridiculous war this is! I feel it can't last much longer. What to do when it is over is the great question. I feel I should like to farm in S. Africa, but doubtless I shall never do it …

In another letter to his parents written a month later, David wrote about the hazards of the desert wildlife:

There is no trouble with fleas, ticks or mosquitoes, but flies have been perfectly awful. Fortunately the cold weather is gradually killing them off & soon there won't be any. The only other things are scorpions & snakes, of which the KRITE

---

*   The military term for camp.

is the chief one to avoid. I have not come upon any yet – only one small snake which I killed, but you sometimes get beetles about 2 inches long in your valise at night & think they are scorpions in the dark!

David had always been fastidious in matters of personal hygiene. The following extract from a letter to his parents written on 2 November illustrates just how difficult it had now become for him to keep up even the most basic standards. Having apologised for not writing as often as he would have liked, David continues:

I honestly don't seem to get the time. I have probably never been worked so hard before, but there is a war on, & one must do one's bit. I even had to cut my fingernails by moonlight last week as there was no time during the day ...

It was unbearably hot today ... Flies were just crawling all over my mouth and eyes & everywhere else. In addition I am having a spot of bother with desert sores & crabs of all things!! It is very upsetting! I had to do a surreptitious moonlight shave of the nether regions the other night in a half mug of cold dirty water ...

I have to travel as light as I can, so my wardrobe is very limited, & my only means of laundry ... is when someone goes on leave, which happens about every two months. Pyjamas & sheets have to last 6 weeks to 2 months & shirts at least a fortnight, & last night I had just put on a clean one when someone spilt soup all down my back!

Not a very cheerful letter I'm afraid, but my morale is really very good. Morale is the only word for the situation! I am alive & kicking – there have been a few excitements – & I am feeling fitter than usual, thanks to paraffin every night, plenty of bicarbonate & a fortnightly no 9.*

David's last letter to his parents from the desert was written on 15 November, shortly before the start of serious hostilities. It is a little more cheerful in tone than the previous one, and poignantly sends Christmas greetings, hoping that they would arrive in time:

I am still very harassed & overworked. I was up touring around in the desert all night twice last week, but in spite of everything I am feeling a bit fitter today. My catarrh has become almost negligible; better than it has been for three years anyway. On the other hand my digestion seems to get gradually worse. The desert sores are healing I think, & I have got over the crabs. We are getting a spot more water & I occasionally get in a wash. We have just got some beer up too which is rather nice – the first we have had for many a moon, & a chap coming back from leave has brought a few oranges & grapefruit & some celery & butter. I can't tell you how good they were!

---

*   A laxative pill widely used in the British army at the time.

I wonder if this will get to you by Christmas. If so I will wish you a really happy Christmas, & lots of Good News about then. I hope you will manage a really good Christmas dinner somehow. I wish I could be with you. I expect we will celebrate in some way or other …

David's letters to Pamela from the desert replicate to a large extent those he wrote to his parents, but naturally the tone differs; there are frequent nostalgic references to their snatched time together, and constant gratitude for the letters that she wrote to him. On 5 October he wrote to her:

I have just got back from leave & found a letter from you waiting for me. It was a very old one but a very nice one, June 24th to be exact; you had just heard about my moustache & were not too keen on the idea … It was such a nice letter that I am afraid you liked me more in June than you did in August! I think I will get all your letters in the end, and it doesn't matter how long they take, they are lovely to get …

I had a lovely leave … I spent the first few days in Cairo, where I swam & danced & went to 'the Northwest Passage' & one day galloped on a white arab across the sands from the Mena pyramids almost down to the other ones … It was wonderful to have a hot bath after nearly two months without & also a hot shave & some fresh food & to get all my clothes washed. Also I did a lot of shopping & bought my winter uniform (Bedford cord trousers & a golf jacket lined with camel hair stuff). I also sent you two lovely pairs of stockings for Christmas, which will probably not fit, if they arrive at all … I think I had better send you my love for Christmas now and be sure it gets to you on time. I still think you are quite the sweetest thing I know & very wonderful.

The next letter was written on 27 October, and gives further details of desert life:

This war is a very boring business & a very uncomfortable process, I have decided. As I write I am in our little mess 'tramps dugout' with the side of a lorry as one wall & just room for the three of us at a pinch. It is extremely hot & in a few minutes I shall have to go out & pay the troops in the sun. The wind is blowing much dust about & flies keep settling on my nose as I write. But we have been very lucky last week & had a few pats of butter brought by a friend from Cairo & also a cabbage & last night I even had a bottle of beer. My usual liquid refreshment is tea for lunch, breakfast & dinner, made with tinned milk & out of very salty dirty water & there is usually an eighth of an inch of sand in the bottom of one's mug when one has finished. I am beginning to get very tired of it especially as it is flavoured with petrol fumes in the brewing …

I have just finished my payout & have come back to find 3 letters from you waiting for me. Isn't that wonderful! I have just read them all & feel much better, not that I was depressed, but I was just trying to give you an idea of what this extraordinary life is like.

David's next surviving letter, written on 7 November, expresses deep gratitude for several letters received from her and goes on to reminisce about his and Pamela's time together and English life in general compared to his current circumstances:

You were sunbathing in one [letter] on a day off … & you had been riding in Grovely* in another. Grovely is quite one of the most wonderful names I know. I often say it to myself. It really is too good to be true, but it is.

You talked of lunch at the Cafe Royal & of strawberries & I had to stop reading as I was awfully hungry having had no lunch or tea & as I was waiting for supper …

Life presents rather a dismal picture at present. I am very overworked & there is no beauty to be found in a desert sunrise when we always get up at 5.45. There is no change of scenery – just sand, & one never sees anyone who is not in the army, not even a black man occasionally. There are no papers, no wireless, no news, no water to wash in & sometimes no water to drink … I have been trying to work with flies crawling all over me & dust blowing all over everything & blowing my papers away, & if you scratch yourself it always gets poisonous & you get horrid sores. In short although I have only been 3 months in this part of the country I have had enough & feel like a spot of luxury once more. I am afraid I am too fond of the better things in life & I expect this is all very good for me, but I wish it was all over.

David's final letter to Pamela from the desert, written on 14 November, includes some rather touching homespun philosophy. By then he had received a letter from her describing her guilt earlier in the summer about the patient who had to have a foot amputated. At one point in his letter David replied:

I don't expect you will remember the incident about the telephoning & the man who had his leg off by the time you get this, but you mustn't worry about that sort of thing. You are as bad as me. I always worry myself silly about all my responsibilities, & the mistakes I make & think I may make. I console myself by the thought that I didn't ask for this war or for my job & I am doing my best & can't do more & if I make mistakes, provided they aren't through negligence or laziness, it is really just bad luck. Try doing the same – it is a great help, & if you

---

* Grovely was the wood on the top of the downs overlooking the Wylye Valley from Wilton westwards. It had always been a favourite haunt of courting couples.

ever don't think you are doing your best, I can assure you you are – you certainly were on that occasion, & anyway a few minutes delay wouldn't affect the situation, I don't suppose …

Try to figure out where space ends or think of the speed of light or the responsibilities of generals & admirals & the number of men who get killed by their mistakes & one realises that one's own little worries aren't worth any consideration at all.

This well-meant advice arrived too late to influence Pamela's decision to quit nursing for good. The incident to which David referred had continued to prey on her mind. On 23 August she wrote: 'Feel dreadfully dreadfully depressed about that man again & can't see the wood for the trees. Don't know what to do.' Finally, at her wit's end, Pamela once again off-loaded her worries onto the long-suffering Gertrude Best: 'Went to Matron about Cooper. Never said I told a lie or anything but just more or less explained. She was terribly nice about it. I hope I've done right. Felt much better. Oh dear.'

Her immediate anxieties temporarily assuaged, Pamela switched her concerns to David and his well-being. On 31 August she wrote: 'Today is really the anniversary of my meeting David. Isn't it funny. I wonder just where he is tonight.'

In early September Pamela's diary refers to buying David's Christmas present, some handkerchiefs which she subsequently embroidered in her spare moments; Pamela's typical self-deprecation is again in evidence, even in this small labour of love: 'Did David's present which is very bad & awful stitches.' Despite such perceived imperfections she was anxious to get her efforts in the post to David as soon as possible, for on 16 September she states: 'Put up & sent David's hankies, card & letter.' These reached David just before the beginning of the November offensive, and his letter to Pamela of 14 November shows how gratefully they were eventually received, even if the present was somewhat impractical:

Yesterday I got the longest letter from you & an airgraph (Oct 16) & my Christmas present. Thank you most awfully Darling, they are lovely handkerchiefs & embroidered wonderfully, I think. I would say 'a very useful present' if they weren't far too good to use in the desert.

On 2 September Pamela moved into a new, rather grand, billet, which evidently pleased her: 'Moved into my billet … which is wonderful. The Bainbridges in 27 The Close!' She goes on to record primarily her hospital work but also meetings with various friends, visits to 'the flics', the occasional dance, and time off back at Ditchampton Farm. Exhaustion – both physical and mental – continued to plague Pamela. The principal high points during this period were days when letters arrived from David. One letter in particular delighted her: '*September 16th* Woke up to another letter from David!!!! I think without exception the most wonderful letter anyone could ever have. Oh dear if it could all come true.'*

By now Pamela had new patients to worry about. Her entry for 17 September records a particularly long day which started soon after she accompanied Arthur Street to Salisbury to catch the 6.30 a.m. train to London for one of his broadcasting engagements. In it she refers to a 'probably enteric man'. The next day was equally long with: 'two men querie [sic] enteric. Had to special them. I feel I just can't – get so worried. So afraid I've done something wrong. Do hope I haven't.' The entry for the next day is almost identical, but she added 'might be typhoid for Goldfinch – might not'. Fortunately for Pamela, however, the patient in question was quickly transferred from Tower House: '*September 24th* Goldfinch has gone to the American Hospital – great relief as it was v. worrying looking after him but I do hope he gets better very soon – when you don't know anything it's so difficult.'

Just how personally Pamela took her responsibilities for the patients in her care can be judged from an entry made some three weeks later: 'Went & saw Goldfinch with Susan Copp up at the American hospital. Awfully nice doctor showed us in but it was all against orders & we hadn't got to touch anything – feel simply awful.' Pamela, with her over-active conscience, feared responsibility above all else. A diary entry some two weeks later gives a further example: '*October 9th* Had the jolly old place to myself. Sister was off. It was awful. I can't take it. Had to write the report & everything – oh dear oh dear oh dear.' The following day Pamela had to do the ward round with the senior doctor in charge; she noted in her diary, not without some pride: 'Had to go round with Dr. Burroughs!! Think of it. Me going round with Dr. Burroughs – my goodness – what a hoot – but oh this dreadful responsibility. Can't take it.'

Arthur and Vera Street were painfully aware of how tough their daughter was finding her contribution to the war effort, and did their best to raise her spirits with social gatherings back at Ditchampton Farm on Pamela's days off duty. Her diary records one particularly happy occasion which took place on Sunday 21 September: 'We had a lovely party. Two friends of Pop's from Upavon & 2 more airforce people came and Tom from Larkhill – Di Schreiber, Kay, Bridget & Hazel – Sybil. Tom & Sybil stayed to supper and we went egg collecting & it was quite like old times.'

However a sad family event overshadowed such jollifications. Pamela's diary for September contains several references to visiting her grandmother Foyle during the latter's final illness, and on 27 September she records simply: 'Granny died yesterday morning – did not know till this morning when I rang Mummy.'

★   This was almost certainly the letter about the fortune-teller that David had met at the foot of the Sphinx, during his time at base camp outside Cairo, foretelling his and Pamela's marriage the following year.

Pamela had for some time been longing for a proper break, encouraged by Vera Street who, following her own mother's death and funeral, was now free to accompany her. Mother and daughter cast around, initially in vain, for a West country hotel with a vacancy (at the time hotels in the area were almost permanently occupied by military personnel and well-to-do townsfolk escaping potential bombardment). No doubt sensing Pamela's disappointment, on 15 October Arthur Street took Pamela to London on a rare treat: 'Pop & I London ... Lunch at the Savoy. Saw Blithe Spirit – Noel Coward – then Scotts where had my first oyster. Lovely day.' A few days later a vacancy finally arose at the Branksome Towers Hotel near Bournemouth, where Pamela and Vera spent the best part of a week. Pamela and her mother returned home on 24 October. That same evening Vera took her daughter to see the family doctor, with the following result: 'Mummy took me to Dr. Stratton in the evening and what with everything I have decided to resign from the hospital! It is going to be very difficult.' Pamela was initially obliged to return to work, but on her first day back only managed a brief word with the matron: 'Saw Matron by accident & produced [the doctor's] note & told her I wanted to resign. She asked if I was going to get married silly old thing.' Pamela had to wait a further day before she could talk matters through and officially give in her notice:

> Had my talk with Matron & it is all over. I am leaving next Monday. Well well well. She was awful & went on & on about it all & I said all the wrong things & that it was too hard work & heaven knows what which is ridiculous but anyhow I've done the interview.

Once Pamela's week's notice was up, Gertrude Best's attitude seemed to have mellowed, causing Pamela guilt of a different kind. On 3 November she wrote: 'The most dreadful day – waited until 6 o'clock to wish Matron goodbye which was painful in the extreme as she was nice – was very very busy most of the day – I've left now – it's very odd – after 15 months it's unbelievable.' Not surprisingly, Pamela's diary entry for the next day records her relief and gratitude to be back at Ditchampton Farm: 'Well here I am at home. It seems too wonderful for words at the moment... Wrote to Mrs. McCormick this afternoon & then we all went to the flics which was great fun. It is lovely to be home like this for a bit.'

Another treat was soon in store for Pamela. Her best friend, Sybil Edmunds, was due a couple of weeks' leave from the ATS, and the two girls began to plan a trip away together. London was considered comparatively safe from bombing at this stage of the war, with Hitler concentrating so much of his fire power on the Russian front, and the girls managed to wangle a room at one of the hotels owned by the Streets' friend George Cross. On 16 November Pamela's diary records:

Sybil & I actually came to London. Phil, a Fanny, brought us in an Army car as we both wore uniform – we got the complete giggles on arriving and it was the funniest thing seeing Sybil barge through swing doors in uniform + suitcases … It is a terribly nice place.

During the next few days the girls packed in as much as they could of London's cultural life then on offer:

Went to Leicester Square first thing to find out about 'Gone With The Wind'. It was quite booked up except for standing at 10.30 this morning & the 90th week! Went in and chanced it – stood for 4 hours & it was well worth it although most people would have thought us crazy.

The girls went on to see 'A Quiet Weekend' at Wyndhams, the Russian Ballet at the Garrick (about which Pamela wrote: 'which I didn't enjoy frightfully – never have – but Sybil liked it'), a Vic Oliver review entitled 'Take a Load of This', plus visits to a Sickert exhibition and also one of war paintings at the National Gallery. Pamela even found time to have her hair permed at Harrods,* and at one point commented: 'I love London – if only there wasn't a war on, & you could do what you wanted but I'm very lucky anyhow.'

---

* This was by no means as extravagant as it might appear to today's readers. Although already considered London's most upmarket department store, it was still well within the budget of families like the Streets.

Eight

'Operation Crusader' (November–December 1941)

Despite Pamela's brief taste of London's high life, news of the start of hostilities in the North African desert had not been lost on her. On 20 November she wrote: 'Sent David an air graph – the new offensive in the Middle East is terrific & he must be in the middle of everything.'

According to her diary, the first reports to reach England about 'Operation Crusader' were all positive:

November 21st We seem to be doing well in Libya and have taken them completely by surprise. Wonder where David is.

November 23rd The news from Libya is v. good.

By now, however, having received yet another of David's letters from the desert, Pamela's over-active conscience was at work again; she goes on to reflect on the differences in their current respective lifestyles: 'I feel awful about writing him goodness knows what about London & everything & there he is terribly depressed going without everything & probably thinks me just a good time girl which is probably quite right.'

Pamela need not have worried; the letter in question could never have reached him. After all the months of preparation, David's regiment was already in the thick of military action. David's detailed and fast-moving account of his role in 'Operation Crusader' and subsequent capture, written in his post-war memoir in an understated, somewhat self-deprecatory manner, with frequent flashes of dry, period humour, is too long to reproduce here in its entirety. The following excerpts, however, provide vivid insights into the nature of the fighting. The overall impression is that of the general chaos and swiftly changing fortunes of desert warfare. Examples abound of narrow escapes, individual bravery and personal initiative. Almost as treacherous as the enemy forces was the deceptive terrain itself, in which vehicles constantly floundered. As with any rapid military advance, much depended upon the reliability of the supply chain bearing vital fuel and ammunition, not to mention the availability of reinforcements at scenes of heavy fighting.

'Operation Crusader' began on 18 November, only a few days before Rommel's own planned offensive, which gave the Allies the benefit of the surprise factor, as David's memoir explains: 'I heard later that Rommel had planned his attack … for the twenty-third, five days later. This was quite an advantage to us as his troops were more prepared for attack than defence.'

David goes on to describe the last-minute preparations as follows:

The two days before 'D' day were the complete pandemonium which the older hands told me always occurred before an attack. Everything had to be done at the last minute. Maps, new codes, and orders were handed out, trucks had to be handed over to other regiments, and other trucks came to us. When we finally started off we had that uneasy feeling which you get when you set out for your holidays and feel sure that you have forgotten to pack some essential object.

Such misgivings notwithstanding, the regiment set off in high spirits. Having been told that they had a vast superiority of tanks and aeroplanes, all sections had every confidence in their eventual success. The beginning of the advance was for David, a novice to the battlefield, an awesome sight:

The desert was alive with guns, tanks and lorries all moving westwards in a cloud of sand raised by the thousands of wheels. Wherever one looked one saw military might. Fighters were sweeping round in circles overhead and groups of bombers kept passing over. There was a continual roar of engines. Our guns were rattling along with rows of tanks on either side. We felt so powerful that nothing could stop us.

They continued westwards unopposed all day, crossing the 'wire' between Egypt and Libya in the early afternoon at a point just above Fort Madalena, which David described as a 'real P. C. Wren fort where you expected to see the foreign legion keeping guard on the mud turrets'.

Not everything went exactly to plan on that first day. Arriving late at a pre-arranged refuelling point which should have had overhead air support, and finding neither fuel nor fighter planes there, they continued on until darkness fell and they were obliged to camp for the night. The gun-towers were almost out of petrol, and much of the night was spent siphoning fuel from the smaller to the larger vehicles so that all would have sufficient to cover 20 miles the next day. Fortunately their 'B' echelon with fresh supplies caught up with them the following morning, so their advance westwards was able to continue.

David's first narrow escape came on the second day. Major O'Brien-Butler, at the time at an observation post some 2 miles ahead of the main force, radioed instructions to David to take a gun-tower and rescue his armoured observation truck, which had floundered earlier in boggy ground, giving him fifteen minutes in which to complete the task. David duly succeeded in pulling out the Major's truck, but halfway back it ran out of petrol. With enemy tanks approaching and Allied troops to his rear David found himself potentially in the middle of a battle, but luckily managed to radio back for another gun-tower to pull him back to their gun position. Fortunately the enemy column in question, composed largely of non-fighting vehicles guarded by a few tanks, realised that it was vastly outnumbered and consequently withdrew.

That afternoon the Allied advance changed direction northwards towards the coast and Tobruk, reaching the Benina aerodrome at Sidi Rezegh, where enemy aircraft were still landing, oblivious to the rapidly approaching Allied forces. David's battery prepared for action, but was overtaken by the 6th Tank Regiment, which raced ahead to take the airstrip by surprise with practically no opposition. David's battery followed on down to the aerodrome where they 'shuffled around for an hour or so' before settling for the night on the north-west corner, the guns surrounded by the Sixth Tank regiment.

In the small hours David was awoken by the rumbling of tanks and shouting of orders in German. It turned out that they had leaguered for the night only a few hundred yards from a well dug-in German anti-tank position, and during the night German troops had surrounded them on three sides. The Germans opened fire, and David described his first experience of being thus targeted as follows:

> Mortar, shells and solid anti-tank shot came at us from three sides. The enemy used tracer shell of all colours, red, blue, green, yellow and white, which made a really beautiful firework display in the dark. You could easily watch the shells coming and they all appeared to be coming straight towards you personally.

The regiment retreated hastily some 5 miles south, where they dropped into action and returned the enemy fire. Only one of the gun-towers was lost, but a few tanks were set on fire. Most members of David's regiment survived unscathed, though two fellow officers became separated from the unit during the night and were later reported prisoners of war.

The following morning David's brigade went on the offensive again, led by their tanks, which overran the German anti-tank gunners. David described – with naïve amazement – the duplicitous nature of the enemy artillery:

> They stood up with their hands up, and after the tanks had passed, got down to their guns again and shot up all our bren carriers who were following the tanks.

We kept up a continuous fire, helping to repel enemy tank attacks from every side, putting down smoke screens to assist our tanks, and firing at the German infantry and supply vehicles in the distance. The desert all around us gradually became so covered with knocked out tanks and burning vehicles that a great deal of skill was required to recognise which ones were knocked out and which were not. One had to look in every direction in an attempt to observe enemy tanks before they observed us, and one had great difficulty in distinguishing our own from the enemy's. We were bombed and shelled continually.

By nightfall things were looking bleak for David's brigade, with several units severely depleted. Major O'Brien-Butler gave his men a particularly grave pep talk, which David remembered almost *verbatim*:

The Major called the troop round him and spoke to us somewhat as follows: 'I want you all to know the situation. As you know the Brigade has had a pretty rough time here and out of three regiments, a hundred and sixty-five tanks in all, there are only about fifteen left in their tracks. There is a thin line of infantry in front of us and nothing behind. It is thought that the enemy are preparing for a night attack. I want you all to understand there is no withdrawing from this position. If the enemy come in during the night we won't use small arms, as we'll only shoot each other in the dark, but I should like everyone to arm himself for the night with a pick or a spade and we'll bash the Germans over the head. Of the two supporting brigades the 22nd is stuck in the mud to the south and no one knows where the 4th is. To your posts dismiss.'

Having been given guard duty from midnight to 3 a.m., David saw little point in setting up his camp bed, but instead spent the night in the front of his truck, reviewing the situation:

It was obvious the battle was not going according to plan, and it struck me that some-how or another it looked as if we were the 'suckers' … Just then the Major appeared at my window. 'Hello David,' he said. 'Well Sir,' I said by way of conversation, 'I take a pretty serious view of this.' 'Yes,' said Terence, 'sometimes things become so serious that they are just laughable,' and we both laughed, but it was pretty forced.

Up until this time I had not been in the least worried about the possibilities of death, but now that it seemed almost probable I suddenly discovered that I did not want to die at all, and as I sat in my truck I found myself saying a few short prayers.

David spent the remainder of his period on guard on high alert, experiencing several false alarms, partly due to a curious feature of the North African desert at night:

The desert around us was strewn with large white snail shells, each nearly the size of a hen's egg. Whenever vehicles moved near us in the dark these shells were squashed making a loud crunching noise. Several times I thought I heard noises of approaching enemy, and wandered out with one hand on my revolver and covered by a couple of sentries, but the Germans never attacked.

Better news reached David's battery shortly before dawn; the 4th Brigade and 5th South African Brigade were reported to be drawing near, and that by 10 a.m. the battery would be relieved. In the event neither brigade turned up at the appointed time, but David's regiment was spared the expected attack and instead managed to regroup and take part in another attempt to retake the airstrip at Sidi Rezegh later that day, during which David experienced a particularly narrow escape. In the afternoon he was sent to relieve a fellow officer, Hugh Barrow, at an observation post overlooking both the airstrip and nearby road, along which enemy vehicles were moving back and forth. Whilst Hugh was grabbing a bite to eat in the gully below, David watched as seventy German tanks refuelled and moved slowly out of sight westwards; David duly reported this back to head-quarters on Hugh's wireless. What happened some twenty minutes later took him completely by surprise:

> A terrific noise started on my left, and several anti-tank portées* and other vehicles rushed past me firing behind them. The tanks had moved round in a wide arc and were attacking the aerodrome behind me from the west. I ran quickly back to the gully, winding in the wire of the remote control as I went, and Hugh and I drove out of the gully and over the next ridge with bullets and shells whizzing past us ... Then I discovered that the Fourth Brigade had arrived, were coming onto the aerodrome from the east, and beginning to engage the Germans. Realising that I was on the wrong side of a tank battle, and being of no use to the troop without a wireless set, I decided to make my own way back across the aerodrome. We [i.e. David and his driver] drove as fast as we could straight through the middle of a tank battle, which was by then well under way, and thought ourselves very fortunate to arrive at the troop position undamaged.

David's fellow officer Hugh Barrow remained behind enemy lines, dodging from gully to gully with his wireless set, reporting valuable information about the ene-my's movements, for which he was later awarded a Military Cross. This was also the well-documented engagement in which their Brigadier, Jock Campbell, was awarded the Victoria Cross. for outstanding bravery, as David's memoir goes on to explain:

---

*   Trucks carrying anti-tank guns.

He led the tanks into action in an open staff car; then finding a troop of the Sixtieth Field regiment, who were having a hard time on the east of the aerodrome, he fired a gun, whose crew had been wiped out, continuing after he was wounded until he was carried out of the action on the back of a tank.

For David, these first few days of battle preceded a further three weeks of skirmishes and at times heavy fighting. On the one hand he clearly experienced the adrenalin rush of battle: 'Then followed the most hectic and exciting days of my life.' On the other hand, however, he quickly discovered the disadvantages of being in the artillery – as opposed to being in a more rapidly mobile unit of a regiment – in a desert environment:

I had always imagined that when the artillery went into action, they would choose some nice quiet spot, protected from the sight of the enemy by a good big wood or hill, and would fire over the heads of the infantry with nothing much to fear except the shells from retaliating batteries. During the following days I was very disillusioned. In the desert there were no friendly hills or woods, and being members of the Seventh Armoured Brigade there was usually no infantry in front. In battle we seemed to be the least protected and mobile of all. Tank battles in the desert were like naval battles. As in naval battles there was a great advantage in catching the enemy silhouetted against the rising or setting sun, where you could shoot them easily and they could hardly see you. Consequently there was much manoeuvring and you never knew from which direction the next attack was coming. The tank crews were protected by a certain amount of armour and could quickly advance or retire or change direction according to the tide of battle; we had no protecting armour, and if we wanted to advance or retire we must first bring up the gun-towers and limber up, packing up all the shells, charges and paraphernalia lying round the guns. If we were in a line facing, say, north, and the enemy attacked from the south, we had to turn the guns round and quickly bring up all our 'soft stuff', gun-towers, ammunition lorries etc which were dispersed behind the guns through the guns and disperse them on the opposite side. If the enemy attacked from the west we could not just turn our guns to the right as each would find itself pointing straight at its neighbour, but we would have to manhandle them round in wide arcs so that the whole troop could fire to the west unobstructed. During the following days although the troop remained in the same position we were made to spin round like a circus.

By now David must have appreciated the relevance of his training in the English West Country almost a year previously, much of which consisted of moving his troop's guns – frequently at night – from one muddy field to another.

Other divisions, however, were not so well trained. After the arrival of the 5th South African Brigade, David was ordered to obtain from them a quantity of much-needed ammunition. It quickly became apparent to him that the South Africans were woefully ill-prepared for the ensuing fighting. Even at the height of battle, bureaucracy was one of the problems; once David had – with great difficulty – tracked down the troop Sergeant-Major in charge of supplies, he was obliged to sign a great many forms before two ammunition trucks were released into his care. Worse was to come, however, as his memoir describes:

> The lorries were driven by negroes, who were deep down in slit trenches, and it was quite a job to get them both out at the same time. I discovered that the ammunition in the lorries was buried beneath a mass of water tanks, cooking apparatus and spare clothes. I told the drivers to pull it all out, and I led them off to our troop … On unloading I discovered that a great many of the cartridges were used. When I asked one of the drivers if he knew about it, he rolled his eyes and said, 'Yus, Sah, dey bin like dat since Abyssinie; we don know why we lug dem round' … After I had taken the black men back to their own troop, I told Pip Crane [a fellow officer] that they would all be wiped off the face of the desert, which prophecy was fulfilled later that day.

Indeed, that afternoon the South Africans were taken by surprise by Rommel's column, which attacked their poorly guarded 'B' echelon. Although nearby, David's troop could only watch helplessly as the Germans took prisoners and looted vehicles, for fear of hitting the South African troops, who now came streaming back through the British guns. Once those able to make their escape had done so, David's troop opened fire, David taking over from another gunner who was unable to distinguish between German and South African tanks in the smoke and dust. David reported having the satisfaction of seeing two tanks, at which he had been firing, burst into flames. Meanwhile the Germans launched a secondary attack under the cover of some abandoned South African ambulances, of which David's regiment's 'C' troop bore the brunt, with heavy casualties.

Once again the outcome of the fighting was inconclusive, with David's unit being obliged to withdraw. The following day they received orders to come to the aid of the Allies' advanced divisional headquarters, which were being threatened by Rommel's column some 20 miles to the south. They set off, with David positioned at the rear with instructions to pick up any 'stragglers'. At one point the Major radioed back to him to bring in an abandoned lorry which looked in good condition. Whilst obeying orders and roping the lorry in question onto another lorry, David got left some distance behind; to make matters worse his own truck then developed a petrol stoppage. Whilst his driver was cleaning out the petrol filters, they came under friendly fire from two Hurricanes who fortunately missed them. This, however, alerted David to the fact that there were enemy troops in the vicinity.

Once David and his driver got under way again they came across another 'straggler', a young Rifle Brigade officer and three men whose truck had lost a wheel. The young officer waved frantically for David to come to their rescue; David's car was already carrying four men, but somehow he and the others managed to cram them on board and they set off once more to catch up with their troop. At that moment, David became aware of a huge enemy column advancing in the same direction on their right. Despite David's driver's best efforts to bear left with all possible speed, they were too weighed down to put any distance between themselves and the enemy column, who had by now noticed them. Two German cars detached themselves from the column and raced over, opening fire. What occurred next was another of David's lucky escapes, as his memoir describes:

Unfortunately I was prevented from returning fire by the young R.B. officer, who had been sitting on the roof behind me with his legs hanging over my shoulders, and who, when the shooting started, evidently decided that the top of the car was a bad place to be, and clambered over my head onto the left mudguard. His feet slipped and he was left clutching onto the mudguard with his legs bumping along the ground, and yelling frantically to me to rescue him. I leaned over the door and managed to catch hold of the bottom of one of his trouser legs, and we proceeded thus until we drew out of range and I was able to order a halt and pull him in again. We were barely on the move again before the motor started to choke and splutter and once again the car stopped. At this moment a Bren carrier, which had apparently also been left behind our column, appeared like a saving angel. I waved frantically at it, and when it drew alongside us I asked the officer in charge if he would take all eight of us on board. He replied that we could but try, and there didn't seem to be any alternative, so the twelve of us limped along in the Bren carrier and managed to rejoin our column.

David made use of a temporary lull in the fighting the following morning to take some wounded men to the first-aid post, where he took the opportunity to have the desert sores on his hands dressed. That afternoon David was granted a temporary reprieve from front-line action and an opportunity to use his initiative. The major told him that the regiment was preparing to seek out and destroy a German column to the north, but that there was little point in taking along the severely depleted 'C' troop. Instead David was instructed to stay behind to look after them, collect any missing men and try and bring in some abandoned trucks. The following day, having got food and water for the thirty men in his charge, David was on the point of setting off to find the abandoned vehicles, when he received a chance visit from Brigadier Jock Campbell. The brigadier advised David that the direction in which he was heading was too risky, and that if he was supposed to be re-organising a troop, he probably had more pressing things to do.

David decided to get more guns, a tall order for a lowly Second-Lieutenant, but one in which he was ultimately successful. First he made contact with advance army headquarters, and requested guns and vehicles for an entire troop. On David's assurance that he had the requisite number of drivers, arrangements were made for four guns to be sent to the railhead and for David to be granted the necessary support vehicles. Having selected fourteen drivers, David set off immediately in the salvaged lorry, leaving the other men in the charge of the Sergeant-Major. The following morning they reached the army headquarters just inside the Egyptian border near Fort Madalena, where David reported to the authorities and met the generals, who seemed pleased with the progress of the advance. Then began a few days of feverish activity, which David described thus:

> During the next few days I worked harder than I have probably ever worked in my life. I was up at dawn and busy till after dark, never finding time to have a proper meal or even a shave. I was afraid that I might have perhaps overstepped myself by ordering equipment for a whole troop without consulting anyone … At rear army headquarters I learned that there were only four 'pick-ups' (8cwt* vehicles equipped with wirelesses) in reserve for the army, and that I was not important enough to have two of them. This meant that I had to collect vehicles in one place, wirelesses in another, and have them fitted in yet another, and there didn't seem to be any batteries or head-phones available. The guns duly arrived up from Matruh, but had no sights or gun tools … All the new vehicles which I collected had to be equipped with three days' reserve food and water for the number of crew which they would eventually contain. The officers in charge of food and water points were very reluctant to grant me this, and I had great trouble in obtaining sufficient water cans.

Worse was to come; whilst collecting rations one evening in semi-darkness, David drove over some barbed wire which wound itself round his car's rear axle and ripped open the petrol tank. He managed, with great difficulty, to have it repaired the following morning; however his driver had by this time developed an extremely painful poisoned thumb, and David was obliged to leave him at a field hospital and take over the driving himself.

David had one stroke of luck in the midst of these frenetic three days. Whilst driving through a desert transit camp *en route* to the railhead, he came across a further fifteen men from his regiment who had been on leave when the battle started and had been unable to rejoin their troop. David divided these extra hands

* hundredweight.

between his new vehicles and, finally, with justifiable pride, was ready to lead them back into action:

> By the end of the third day I had gathered together everything obtainable, and set off as night fell with my fine new troop laden up with petrol, water, rations and ammunition. On the following afternoon I was once again with the sergeant-major and fifteen men who I had left behind.
>
> I now had forty-five men and was able to form them temporarily into sections to make a fighting troop. I was able to collect a few more gun sights and tools, some old clothes in lieu of cleaning materials for the guns, some German spades from an abandoned lorry, and pick-helves* to be used in place of ramrods. Next day we drove the last lap of twenty miles across deserted desert to report to Brigadier Campbell, and then accompanied the 'B' echelon in the dark to rejoin the battery, where I was welcomed very enthusiastically by Terence [Major O'Brien-Butler], who immediately inspected the new guns and vehicles.

Almost inevitably, pride came before a fall. The following day David discovered his new wireless did not work because the batteries were flat, nor could he start his car for the same reason. As luck would have it, the colonel drove over to find David having his car pushed round in circles by a lorry behind the guns in an effort to start it. David admitted in his memoir:

> I was secretly expecting him [the colonel] to give me a pat on the back for producing a renovated troop at such short notice, but instead he gave me a good dressing down for allowing my guns to be in too straight a line, thereby making a fine target for a strafing enemy plane.

Happily this reprimand failed to dent David's pride entirely, for despite their various technical shortcomings, his new munitions evidently added to the regiment's fire-power, as his memoir goes on to explain: 'During the next three days the troop averaged eight hundred rounds a day, and I had the satisfaction of knowing that these rounds would not have fallen among the enemy but for my efforts.'

It would not be long, however, before David's luck ran out.

---

* 'helve' means 'handle'.

Nine

Capture
(December 1941)

On 7 December 1941, an event took place that was to change the course of the war. Over the past few decades Japan had become the dominant force in South-East Asia, with an increasingly aggressive expansionist policy. Tensions between Japan and the USA had been building steadily, and by December 1941 relations between the two countries had reached an all time low. Though Japan was not yet technically at war with the USA, Japanese attacks on the colonies of the Western Powers in the Far East were feared. Nevertheless the Japanese bombing of the US Pacific Fleet at its main base on Oahu Island in Hawaii, within US territory, came as a complete surprise to the forces stationed there, and shocked the world. However calamitous, this proved a pivotal point in the fortunes of the war. Up until then the USA, whilst offering aid to the Allies in the form of convoys and munitions, had yet to declare war on the Axis forces; now its hand was forced, and within a matter of days America formally joined what had now become a global conflict. On this side of the Atlantic, Britain no longer stood alone, as Prime Minister Winston Churchill made clear in his broadcast to the British public on 8 December. The tide had finally turned in the Allies' favour.

★ ★ ★

Meanwhile, David's regiment continued to fight inconclusively in North Africa until, in his own words, came 'the dreadful night when I was captured'. The official history of DD Battery records the event briefly as follows:

> 12th December – During the night enemy columns passed close to the Column's leaguer. Lieut. McCormick had broken down within a mile or two at dark (he even returned once to the leaguer to collect M.T. spares and had gone out again). He and his crew bedded down where they were, intending to come in in the morning, but they were never seen again and were later reported prisoners of war.

In his memoir, David elaborates on this episode in far more vivid and detailed terms. It was yet another example of the rapidly changing fortunes of war, for David was to find himself both captor and captive within a matter of minutes. At this stage in the fighting, the Germans were being pushed back from Tobruk, and on the day in question, David's unit had advanced some 100 miles westwards in order to attack the enemy's communications. They had managed to destroy a number of German supply vehicles which, in David's words, 'fled first to the right and then to the left in a vain attempt to avoid our shells, like frightened sheep being rounded up by a sheepdog'.

By evening, however, it was decided that David's unit had advanced too far behind enemy lines and needed to withdraw some 10 miles, with David at the rear with instructions to pick up any 'stragglers', on this occasion an ammunition lorry which had suffered a petrol stoppage. Once the problem had been fixed, David and his party set off back to the leaguer; however ahead of them at one point was what, on first sight, appeared to be a patch of white sand; this turned out to be a pool of water, in which the ammunition truck foundered. David and his men were unable to pull it free without further assistance, and he radioed back to his unit to explain his predicament, eventually receiving orders to return to the leaguer in the smaller lorry, which he managed to do in the dark with some difficulty. It was decided that he should then return to the bogged down ammunition lorry with a spare gun-tower, and make another attempt to free it. It took until 3 a.m. for David and his team to unload the ammunition onto firmer ground and eventually pull out the beleaguered lorry. Finding their way back to their unit a second time, however, proved even more difficult, largely because the magnetic compass David was using to take bearings was variously affected by the different vehicles in which he made each journey. Unable to find the leaguer, he and his men received radioed instructions to stay where they were for what remained of the night, and rejoin the column at first light.

It was now 4 a.m., so David told his men to get some rest whilst he himself waited up in the front of his car. Half an hour later, he became aware of the rumbling of an approaching enemy column. Being already lost and not knowing in which direction to move, David decided that he and his men should stay put and hope the column would pass by without spotting them.

Just then, however, a small car appeared out of the night, and stopped some 20 yards away, its occupants peering at them intently. David's memoir continues:

I walked over to it, and looking through the window asked, 'Sind Sie Deutsch?' in my best German. The answer was something quite incomprehensible; so I drew out my revolver from under my greatcoat and waggled it at them. Three Italian officers and their drivers hurriedly jumped out with their hands above their heads, and my men came over and relieved them of their weapons. They looked very frightened and one produced a bottle of cognac to pacify us.

The rumbling of the enemy column was growing ever louder, so David decided that it would be prudent to move after all, taking with them their new prisoners, who he considered to be of possible use to Allied Intelligence. Finding room for them all was the first problem, but by distributing the Italians amongst David's vehicles and commandeering the Italian car, it seemed just feasible. Unfortunately, at the very moment that one of David's men was trying to start the Italian car, a bright moon broke through the clouds, revealing two enemy columns, one to the north and one to the south of David's little party. Three vehicles were rapidly bearing down on them, and the tables were about to be turned. This is how he described the actual moment of his capture, for which he later blamed himself:

> I have often thought that if I had thought quickly enough and we had run to our cars, we could have started up by the time the cars reached us, and dashed off into the desert with a good chance of escaping and rejoining our column sometime during the day. But tired as I was, and not knowing which direction to take, I stood hypnotised by the situation during those vital seconds quite unable to make any decision at all.
>
> The lorries stopped. Each contained about fifty soldiers, sitting half asleep with blankets round their shoulders. From the leading lorry stepped a tall Italian captain with a bandage round his head. He spoke to the former prisoners, then turning to me asked, in good French, how many men I had with me. I told him there were seven of us. He told me that we were entirely surrounded by thousands of Italians and Germans, and that we had the choice of surrendering or fleeing. If we chose to surrender we would be well-treated, we would go to Italy where we would have wonderful food, sunshine, and live in a beautiful villa for the rest of the war; we could keep all our personal possessions. If we attempted to flee, he could not guarantee that we would not all get shot. I told him I would consult my men. Six of us, including myself, thought we were in the bag; the seventh, a Londoner … who had recently joined the regiment, suggested that I put *them* all in the bag. I told the captain that we were his prisoners and handed him the butt of my revolver. He said I had made a wise decision, and that we were very fortunate, for 'for us the war was over'. 'For us' our troubles were just beginning, and I think we all realised the fact.

Thus began David's uncomfortable and frequently perilous journey to an indeterminate period of captivity in Italy. The Italian soldiers, by now fully awake, immediately started looting the British vehicles until ordered to stop by the Captain, but not in time to save David's first significant loss, 'my treasured box of chocolates, which I had ordered a month before, and which had arrived on the previous day'. His memoir continues:

I was told to get in the front of my own car. The Captain got in the driving seat, my men were put in one of the Italian lorries, and the whole column slowly turned round and set off in the direction whence it had come … The Captain was full of admiration for the Ford pick-up, and I couldn't help telling him how to drive it properly when he made mistakes. It seemed a crime to see a car so abused. He asked me if there were many British in the neighbourhood and if I thought there would be a battle the next day. I told him there were thousands of British all round and he would almost certainly be dead by this time tomorrow. He swallowed once or twice but said nothing.

The Italian column with its new prisoners eventually came to a halt between two groups of small guns, and almost immediately came under fire from two British armoured cars that had appeared out of the half-light. The Italian captain leapt out and fell flat on his face, ordering David to do likewise. As shells fell all round them, David's reaction was understandable: 'As I lay on the ground … I felt quite appalled at the idea of being hit by my own people.'

Once the firing was directed further down the line, David was ordered back into his car, and the captain drove back at high speed through the Italian lines, all the while leaning out of the window and exhorting the Italian gunners to stay at their guns. David's memoir continues:

A small car full of officers dashed past us in a panic, blowing its horn and shouting at a few lorries to get out of its way. It appeared that the great advantage of being an officer in the Italian army was that you had a faster car and could get out of the way of danger quicker.

Once safely out of the firing line, David was ordered into a small car with three Italian officers who were instructed to take him to the Italian Commandant. For several hours he was driven round in a half-hearted manner, with frequent stops, until some Allied 25-pdr shells landed in the vicinity. At this point the search for the commandant was abandoned, and David was returned to his men, whom he now found sitting in a lorry below an escarpment.

The little band of British prisoners was by now in the hands of a new group of Italians. There seemed to be only one officer in charge, whom David described as follows:

He was a huge good-looking man, who reminded one of the hero of some Hollywood military film. He managed somehow to keep himself looking smart, providing a marked contrast to the others, whose appearance was little or no better than that of a gang of beggars or gypsies. He seemed to be in charge of all the Italians within a radius of about a square mile, including fifteen midget tanks, several guns, and a horde of infantry, which he ruled by yelling and gesticulating at them, and, when this produced no effect, which it never did, by going round kicking them with his beautifully polished riding boots.

As the day progressed, David's contempt for his captors intensified. Shells were still falling intermittently in their midst, causing the Italian lieutenant to move his 'mixed flock' further along the escarpment accordingly:

Then ensued all the usual yelling, arm-waving, and kicking. Tanks and lorries were started up, guns were fastened onto the rear of the lorries, the infantry all clambered in, and the whole cavalcade moved about two hundred yards along the base of the escarpment. Then more yelling and kicking, and out they all got again, each man with his wretched rifle and spade, each man to choose his own position, which was usually in some natural hole or gully ... where he could get no view of the enemy, and would be useless in the event of an attack, but felt fairly protected from shells or bombs. They all dug themselves little troughs, and collected boulders and rocks, which they lay round their edges, giving the impression of gardeners making little rock gardens round little pools. But instead of pouring water in the troughs they lay in them themselves until the next time they would be kicked out for a new move. They were completely apathetic.

It seems that one of the missing elements of David's military training was instructions on what to do with his personal possessions in the event of capture. By now he and his men were under the immediate control of a sergeant who clearly hungered after David's field-glasses, which were still hanging round his neck under his great-coat. With the benefit of hindsight, David described what he should have done next:

I know now that I should have smashed them as soon as I got an opportunity, but capture was a thing I had never anticipated or thought of, and I had no idea of the correct drill. If I was ever to be captured again I should now know exactly what to do. I should first arm myself with detailed information of all the news of military and general value for the benefit of older prisoners of war, who I should later join, then have the biggest meal of my life, put on all my best and newest clothes, including two sets of shirts and underclothes, fill my pockets with spare socks and toilet kit, and have cans of petrol handy to throw over every other piece of army and personal equipment and be set alight. As it was I was foolish enough to believe that I really was going to be allowed to keep my personal kit, as I had been promised, and apart from tearing up a few notes and maps, which I thought might prove of interest to the enemy, I destroyed nothing, even being short-sighted enough to change into a very worn pair of boots and socks instead of the good ones that I was wearing.

The Italian sergeant kept pestering David for his binoculars, at one point telling him that his commanding officer had ordered David to hand them over. David countered by saying he would do so only if the officer gave the order in person. After much sulking on the part of the Sergeant, a compromise was reached whereby David agreed that when he and his men were handed on to someone else he would give the sergeant his binoculars, provided that in the meantime the latter had done everything he could for the little group of prisoners: 'From then on he was quite subservient, fetching bread and water for us, allowing me to fetch some rice porridge and condensed milk from my car ... and allowing us to get out of the truck and cook it.'

A crowd of Italian soldiers now gathered round, intrigued by such proceedings. David soon realised that they did no cooking for themselves, but relied on one hot meal a day brought round in a truck, consisting of a soup of vegetables and macaroni; for the rest of the day they made do with dry bread, a tin of inferior bully beef, and water.

That night David slept for the last time in his own camp bed, 'tucked up by the binocular-struck sergeant'. At this point he experienced a reaction evidently common to many newly captured prisoners of war. Instead of lying awake worrying about the horrors awaiting him, or fretting about how he might have avoided capture, in his memoir he describes how he felt:

> That night I slept the sleep of the just ... For many weeks I had started the day at 5 a.m., been on the go without time to rest for a proper meal all day, and after dark often had to spend most of my valuable sleeping time groping my way over the desert to some other unit to collect guns, petrol or spares. And of course the previous night we had no sleep at all ... Now that I was a prisoner ... instead of being miserable and dejected, I felt a great sense of peace and relief, as if all my troubles were over and an overwhelming weight had lifted from my shoulders. I must have gone to sleep at about eight o'clock and slept till after ten the following morning.

David was in for a rude awakening the next day when the reality of his new situation truly dawned on him:

> The fact that I was a prisoner really sank home however when Nature called me. I was allowed to go a few yards from the truck to take my trousers down, and one of our guards was instructed to stand almost on top of me with his rifle at the ready.

Later that day David and his men began their journey to the coast in earnest. They were taken by lorry some way westwards through heavily shelled lines to a hollow where David received his first proper interrogation through the medium of an interpreter. His refusal to reveal anything other than his name, rank and number exasperated his interrogator:

> [He] went right up in the air and raved against the British so-called sense of honour. It seemed that we thought nothing of bombing hospitals and hospital ships and raping our enemy's womenfolk, but when asked a simple straightforward question, this sense of honour forbade us to answer.

David next saw the rest of his men being led off to be similarly interrogated, and shouted a reminder to them that they need only state their name, rank and number. Then followed a particularly sinister development:

> I was led out of the hollow to rejoin the others, who were paraded in a line with their backs to a group of tough-looking men armed with tommy guns. I was told to stand at the end of the line. The others were all looking a bit green, and the man next to me whispered that he thought they were going to shoot us, a thought that had already occurred to me. An Italian officer came up and asked if we were still determined not to answer their questions, saying that it would be much worse for us is we didn't. I told him we were, and after he had a short conversation with the men behind us, to our great relief we were ordered to get into a nearby truck.

At this point David and his companions were parted from their personal belongings, which were still in the truck that had carried them to the hollow. David protested in vain to a 'tough individual in silver braid and stars' that he had been promised they could keep their kit; the latter replied that he knew all about it, but that their possessions were now his. He then proceeded to search David and relieve him of his binoculars and last cigarettes. David's memoir continues:

> I discovered later that he was a *brigadiere*, equivalent to a sergeant in our army. I am not a revengeful person by nature, but many were the times later on when I had no socks or toothbrush, or a bad cold and no handkerchief, that I imagined myself shooting that *brigadiere*.

As night was falling the British prisoners, guarded by three Italian soldiers, were driven off in another small truck filled with motor tyres. Their driver promptly lost his way in the dark, and they were obliged to spend a very uncomfortable night in the truck with no room to stretch out. David recalls in his memoir that to make matters worse, 'a host of fleas left their Italian hosts, evidently preferring British blood'.

At daybreak the following morning, having had no breakfast, they resumed their journey, stopping after a few hours at a rear headquarters where David was forced to relinquish his cap badge to an Italian officer, about whom David wrote wryly in his memoir: 'I expect he took it back on his next leave as a souvenir of the British officer who he had captured single-handed.' The party then continued as far as the main coast road, where they were herded into a small pink hut to await yet another truck. David described his amazement at their new guard's behaviour, quite unlike that of any soldier he had previously encountered:

[He] was a fine-looking tramp with a black beard, who sang pieces from various operas in a fine tenor for about an hour while we waited. I had never imagined such a soldier in my wildest dreams, but later on I was to discover that he was not such a rarity as I imagined. The Italians are a music loving race, brought up on their famous operas, and even the simplest peasants seem to have a fine knowledge of music. When they are happy they sing, and don't appear to be the least bit self-conscious about it.

An open-sided truck now transported the prisoners westwards along the coast road, with David sitting in the front beside their driver, 'a gnarled old peasant in civilian clothes'. During the journey David noted with dismay the number of German and Italian tanks and other transport either moving up to the front or lying hidden from aerial view in the orchards alongside the road: 'It was apparent to me that the enemy had a great many reserve tanks, which our intelligence knew nothing about.'

As they neared their destination, David could not help becoming increasingly impressed by the neatness and efficiency of Mussolini's colonisation scheme: 'The road was excellent and along the sides were well-cultivated little farms with modern pink villas with the words of the Duce scrawled across their sides.'

At midday they reached a village with a small square building in the centre, into which they were shepherded whilst all but one of their guards left – as David presumed – for lunch. There they soon received a visit from a German officer who spoke good English, and enquired whether they needed anything. David replied that he and his men had eaten nothing since breakfast the previous day save a small piece of dry biscuit; his request for food fell on stony ground, for after the German left they never saw him again. They were visited next by an Italian officer, who had heard that there was a British officer amongst the prisoners. Once David had identified himself, the Italian apologised profusely for having shut David up with his men, and offered to take him to better accommodation. Suspecting that this was a ruse to pump him for information, David replied that he was not interested in any other accommodation, but that he and his fellow prisoners would very much appreciate something to eat. He was eventually persuaded by the others to go with the Italian officer and take whatever he could get, and he ended up in a small office, being treated courteously by two Italian officers who gave him a tiny cup of coffee, a small glass of very good brandy and a Turkish cigarette. They appeared keen to demonstrate how well Italians treated their prisoners, and when David told them about how he and his men had been parted from their possessions, vowed to investigate and track down the culprits. At this point, however, a soldier entered the office to announce that the lorry was waiting, and David was ushered out. As he got into the lorry, one of the officers slipped a small package into his hand, which he found to contain a roll of bread, which he divided with the others – barely a mouthful each.

The day's journey ended after dark at Derna, where David was once again separated from his men and led to a tent, where for the first time since his capture he met up with three fellow officers: a British doctor, and two Hurricane pilots, one British and one South African. There was a fourth occupant of the tent whom the others suspected of being a 'stooge', so their conversation was guarded; it seems their instincts were correct, for he disappeared the next morning never to be seen again. It was pitch dark in the tent, so David had no idea what his new companions looked like until the next day. By the time he joined them, they had already been given something to eat, so David pestered their guard for some time, eventually being given a can of stew. Though ravenously hungry, he found that after only a few mouthfuls he felt sick and could eat no more; instead he found a corner of sand in which to lie down and soon went to sleep.

The following morning David and the other three officers rejoined his men in the open lorry, David giving up his place in the front to the South African pilot, who had been shot down in only shirt, shorts and flying boots. The day was cold and wet, and to make matters worse there was a large hole in the floor of the truck, through which a continuous cloud of dust poured upwards. Eventually the group of prisoners completed the final leg of their uncomfortable journey to Benghazi. David describes their highly insalubrious destination as follows:

> … a large walled-in white building, which looked like some warehouse or jam factory. Two huge gates were thrown open as we arrived and in we drove …
>
> This transit camp at Benghazi* was a horrible place. It was just a small sandy yard surrounded by a high wall. Inside were crowded hundreds of prisoners at times with nowhere to sleep but the very filthy ground. The place was full of lice and fleas and dysentery was rampant. The sanitary arrangements consisted in two long ditches dug along the far wall, with logs slung above them for people to sit on. The British had marked one ditch for people with dysentery, the other for people without. The whole camp stank of sewage and was crawling with flies …

The newcomers were met by a small but efficient group of British officers who recorded details of their names and addresses, produced a meagre meal for them,

---

* Known locally as 'The Palms'.

and issued them with Red Cross postcards for their signature which stated that they were prisoners of the Italians and being well treated. David duly filled in his postcard to his parents, but in his memoir added wryly, 'Needless to say, it was never received.' Fortunately for David, he was only obliged to spend one night in what he described as 'this Benghazi hell-hole'. The following day he and the British pilot officer, Keg Downing, were issued with rations for a three-day crossing to Italy, consisting of three small loaves of brown bread and a tin of bully beef. David later recorded his stupidity at not accepting the proffered tin, on the grounds that he had disliked the contents when previously sampling them: 'I was a very inexperienced prisoner at this period, and had not yet learnt the most important lesson, to take every scrap of food that came one's way.'

David next endured a mortifying drive to the docks, along with three other officers and some 200 non-commissioned troops, being jeered at and spat upon by local crowds. On arrival, he and Keg were singled out and put on a tiny tug, along with a dozen Indian troops, and steered round a jetty to where a small, dirty submarine lay moored. Surely, he thought, they were not going to be transported to Italy in such a vessel? Next, however, he and Keg were made to walk across a plank and down some metal steps in the conning tower, then crawl through some little watertight doors until they found themselves in the front compartment of the submarine, the Indians having been taken to a larger compartment in the rear.

David discovered that his and Keg's accommodation for the forthcoming voyage was in the non-commissioned officers' quarters, down the centre of which ran a row of bunks that folded upwards when not in use. Where the row of bunks ended stood a small mess table flanked by wooden benches, and forward of these lay the submarine's torpedo tubes. Initially the two British officers were told to make themselves comfortable on the floor on either side of the table, but since this was covered with grease and dirt David protested, eventually reaching a compromise with his captors that allowed him and Keg to share between them one bunk and one camp stool in three-hour shifts.

As night fell, the submarine left its mooring and prepared to submerge, a process which David and Keg, neither of whom had previously been in a submarine, found quite alarming, but with which – as the voyage progressed – they would become familiar:

Once out of the harbour a sort of air-raid system went off … and the submarine proceeded to submerge. It was a very exciting affair for us as we had no idea what was happening or why we were going under. There was a speaking tube in our room. A bell would ring, the nearest person would pick up the tube and answer 'Pruro' (prow), then down would come an excited jabbering in Italian. People would quickly pull levers and turn knobs and wheels, the front of the submarine would point down, all sorts of gurgling and splashing noises would come from the sides of the ship, and down we would go … We became quite used to it after the first few times, but this first time took us by surprise. I managed to discover that it was a routine practice which they always did at the beginning of every trip …

Once the initial practice was over, David and Keg had the dubious pleasure of watching their Italian room-mates tucking into a very good meal, while they themselves were forced to make do with a small portion of stale bread. Later the next day, following David's protestations, their Italian captors gave in, and David recorded that for the remainder of the voyage he and Keg shared with the Italian NCOs two extremely good meals daily, consisting of 'soup, a meat or egg and spaghetti course, fruit, cheese and biscuits, supplemented by a good Chianti wine and vitamin pills'. As the journey continued, the two British officers became on increasingly friendly terms with their captors, learning more about the submarine, which – despite having been in service for some fourteen years – had yet to fire a torpedo in wrath. One of the NCOs even took David once a day to the engine room to smoke a clandestine cigarette.

All went smoothly until the third day out, when the ship suddenly received radioed instructions from Rome to go to a certain position in the Mediterranean, where they surfaced gingerly for observations to be made through the periscope. David described in his memoir the ensuing confusing events:

Then followed a stream of orders, including the word 'attacco', which was mentioned several times. We didn't know whether we were going to attack or be attacked, and we didn't know which we would prefer … We proceeded down to our maximum depth, shut off the engines, and waited. One of the crew came along and said we mustn't talk. Then suddenly we heard some muffled explosions in the distance. There followed a silence of about twenty minutes' duration and then came some more explosions, this time much nearer. These explosions continued for several hours

Most frustratingly, at this point, David's war memoir suddenly breaks off mid sentence. The only other family record of what happened next is the following (somewhat badly) typed copy of an extract from a letter he wrote to his parents from Oflag VA in Germany on 27 October 1943:

I don't think anyone will now object to me telling you that I was taken from Benghazi to Taranto in Dec '41 in a small 1941* submarine with one other officer. We got an awful message from Rome on the second evening telling us to go

---

*   Obviously a typing error, since in his later memoir he wrote that the crew had told him it was 14 years old.

somewhere in the Med. When we were there we were depthcharged, and spent all day as far down as possible in complete silence, with the engines turned off.

It was quite an interesting experience, and one which I would rather have missed.

After the war, David discovered the reason he had been singled out for transport to prison camp in Italy via submarine. Following the Pearl Harbor debacle when the United States formally entered the fray, his surname would have been picked up by Axis intelligence, since the influential McCormick family in America had diplomatic connections. Edward McCormick's first cousin, Leander McCormick-Goodhart, was David's godfather, owner of Langley Park and private assistant in Washington to the British Ambassador, Lord Lothian, until the latter's untimely death in December 1940. Thereafter throughout the war Leander continued his work at the British Embassy, concentrating on aid to the United Kingdom, in particular the development of the Lend-Lease programme. Consequently David would have been classified as a '*prominente*' (a person of particular importance), a potentially useful bargaining tool. For such prisoners, transport by air or submarine was considered safer than by ordinary surface troopship.

★ ★ ★

It goes without saying that once 'Operation Crusader' was under way, David had no time for writing home, and any letters received from him between then and the new year would have been written before the fighting began. It was a desperately anxious time for Pamela and his parents, who had to make do with news bulletins and newspaper reports. At least, for the sake of public morale, these were for the most part upbeat.

Having quit nursing for good, Pamela was now back at Ditchampton Farm regaining her strength and already considering her next wartime occupation. Her diary entry for 8 December shows how closely she was following the course of the war: 'America is now at war with Japan! The Japs went & bombed the Pacific Islands to smithereens without warning & it is all U.P. The whole world is fighting now but as Churchill says, 4/5ths of the world are with us.'

Since their meeting in Weston-super-Mare prior to David's embarkation, Pamela and David's mother had kept in close touch, both women immediately informing the other if either received any news from him. Although their personalities were very different, Phyllis McCormick liked and approved of Pamela as a prospective daughter-in-law, and now issued an open-ended invitation for her to come and stay with her and her husband Edward at their home on St George's Hill, Weybridge: '*December 9th* Mrs McCormick wrote me an awfully nice letter and has asked me to spend a night with her anywhen [*sic*] and go to a movie or something. She evidently thinks I'd be bored to sit!'

As the year drew to a close, Pamela's diary reveals that her conscience was once again troubling her, and she was becoming increasingly impatient to start new war work:

December 10th Feel I must get into the A.T.S. soon or I shall bust …

December 22nd Talked over the A.T.S. with Pa and shall see about it tomorrow. Do hope I can go and see Mrs. McCormick before …

December 23rd Pop & me Salisbury. He went in & saw the recruiting girl who was nicer than yesterday & I went in & put my name down to apply. Well that's that. Have to go for medical on January 1st.

On 12 December when, unknown to Pamela, David became a prisoner of war, her diary entry records further encouraging war news: 'The war goes well in Libya … The Russians also are doing fine …'

On 15 December Pamela received the last two letters that David wrote to her from the desert. The contents of one did not altogether please her:

Two lovely letters from David. The last written Nov 14th. He's thinking of migrating to S. Africa after the war to grow grapes — well what does one say to that. Wrote a long & very definite letter back saying I don't think I could say goodbye 5 times & what about it! Oh lor I hope it's all right.

Whatever Pamela may have written in reply obviously never reached David; this remained an issue to be resolved once the war had ended.

Meanwhile in south-west Wiltshire life went on as normally as possible given the strictures of the time. Local dances for the festive season continued to be organised, though for obvious reasons, male partners were becoming increasingly difficult to find for young women in Pamela's position. Her heart was in any case elsewhere, and she took little pleasure from such events: '*December 13th* … Dinah and I went on to Mrs. Siveright's dance which was <u>awful</u> …'

At least Christmas day itself in the Street household seems to have been a happy affair: '*December 25th* Lovely Christmas Day … Mummy & I went to Holy Communion early which was very impressive as all candlelight. Mummy gave me gloves, & Pop money — it was all very nice. I wonder where we'll all be next Christmas. Wrote Mrs M & David.'

Pamela's contemporary writings make it clear that the Streets were ardent admirers of the prime minister and listened avidly to his broadcasts. One such, delivered on 28 December, caused them considerable surprise: 'Churchill has been in America all the Christmas!' A couple of days later Pamela was in for another pleasurable surprise:

'*December 30th* Mr McCormick rang up & it is all right for me to go next Sunday with Pop!! Wonderful. Dreading my medical Thursday! Listened to Churchill again.'

Pamela had been having the usual problems in finding a suitable escort for a New Year's Eve dance to be held at the White Hart Hotel in Salisbury. Tom Jago, a family friend in the military and former billetee at Ditchampton Farm, had been approached, initially unsuccessfully, but at the last minute he made himself available. Consequently Pamela's last diary entry for 1941 ends on a happier, cautiously optimistic note:

December 31st Major Jago came to take me to the New Year's Dance at the W.H. He was awfully nice ... Here's another year over and tomorrow is my medical for the A.T.S. Well, well, well. Perhaps the war won't last all that time & we shall be able to live again.

Ten

Unaccustomed Activity and ATS Training (Late 1941–February 1942)

Once the Blitz began, as already noted, Edward and Phyllis McCormick had sought temporary refuge in the latter's family home, Breckenbrough Hall near Thirsk in Yorkshire. The Breckenbrough estate included some tenanted farms and a home farm that supplied the main house with meat and dairy produce. Presumably, as in the case of Ditchampton Farm, many of the farm hands had been called up for military service, for David's parents' letters to their son while he was in North Africa in the autumn of 1941 reveal that they were both involved in unaccustomed agricultural work to help with the war effort. It is probable that – again as was the case at Ditchampton Farm – much of the pasture was ploughed up in the 'Dig for Victory' campaign. An enthusiast for all things mechanical, Edward seems to have relished mastering the art of ploughing; in a letter to David dated 29 September 1941 he wrote:

I have been doing some of the ploughing with the new Fordson & a two-share plough. I have done as much as 6 hours of it in a day, pretty strenuous! It is really quite exciting when you get to the end of the furrows as you have to lock over on full lock with one hand, to avoid running into a ditch or fence, and with the other hand you have to reach far back and pull a cord attached to a lever which raises the plough out of the ground or puts it back again … I enjoy doing it …

Not all farm tasks proved equally congenial, however, to such a novice labourer; a month later Edward wrote to his son:

I have done much ploughing & harrowing now … I have assisted in leading the harvest and aftermath for the silo, threshing and finally lifting mangolds. This latter

I found the toughest job of the lot as it has to be done in a bent position and I have always had a weak back. It is quite a hazardous job as having pulled your mangold which weighs from a few ounces to something over a stone, you have to flip it sideways and cut its leaves off without, if possible, cutting the root itself, your tool is very sharp and it is by no means difficult to take a bit of your hand off …

By late October 1941 the female members of the family were also called upon to 'do their bit', David's mother included. On 1 November Phyllis wrote to David:

We are working really hard getting in the potatoes – a whole large field of them – the tractor roots them up & we follow with buckets which we fill frightfully quickly & empty into a horse-drawn cart which keeps walking away, so one is always trying to keep up – and the buckets are very heavy. It has to be done before the bad frosts …

Fuel shortages meant that as the autumn of 1941 progressed, the large, draughty rooms at Breckenbrough Hall became increasingly cold; its occupants were only allowed one small coal fire in their bedrooms just before bedtime. To make matters worse, throughout their stay the eccentric Evelyn Samuelson had been rather less than welcoming to her sister and brother-in-law, and had been increasingly getting on the latter's nerves. Once the essential farm work had been completed, David's parents were more than ready to return to Weybridge. Back in her own home, however, Phyllis had little to distract her, and her letters to David during this period reveal the full extent of her anxiety over his safety and well-being, particularly once reports of the Libyan campaign began to reach England:

November 22nd
Darling Dave
As I write the battle of Libya is raging, & I can't tell you how frightfully anxious we are about you. It was a great shock when it all started …
    It is nice to be back in our own home, but I miss you both more here …

December 2nd
I always think of you when I'm in bed especially – it must be so awful never to have a decent night's rest – when civilians talk of 'being in the front line' I'm afraid I become very rude indeed …

December 13th
How I long now to hear from you that you are safe somewhere. It is all I can think of – when people talk to me, half the time I have no idea what they are saying – they must think I've gone a bit bats!

January 2nd 1942

I've been having flu & am just up & feeling pretty mouldy. I do hope I'll be all right by Sunday as Pamela is coming for a couple of nights. Her father is bringing her along to lunch – it is the last chance for her before joining the A.T.S. so I don't want to put her off unless I'm really ill.

 Dad & I are in a constant panic about you, darling – I don't see how we can help it …

It was probably just as well for David's sake that these letters never reached him, but were eventually returned to his parents unopened, their original envelopes having been stamped with the stark, uncompromising words: 'UNDELIVERED FOR REASON STATED. RETURN TO SENDER. Addressee Reported Prisoner of War.' At least Edward McCormick had new occupations to take his mind off the constant worry, as his letter to David written on Christmas Day 1941 explains:

I have just taken on the job of Senior Warden here … It is a nuisance for me as it will mean quite a lot of chivvying around and calling on people and arranging meetings etc, and in addition to this I am expecting to start work in the office of Vickers* on Monday. Office hours are 10–12 hours a day starting at 9 or perhaps 8. I don't expect to enjoy it a bit … However, I feel that unless most of us try to put 99% of our energy and ability into winning this blasted war it will take a hell of a long time to win it, so I may as well try, regardless of how much I hate the effort …

In the event, Edward's employment at Vickers kept being delayed as he was constantly thwarted by red tape; being an American domiciled in England he was technically an 'alien', and needed special permission from the Home Office, which was slow to come through. In fact this was probably a blessing, as during the early part of 1942 he was needed at home by his wife, whose illness went from bad to worse. Waiting for news of David was becoming increasingly unbearable for Phyllis McCormick, adding considerably to the severity of her illness.

★ ★ ★

At the beginning of January 1942, Pamela started a new, larger, one-year diary in a 'page per day' format. This allowed her to record more of her activities and feelings on each day than did her previous, cramped, diary with five days' worth of entries on each page. On 1 January she had enough room to write not merely about signing up for the ATS and her concerns about her ear trouble that had recently

---

★ The nearby military aircraft manufacturers.

recurred, but also – intriguingly – about the favourable impression that Major Tom Jago had made at the New Year's Eve dance the evening before:

> Went for my Interview and Medical for the A.T.S.! Rather a New Year. Passed and have to go to Honiton on the 16th for my month – and how – The officer A.T. was awfully nice and I put my name down for Radio location though anyone less logical I suppose you couldn't find but if that's hopeless perhaps can do camouflage. The medical wasn't bad except for a wretched little ear man who thought I was swinging the lead and took no notice of my exma [sic] return and buzzing ...
>
> The dance last night was fun & I did enjoy it and Major Jago is very nice – poor man coming all that way and staying at the Old George. Hope he thought it was worth it. What ho she bumps.

This was perhaps the first time Pamela's loyalty to David was put to the test. A couple of days later she records posting a letter to 'Tom', which evidently crossed one he had written to her, about which she wrote on 6 January:

> There was a letter from Tom Jago waiting for me which was rather sweet of him as he hadn't got mine. He's going to Chelsea to live at home on the 12th because he's got a job at Whitehall amongst the High Ups!! Well well well. Basil Hale rang up to ask me to a dance on Saturday at Stockton.
>
> Thick and fast they come at last
> If you don't go working – blast!

Pamela's opinion of Tom Jago swiftly changed as a result of this second dance. Her diary entry for the day in question, 10 January, was written in a fit of pique:

> Went to a lovely dance at Stockton House ... King Peter of Yugoslavia was there and it was in his honour more or less. Tom Jago was there!!!! He is the limit and I'm furious – he always laughs at me and yet he's nice except that he needs someone like me to keep him on the straight and narrow because he ran off with another of those out of sheer hellers I think – well he goes on Monday to Whitehall & it's probably a jolly good thing.

Tom Jago was to disgrace himself yet further in Pamela's eyes by failing to turn up the next day at Ditchampton Farm, where presumably she had invited him by way of farewell before he left for his new job in London. On 11 January she wrote:

> Tom didn't come even though I asked him and dressed up in my best & only sort of thing. He's a nasty bad wicked man and I feel furious with him ...

Feel so cross with Tom after a letter like that. He'd lead anybody an awful dance if they let him – well he won't lead me because he probably won't see me again except I should like to just to get quite straight with him.

On Sunday 4 January, in between the two aforementioned dances, Arthur Street drove Pamela up to Weybridge for the long-awaited visit to David's parents' home on St George's Hill, where she spent a couple of nights. Her diary entries chronicle her impressions of this visit, not all of them entirely favourable. It was clearly a very alien environment, and would have been her first experience of the privileged lifestyle of people who, in those days, enjoyed a sufficient private income not to be obliged to work for a living. Edward (Ted) was a slightly built, mild-mannered man, deeply averse to any kind of unpleasantness, and it would have been immediately clear to Pamela that his wife was the dominant force in the household, who demanded her husband's constant presence and would have made it difficult for him to go out to work even had he so wished. The contrast between Pamela's larger-than-life, hard-working, authoritarian father A.G. Street and her prospective father-in-law could not have been more marked.

January 4th Went!!! Pop and I had lovely drive up and went along the hog's back. When we got to Weybridge we couldn't find the house anywhere as St. George's Hill is a vast residential sort of estate place. Pop rang up in the end and they came down in their car and then we went to Shaws & then to the Golf Club to lunch as domestic arrangements weren't good or something. Pop went off at 3. Another man came to tea and we went to cocktails at the tennis club. Shaws is a lovely house and a lovely garden but David's dog [Rigo, a rough-coated collie] beats everything. He's wonderful. They gave me the boys' room which was sweet of them and were very kind. Oh it seemed so strange being here – echoes of David. I could imagine him here so well though but gracious how lovely it must have been before the war. I know now about his love of parties. You couldn't help it here but somehow I seemed awfully dull.

January 5th Took Rego [*sic*] for a lovely walk except it is so lost-making here. He is a wonderful dog. Mrs M then came too, but Mr M cut down trees all day. He's a funny man. I like her better than him because somehow he seems a bit ineffectual. I don't think either of them are good enough for David which is terrible of me and I shouldn't say it. Somehow though Mr M seems a bit lost in his own house. Mrs M is very talented – painted lovely portrait. Saw a wonderful settee David designed for his flat. Took Rego through Weybridge & everyone stopped and admired him. Also the soldiers + my red coat. We went quite well together though I say it myself. Went to an awful film which they thought quite good called Moon Over Miami …

January 6th Mrs McCormick was ill this morning and had to stay in bed so we couldn't all go to London so he put me on the train and I came by myself. After I go to town it seems silly to go home with my wonderful London waiting for me so I tubed to Piccadilly and thought it was lovely. Went to Swan & Edgar and to Harrods for lunch & Fortnum & Mason. Caught the 2.50 home so went to the News Theatre at Waterloo. Mummy had a very bad cold when I got home but very pleased to see me & vice versa as it was a strain somehow without David …

Pamela was not to know it, but her stay must have been even more of a strain for her hosts, neither of whom had fully recovered from a flu-type illness, but had been unwilling to cancel Pamela's visit since it was their last opportunity to entertain her at Shaws before she began working in the ATS. Both parents would have realised the importance of Pamela's attachment to David for their son's morale whilst he was serving overseas, and were doing their best to foster the relationship. After Pamela's departure Phyllis McCormick's illness took a turn for the worse, as family letters later revealed.

★ ★ ★

Following her return from her stay at Weybridge, Pamela spent her last few remaining days of freedom getting ready for her ATS induction course, with visits to the dentist, doctor and hairdresser and saying her goodbyes to various friends and family. A few days before her departure her orders came through, though in the haphazard way that such postings were being organised at the time, they were clearly not what she had been expecting: '*January 10th* My orders came. Ha! I'm going to Aldermaston and not Honiton after all.' Finally, on 16 January, Pamela left Ditchampton Farm:

Nearly the longest day of my life. Left Salisbury at 12. Mummy & Daddy saw me off. Met a very nice girl at Basingstoke and we kept together. Got met at Aldermaston and arrived in a lorry – the most awful herding this way and that as we were issued with uniform & interviewed and head-inspected that night. Then we all got pushed into a hut called Ironside & that was that. Well where do we go from here!

Pamela's diary entries for her time at Aldermaston paint a sketchy picture of what life was like for the new recruits, many of whom had never lived away from home before. They record friendships quickly made, sympathetic members of staff, but also the sheer drudgery and monotony of the daily routine and the homesickness shared by nearly all the course participants. Just like boarding-school pupils, the girls keenly awaited periods of leave or visits from family members. To boost their morale and provide entertainment, the girls were encouraged to take part in an amateur revue, which would take place towards the end of their period of training.

First of all, the girls were obliged to take an intelligence test, after which they were interviewed to establish their aptitude and preferences for different types of ATS duties:

> *January 17th* Had the most awful Matrix test in the morning – apparently it finds out how much you have up there. Obviously I haven't any as my head went round half way through. Just continuance of herding – an interview – said camouflage but I don't think there's going to be much hope somehow. Oh dear. Lor what a life.

Boredom and despondency quickly set in as the new recruits awaited the results of their tests: '*January 18th* Feel very depressed today somehow. Meals are the worst – hundreds of us just eating and eating. Nothing to do all day really except sit in the hut and mope. Pamela Pamela Pamela …'

How good or bad Pamela's results were is unclear, but in her usual self-deprecating way she feared the worst:

> *January 19th* Better day except until talk of employment this afternoon and as far as I can make out there isn't any for me. Some people did wonders in that Matrix test but I must have been one of the also-rans – dud – I haven't any brain at all. Shall I be a clerk or not. At the moment I feel anything to get back to Salisbury but perhaps it won't be as bad as that I hope. My ears aren't too good which is a curse. Oh dear – will it have been the right thing to do or not I wonder.

More military uniforms and other standard items of clothing were now being issued to the new recruits, and square-bashing became the order of the day: '*January 20th* Cannot remember very much except the usual drill I believe & issued with clothing etc …'

In light of her brief training at the Salisbury College of Art, Pamela's first choice of occupation within the ATS was camouflage, where she hoped to put her artistic talents to good use. Failing this, however, her second choice was to become a clerk, which required a further competence test. Once again, Pamela doubted she had made the grade: '*January 21st* Took a clerks test which was hopeless at – was inoculated once more for tetanus – wrote to Mummy I believe. Parades, snow and colds …'

At the end of their first week the girls were allowed an outing to the nearest main town, a welcome respite from the claustrophobic atmosphere of the training camp:

> *January 23rd* Went to Reading in buses – great event – like a Sunday school treat. Rang Mummy up which was wonderful. Raining now so snow is thawing thank heaven. Was told today that have passed the Clerks test so if I can't get to the

camouflage school shall probably have to start by that. I'd sooner than stay here which am terrified of.

The main feature of Sundays at Aldermaston was the church parade, for which the girls had to appear at their smartest, shoes and uniform buttons shining brightly. Evidently family members were encouraged to attend, and on the first occasion Pamela had hopes that her parents might have been able to make the journey: '*January 25th* Terrific church parade – all spit & polish. Nice day. Wish really Mummy & Pop could have come. Joan [a new friend who lived not far from Wilton] and I are just terrified of being sent to Strathpeffer.'* By now the girls had settled into a familiar routine, one day being more or less indistinguishable from the next: '*January 27th* Day after day – really can't remember very much except the continual parades and lectures & fatigues. One day is very much like another with hurry up Platoon III.'

Pamela evidently performed better at the clerks' test than she gave herself credit for; on 30 January she wrote: 'We were finally approved today. I'm a clerk with camouflage in view – terrific to do. It is all right about my out of bounds pass for Sunday. Whoopee.'

Pamela keenly awaited her first Sunday visit from her parents, but the fates were against her. The winter of 1941–42 was another exceptionally cold one, and on waking on the morning of Sunday 1 February, Pamela discovered that the weather had done its worst:

Snow!! Snow!! Inches of it. It is 10.20 and am just going to ring Mummy up because I don't think they can possibly come. <u>So</u> disappointed – just when everything was all right. Oh dear oh dear oh dear. What a life. Sunday depression & <u>nothing</u> to do.

Fortunately Pamela had a couple of treats in store. She was now due a weekend's leave, and the girls' show would shortly be staged:

February 4th Went down village with Joan and visited the Holmwoods – rang Mummy as our leave is definite D.V. – lovely. Called for washing. Had supper … then went to a rehearsal of our show … or praps it was last night – doing a swing number back row of chorus. Route march this afternoon – absolutely weird, sang songs etc.

February 6th Very excited about tomorrow. Miss Rush came to our rehearsal and I had to get up and do my unrehearsed dance – it was a hoot – I mean I was awfully nervous – hope it was all right.

* The ATS Clerks' School in Strathpeffer, Inverness.

The next day Pamela began her eagerly anticipated weekend's leave, timed to coincide with her mother's birthday:

> *February 7th* Mumms came!!!! + Noble [the Streets' foreman] took Joan and I home and she went on to Shaftesbury. Wonderful … Aunts, Vivi, me celebrated her birthday by chicken dinner. So sorry about Pop [Arthur Street was away on BBC business] but he's hoping to get home tomorrow.

Pamela's entry for the following day was significant in terms of her next wartime occupation:

> *February 8th* Major Seago and another boy (air force) came to tea to see my drawings. I'm sorry Daddy asked him really as I could have quite well gone down and he was terribly off-hand and snooty and asked for landscape paintings which I didn't have. He didn't seem to like anything including me and I thought he was going to cut up rough – however he offered me a 2 mths trial and went off and all the time I felt he thought he ought to but not that he wanted to – it was terrible. However. Had a lovely day and Pop returned to see me special on the 9.30 which was wonderful.

This last diary entry requires some elucidation. 'Major Seago' was the already acclaimed artist Edward (Ted) Seago, who went on to become one of the foremost British landscape painters of the twentieth century, and a favourite of the Royal Family. Despite a recurring heart condition which from childhood had caused him to suffer frequent 'turns' that left him debilitated and bedridden, Seago's single-minded determination to enlist at the onset of the Second World War – albeit with an element of subterfuge regarding his health record – led to a mobilisation commission in the Intelligence Corps. It was only natural that his talent should have been put to use in the wartime art of camouflage, and by the time of his visit to Ditchampton Farm in February 1942 he had been appointed Camouflage Officer, 5th Corps, Southern Command. He was on particularly friendly terms with two of his consecutive commanders-in-chief at Wilton House, firstly General Claude Auchinleck, and after the latter's appointment to Commander-in-Chief in India, with his successor, Lieutenant-General Harold Alexander. Both generals were amateur artists who, when strolling in the glorious grounds of Wilton House, found Ted Seago's company a refreshing change from that of the majority of their more deferential junior officers. General Alexander even went so far as to make available to Ted Seago a hut in North Street, Wilton. This was divided into two halves, one for the use of his camouflage team, and the other as a private studio, where Alexander himself would come to paint whenever possible during off-duty periods. This hut would become Pamela's workplace for the next few months of the war.

Arthur Street would have been aware of Ted Seago's reputation and position through his connections both with Southern Command and local cultural circles, and clearly used his influence to persuade Seago to visit Ditchampton Farm and give Pamela an informal interview regarding her suitability to join his camouflage unit. Following her somewhat ignominious resignation from the military hospital, her father obviously hoped that her artistic talents could be put to use in a more agreeable form of war work. An additional benefit of working in Seago's unit, situated a short walk away in North Street, Wilton, meant that Pamela could be billeted at home.

Unfortunately, however, Pamela and Ted Seago, on first meeting, did not 'hit it off', Pamela immediately realising that the latter had come to Ditchampton Farm under a sense of obligation. What she failed to understand was that Ted Seago was – to use the parlance of the day – 'not a ladies' man'. With a handful of exceptions, Seago found women difficult to deal with, and the naïve Pamela – who at that stage had never even heard of homosexuality – would have been mystified by his lack of normal chivalry. It is also quite possible that he was about to undergo, or was recovering from, one of his heart 'turns', and was not at his best. In any event, whilst he agreed to give Pamela a two-month trial at his camouflage unit, this new period of Pamela's life got off to an inauspicious start.

At the beginning, however, Seago's offer to Pamela was by no means a *fait accompli*. The following morning Arthur and Vera Street drove Pamela and her friend Joan back to Aldermaston for the remaining few days of their ATS course. Pamela's orders came through later that day, though they were not what she had been expecting: '*February 9th* To my great disgust I have been posted as a filing clerk to Bulford even after my interview with Miss Brittain this morning ...' Pamela's spirits were raised in the evening by the end-of-course show, however, which evidently went far better than she had expected: 'We had a drill competition which we lost – and then a final inspection and then the concert which was a huge success, which was surprising seeing that we hadn't rehearsed.'

Two days later Pamela set off from Aldermaston to take up her new posting at Bulford Camp on Salisbury Plain, but on arrival she found that – yet again at the last minute – her orders had been changed:

February 11th Got up at an unearthly hour and wetted the hut – can't say scrubbed because there wasn't any soap[*] – also my box. Caught the 9.30 ... Terribly long day with masses of changes. Reading, Basingstoke, Porton and then Bulford. It was grim but when I arrived a telegram had arrived cancelling my posting. It seemed too wonderful but they wouldn't find out about it for ages but finally

---

[*] Soap rationing was introduced in February 1942, since the fat content was deemed more essential for the preparation of foodstuffs.

put me on a bus to Salisbury!!! … then, heaven, they sent me home to sleep!!!! It was like a dream …

The very next day saw the beginning of Pamela's two-month trial under Ted Seago:

February 12th Started at Major S's camouflage hut in North Street!!!!!!! It seemed so queer – he didn't say a word and looked as though he hated me being there. Apparently he wasn't feeling well but he's terribly touchy. Made models and things and Helen V V [*sic*] was awfully nice and a girl called Judith Buxton, Vera and Pat and Tim the batman.

The last mentioned member of the team would have been Alexander (Tim) Parker, an old school friend of Seago's; a keen amateur jockey, he had been demoted by the army for having gone absent without leave to take part in a race meeting. Ted Seago made it his business to surround himself with loyal friends and colleagues who would willingly conceal from the authorities the severity of his heart condition, of which his old schoolmate was well aware. Disillusioned with army discipline, when asked by Seago to become his driver/batman and cover up for him during his heart 'turns', Tim was only too happy to oblige.

On Pamela's second day at the 'hut', things were marginally better, chiefly owing to Ted Seago's absence. Later she had a reunion with an old friend who had now become her ATS commanding officer, much to both girls' amusement:

February 13th Major Seago out most of the day which was a relief. Carved etc. Have to be told twice about things … We work from 9 till 6 … Saw Prudence Perkins. She's in charge of me – it does seem odd. She threw her arms round me!! How can you 'Ma'am' anyone like that??? It's too ridiculous …

The Allies had recently suffered a number of setbacks, and Pamela goes on to chastise herself for not recording more about the progress of the war: 'I never put down about the news these days but it's too ghastly. Singapore is nearly lost and 3 German ships got through the Straits in spite of us – only 20 miles to play in. It's awful.' Pamela was referring to an incident that became known as the 'Channel Dash'. On 11 February 1942 three German warships, *Scharnhorst*, *Gneisenau* and *Prinz Eugen*, made an audacious run from the French harbour of Brest back to German-held North Sea ports via the narrow Straits of Dover, whilst British naval units failed to sink any of them, a considerable blow to the nation's morale.

Pamela remained mystified by Ted Seago's attitude towards her, which did nothing to boost her self-confidence:

February 14th This morning went for a ride with Pat to guard the Major's car – don't seem to do any work at all. I do wonder what will happen and if he'll kick me out – he doesn't say a word which is so depressing. They let me have this afternoon off but in a way it is a bad thing because I think they want to get me out of the way …

This unexpected period of leave extended to the following day, a Sunday, when Pamela finally had a chance to write to David and catch up with the latest war news:

Lovely day off. Went for a walk & it was marvellous – all cold and sunny. Everything very clear … Wrote to David – I'm afraid the first since I went to Aldermaston. David where are you? I haven't heard since before Christmas. I do wonder what is happening to him. The news is so terrible. Singapore has fallen. The Japs are overrunning everything. Africa is still [?] and the three German ships walked out of Brest and through the straits of Dover just like that. Winny spoke. It's all so unbelievable.

A surprise announcement was made to the camouflage team when they returned to work on Monday morning:

Started again. The strain is terrific. I only mess about & the Major looks glum and goes into his sanctum … Then he announced we should all fly tomorrow. <u>Fly</u> think of it – and it has got to be very hush hush. Didn't dare tell Mummy so got Pop's permission …

Pamela's ecstatic diary entry for the next day records her impressions of this, her first ever, flight:

February 17th Today we flew. It was the most wonderful sensation out. I would never have believed it. Everything was so clear and concise and showed up like dollshouses and wooden things & not real at all. Anything white was an absolute landmark. Saw this house and it was so funny. Like a little cream villa an 1/8" high. Went downstream to Fordingbridge & back. Think I saw the Bensons' farm at Rockbourne. Saw lots of forestry land and sandy paths – the country houses were lovely – lots of greenhouses. Saw several bomb craters & one filled with water – dark camouflage is marvellous, anything light hopeless. Tracks are amazing – and also places where there's been a haystack. Saw piles of lime at regular intervals on plough showing up like mushrooms – anti-tank ditch is a gift – see it easy as anything. Rivers are dark & light grey according to the light. Paths show even through woods at this time of year …

No doubt Ted Seago's decision to take his team flying was made in order to take advantage of the current snap of clear weather; however he needed little excuse to take to the skies, for this was the aspect of his camouflage work he most enjoyed. Although he was an army officer, Seago's work required close liaison with the air force; earlier in the war he had lived at the School of Army Co-operation at Old Sarum RAF station, where the officer's mess was shared by both army and RAF officers. There he found himself in his element, making numerous friends. Before long, despite his health problems, he became determined to learn to fly himself, and enlisted the help and tuition of an air force friend who frequently piloted him on camouflage reconnaissance expeditions. Although it was highly irregular, Seago was soon making solo flights in the station's small low-level training plane.

As a member of the ATS, Pamela was obliged to attend regular platoon meetings. Her first one took place a couple of days after the flight experience, and proved an eye-opener of a rather different kind:

> *February 19th* Went to a Platoon meeting at Flemings. Prudence [her friend and commanding officer] spoke. It was rather a revelation. The ATS here seem much worse than Aldermaston – awful language & plenty of it. She says it is a very slack platoon & I should jolly well think it is …

Despite the excitement of the camouflage reconnaissance flight, during the coming days Pamela continued to be plagued by misgivings about her competence within the unit: '*February 20th* Did something wrong. Stuck two notices on wrong way round & Pat spent over half the day correcting …'

By now Arthur and Vera Street would have been aware that things in camouflage unit were not going as smoothly for their daughter as they had hoped. This time it was Vera Street who took action, using the now tried and tested formula of inviting Pamela's work colleagues to a meal at Ditchampton Farm, as Pamela's diary entry for 20 February goes on to record: 'They all came to supper excepting Vera who wasn't well & Tim who said he was too shy! And had a cold! Ha! They enjoyed it awfully I think. It was nice having them out. Of Mummy & everything …'

Pamela would soon be worrying about a far graver matter than her competence at the camouflage unit.

Eleven

Missing in Action
(February–April 1942)

Despite the fact that the Japanese bombing of Pearl Harbor in December 1941 had brought the Americans firmly in on the Allied side, for the first half of 1942 the outcome of the war was very much in the balance, with the Axis forces seemingly in the ascendant. The Japanese were taking full advantage to further their expansionist policy in South-East Asia, and the overrunning of the British colony of Singapore in mid February was already being perceived as something of a national humiliation. On the Eastern Front, the fight for Stalingrad was at this stage still indecisive, with huge losses on both Russian and German sides. On the high seas the German U-boats continued to take a heavy toll on Allied shipping. In the African desert, the very territory over which David McCormick had fought so strenuously some months earlier would soon be back in the hands of the Axis forces, who would go on to take Tobruk on 21 June and succeed in forcing the Allied troops back behind the Egypt–Libya border. Later in the year the tide would begin to turn, but for British citizens back home who could only listen, wait and hope, the spring and early summer of 1942 was a particularly harrowing period.

★ ★ ★

Back on the home front, for the McCormick parents and Pamela, February 1942 was the most harrowing time of all. On 2 February Edward McCormick, whose wife Phyllis was still bedridden with pneumonia, received the following telegram from the War Office:

REGRET TO INFORM YOU OF NOTIFICATION DATED 23RD JANUARY 1942 FROM MIDDLE EAST THAT 2/LT D F H MCCORMICK WAS REPORTED MISSING ON 12TH DECEMBER 1941 LETTER FOLLOWS = UNDER-SECRETARY OF STATE FOR WAR +

With admirable self-restraint and solicitude for her well-being, Edward kept this news from his wife, though he felt obliged to inform Pamela's father:

> 5th February 1942
>
> Dear Street,
>
> This is a difficult letter for me to write, and I hope you will forgive me if I blunder. We have had bad news. A telegram from the W.O. to say that David was reported 'missing' on the 12th Dec 1941. Although that was many days ago, one must still hope to get news of him. Prisoners-of-War lists take up to six months to come through, and many strange things happen in this desert warfare.
>
> I am writing to you to ask you to repeat what, in your parental wisdom, you deem it right that Pamela should hear.
>
> David has confided to me that, if all went well, he hoped to ask Pamela to marry him after the war. He is one of those sensitive, and sensible, young men who realise what war is capable of doing to a man, and that it is unfair to hold a girl to any pre-war engagement.
>
> I have no right to presume that there is any understanding between them, but it is obvious to us all that Pamela is interested in David.
>
> My great difficulty just now is that my poor wife has been very ill indeed with flu and pneumonitis. I cannot possibly tell her about David and I am taking all possible steps to prevent her hearing about it.
>
> If you decide to tell Pamela anything, will you please ask her not to write to either of us.
>
> If I hear anything further, I shall write to you about it.
>
> My kindest regards to you all.
>
> Edward McCormick

Arthur Street would have found this letter waiting for him on his return to Ditchampton Farm on the evening of the day on which Ted Seago had called earlier to give Pamela her informal interview. However he kept the news from his daughter for a further fortnight whilst her new posting was uncertain, and then to allow her time to settle into the camouflage unit. No doubt Arthur hoped that in the meantime more definite news might be forthcoming, rather than having to leave her in agonising suspense. However, once the successful supper party for Pamela's new work colleagues was over, he evidently felt the moment had come to break the news to her. On Saturday 21 February she wrote in her diary:

> Daddy told me tonight that David was reported missing on the 12th December. He had had a letter from Mr McCormick a fortnight ago but hadn't told me till now because of everything. I don't know what to think – it all seems so unreal – I just haven't taken it in. His father says Prisoner-of-War lists take 6 months

to come through. I shall just hope and pray that somewhere he may be safe &
sound. Oh David I don't think I was nearly nice enough. If only I'd helped a bit
more before he went – it's awful. I can't believe it – I wonder when they heard.
He hasn't told Mrs McCormick because she's been so ill. It must be dreadful for
him alone like that. He says he will write directly he hears anything. Daddy says
he'll help find out too. If only I knew someone in the regiment who was with
him. It's awful like this.

Pamela's numbed reaction continued the following day. Like so many civilians
whose loved ones were reported missing, she experienced a sense of helplessness;
typically in her case this was tinged with guilt at having somehow let David down
before his departure:

February 22nd I just feel quite sort of blank – it hasn't sunk in. Took Judy for a
walk to Grovely where we went that Sunday – it's nearly a year ago now – it's
unbelievable. Oh God please send him back & look after him. I don't want
Weston ever to fade – it was so wonderful – I want to go and see it again if I
can – if only we could find out about it all. I have sketched a letter to send by
airgraph to the C.O. and to Ian.* After that there is nothing to do but wait except
Daddy's going to find out at the Command. I don't feel worth anything – if only
I'd been more sure and said it then instead of him going not knowing – feel
cold and hard – what he must have been through. I shan't give up hope … Oh
Darling you wanted to marry me after it all and you never said or tied me &
never thought about yourself at all.

On Monday, despite receiving such devastating news over the weekend, Pamela
was back at work as usual in the camouflage unit. Her diary entry reveals that she
and her colleagues were – perhaps mercifully – kept so busy that by the time she
rushed down after work to air-graph the letters she had drafted to Ian Crombie
and David's last commanding officer, the Wilton Post Office was already closed.

Pamela carried on working as normal all week, but after hours made various
efforts to contact family acquaintances with military influence, and clearly derived
support and comfort from several girl friends aware of her plight. Fridays were
paydays for members of the ATS, when they were expected to rise early and
attend pay parade before work. One rare note of humour creeps into Pamela's
diary for the Friday of that week: '*February 27th* Pay Parade so got up early. Have
been paid for lodging allowance too. It seems so incongruous. Mummy makes a
wonderful landlady!'

---

*   Ian Crombie was another newly commissioned officer in David's regiment, whom the
    latter befriended whilst stationed at Weston-super-Mare awaiting embarkation.

On Saturday 28 February Ian Crombie's sister Sheila visited Ditchampton Farm. The two girls spent the time reminiscing about their weekend together at Weston-super-Mare almost a year earlier: 'Sheila Crombie came to tea. The first time we'd met since last March ... She was very sweet. I told her about sending Ian a cable and she thought it was quite all right. She too remembered that evening as if it were yesterday ...'

After such an emotionally fraught week, during which Pamela was still expected to carry on with her wartime duties, it is hardly surprising that she spent much of the Sunday in bed not merely catching up on sleep, but trying to recreate in her own mind the time she spent with David before he left:

March 1st Somehow everything seems so queer and unreal & so odd. I don't take it in. I can't and don't think of David missing. I wonder how long it will take finding out but he must be somewhere – just as long as he isn't suffering too much it will be all right. I want to write down Weston somehow. I somehow think the more you can think remember & imagine it helps because meeting him there did come true on the railway station & if I go on imagining meeting him somewhere here someday it will come true again.

Pamela did indeed write it all down in the blank pages at the end of her diary. Consigning her thoughts to paper was clearly an important emotional release. The resulting essay was prefaced by a quotation from a book she had recently read, *Wild Lone* by 'B.B.', subtitled *The Story of a Pytchley Fox*, which was popular at the time with children and adults alike, and praised in particular for its depiction and intimate knowledge of the countryside:

'The memory fades, to return, perhaps as faintly as an echo, when we lie with our faces buried in the June grass.' – *Wild Lone*.

It is nearly a year now since Weston. The memory has not faded. It is like yesterday but another world. You came to meet me on the station and the sun was shining – there was a nice old porter who carried the suitcases – the new one which Mummy & Daddy gave me – and your car didn't start properly and you had to push – you seemed worried I might not like the place. It is the most wonderful one I know. We met Ian on the way to the hotel – he looked so small with that huge truck. And then we met your parents and you looked in my cupboards in case of bogies. The number of the room was 3 – it has always been our lucky one – and after tea we walked, all of us, along the front and you & I went on and climbed up the fire escape to find Jimmy Miller's flat. And that evening we went to Bleadon & played darts and there were two WAAFS who we had to drive home by 10. And Hamish and I talked about the Seven Pillars of Wisdom in the back – there was you & Ian & Hamish & I in the end & we ate bacon & eggs in The Dug Out.

The next morning was fine again. I shopped with your mother & went for walks with your father because you were busy till the evening. We went out to the pictures – I can't remember what it was – and before that we hunted out horses to ride with Mrs Miller & you thought I'd been bored all day or something very silly – and on Saturday we watched you play rugger & you didn't have the proper shoes – and again the sun was shining – we danced that evening all of us at the Atlantic, not late. There were the Watsons and some others. And Sunday came and I was going – we went for a walk, the four of us, in the morning & looked at the sea and town lying beneath in the sun – it shone all that weekend, and you helped me change my shoes beforehand and said something about wanting to do some other job that was dangerous, as if this wasn't enough.

That afternoon we rode, the two of us. My horse didn't keep up and the sand kept splashing in my face like the mud when I hunted. There were piles of stones on the sand to prevent aeroplanes landing on it & it was like a bending race. I said I looked awful when we got back to the stables but you said girls always said that. I shall always remember those days. They are like a bright green island in a river – it is only for fear a little might fade that I have written them down. I do not want to think they will return only as faintly as an echo, when we lie with our faces buried in the June grass.

March 1st 1942

There is no mention of David in Pamela's diary entry for 3 March, when she reached a new milestone in her young life: '21st Birthday. Funny somehow – it doesn't seem like it– Had lots and lots. Mummy & Pop a wireless!! And money & belt!! & slippers – lovely!!!' Pamela then goes on to record gifts from various aunts, uncles and cousins. However her best birthday present was to arrive a day later. The date, 4 March, is surrounded in her diary by more than a dozen ecstatic exclamation marks:

A TELEGRAM FROM THE McCORMICKS SAYING 'Have received letter from David, he is prisoner in Italy, no address yet, will write.' Feel just so wonderful want to shout – Rang them up. Mrs M said David had said tell Pamela he'd still got the horse-shoe & my photograph – but he'd got dysentry [sic] & was going to hospital. Do hope he wasn't bad and is all right now. What a birthday present. Did anyone ever have any one like it. How I long to get a letter – wonder how much I can write. Wrote him one which will send as soon as I can – if only I knew the address. Hope they give him enough to eat.

Not surprisingly, Pamela's diary entries for the next few days show her passing on the good news to various friends and relatives and making enquiries wherever possible about conditions in which prisoners of war were kept. On 6 March the

Streets were invited to dinner at Compton Park by their wealthy friend George Cross, whose son – also called George – was present. Pamela records: 'Mummy, Pop, me to Compton to dinner. Great fun. Young George was there – he's going to India. He said they never make prisoners work – it's an international law.' 'Young George' was correct up to a point, at least in the case of commissioned officers from the Western European nations that had signed up to the Geneva Convention of 1929. Captured officers were on the whole treated with suitable respect, and segregated into prison camps for officers only. 'Other ranks', however, were often required to work, provided that such work was not directly undertaken for military purposes. Prisoners from non-signatory nations to the Geneva Convention were another matter. On the Eastern Front, Russian prisoners of war were regarded by the Nazi forces as belonging to a sub-human species and subjected to hideous brutality; many were summarily executed or forced to work in appalling conditions in labour camps, which often resulted in death from exhaustion.

On 11 March Pamela received the letter she had been waiting for from David's parents:

> Letter from Mrs McCormick all about David + an enclosed card – we can write to the Italian R.C. [Red Cross] at Rome in the hopes of forwarding – she can write twice a week and is letting me have one of them which is v generous …
>   Wrote David – isn't it wonderful to be able to put that – oh so longing to hear.

Families of prisoners of war were able to obtain special airmail forms on which to write their missives to their loved ones in captivity. Such missives, both to and from the recipients in captivity, were subject to strict censorship. Families and friends back home were encouraged to make light of wartime privations, and do all they could to boost the morale of their imprisoned correspondents. Similarly, prisoners of war, issued with a limited ration of airmail forms and postcards, could not reveal their exact whereabouts, or complain of ill treatment. One of David's early letters to his parents, dated 4 April 1942, evidently fell foul of the censor, the first couple of lines having been heavily deleted in thick black ink. It follows on from this that on first reading, the correspondence between David and his parents and Pamela during his period of captivity seems somewhat bland, though occasionally it is possible to detect certain undercurrents. The first letters that David was allowed to write were – quite properly – to his parents. As before, however, Phyllis and Pamela shared their contents; long before the days of photocopiers, let alone scanners, this involved the physical posting of letters back and forth. Pamela made handwritten transcriptions of certain paragraphs of David's early letters, both to his parents and to her, which makes it possible to continue the chronological narrative, despite the originals of some letters being missing.

A.G. Street.

Vera Foyle and Arthur Street in 'courting' days.

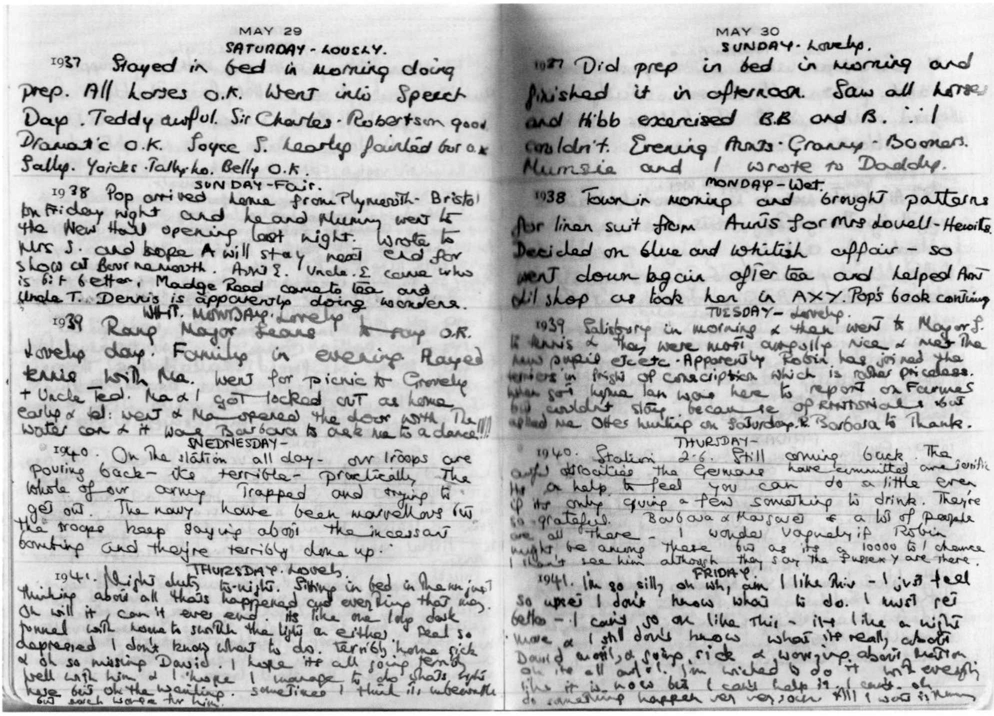

MAY 29

SATURDAY - LOUSLY.

1937 Stayed in bed in morning doing prep. All horses O.K. Went into Speech Day. Teddy awful. Sir Charles - Robertson good. Dramatic O.K. Joyce S. nearly fainted but O.K. Sally. Yoicks. Tally-ho. Betty O.K.

SUNDAY - Fair.

1938 Pop arrived home from Plymouth - Bristol on Friday night and he and Mummy went to the New Hall opening last night. Wrote to Mrs S. and hope A will stay next end for show at Bournemouth. Aunt E. Uncle E came who is bit better, Madge Reed came to tea and Uncle T. Dennis is apparently doing wonders.

WHIT. MONDAY. Lovely

1939 Rang Mayor Leans to pay O.K. Lovely day. Family in evening. Played [illegible] with Ma. Went for picnic to Grovely + Uncle Ted. Ma & I got locked out as home early & Ted: went & Ma opened the door with the water can & it was Barbara to ask me to a dance!!!

WEDNESDAY -

1940. On the station all day - our troops are pouring back - its terrible - practically the whole of our army trapped and trying to get out. The navy have been marvellous but the troops keep saying about the incessant bombing and they're terribly done up.

THURSDAY. Lovely

1941. Night duty to-night. Sitting in bed in the morning just thinking about all thats happened and everything that may. Oh will it, can it ever end. Its like one long dark funnel with nowhere to switch the light on either. Feel so depressed I don't know what to do. terribly home sick & oh so missing David. I hope its all going terribly well with him & I hope I manage to do whats right here but oh the waiting. sometimes I think it's unbearable but much worse for him.

MAY 30

SUNDAY - Lovely.

1937 Did prep in bed in morning and finished it in afternoon. Saw all horses and Hibb exercised B.B and B. [illegible] I couldn't. Evening Aunts - Granny - Boomers. Mumsie and I wrote to Daddy.

MONDAY - Wet.

1938 Town in morning and brought patterns for linen suit from Aunts for Mrs Lovell - Hewitt. Decided on blue and whitish affair - so went down again after tea and helped Aunt Lil shop as took her in AXY. Pop's book coming

TUESDAY - Lovely.

1939 Salisbury in morning & then went to Mayor S. & Annis & they were most awfully nice & met the new pupil etcetc - Apparently Robin has joined the terriers in front of conscription which is rather priceless. [illegible] here to report on Farmers but couldn't stay because of [illegible] but asked me Otter hunting on Saturday. R. Barbara to thank.

THURSDAY -

1940. Station 2.6. Still coming back. The awful atrocities the Germans have committed are terrible & its a help to feel you can do a little even if its only giving a few something to drink. They're so grateful. Barbara & Margaret & a lot of people are all there - I wonder vaguely if Robin might be among these but as its a 10000 to 1 chance I shan't see him although they say the Sussex are there.

FRIDAY.

1941. I'm so silly oh oh, am I like this - I just feel so upset I don't know what to do. I must get better - I can't go on like this - its like a night mare & I still don't know what its really about. David awful, & going sick & worrying about nothing. oh its all awful. I'm wicked to do it with everything like it is now but I can't help it. I can't. oh do something happen very very soon. All I want is [illegible]

Pamela's five-year diary – typical page.

Arthur, Vera and Pamela Street at a puppy show, 1938.

Arthur and Pamela in hunting clothes, Broadchalke, 1938.

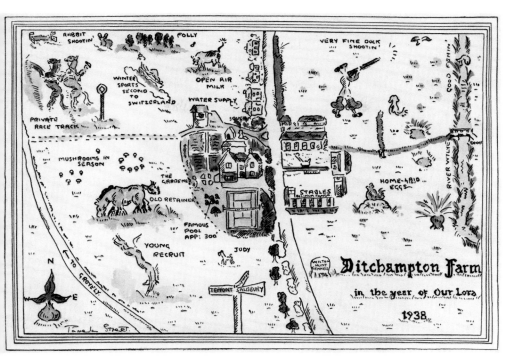

Ditchampton Farm's Christmas card
1938, designed by Pamela.

Pamela, Jorrocks and the float, autumn
1939.

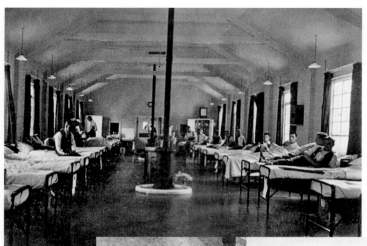

The 'hut', Tower House Emergency Military Hospital, Salisbury.

David and Pamela, Bleadon, Weston-super-Mare, 1941.

Pamela, April 1941.

22.4.41.

This is to say au revoir. I am afraid I can't say a great deal as there is an awful rush going on & I have much to do.

You should get a letter saying that I have arrived safely in about 6 weeks time & a letter from me in about 3 months. What old news it will be!

I am sending his love

& regrets that he didn't know you when he was at Larkhill. Everyone down here who met you thought you were very sweet & much too good for me.

I hope a letter from Cheddar in future is ... 2/4 ... 785/72 ... c/o A.P.

Goodbye darling & thank you for coming into my life ...

David

From now on my address will be:
Destination 'A'. No. ....
Rank 2/Lt. Name David McC ...
72nd Field Regiment, R.A.,
c/o A.P.O. 890
(No.) D E McCormick

David's goodbye letter to Pamela and slip.

Certificate

CROSSING THE LINE

We, Father Neptune, Barber Staff and Bears, do hereby certify that

2/Lt. D. McCormick

was Shaved and Baptised in accordance with ancient order whilst crossing the Equator on Friday May 16th, 1941.

C. A. Slaughter	Father Neptune
John L. Bell	Latherer
A Ratcliffe	Razor Man
John Prior	Bear
H Dennis	Bear
W Drake	Bear
J Butler	Bear

Crossing the equator, May 1941.

David in Cairo, 1941.

David (on left) by the Pyramids, August 1941.

Mess tent at Rakam Bay, August 1941.

David's 'bedroom', Rakam Bay.

David in the desert.

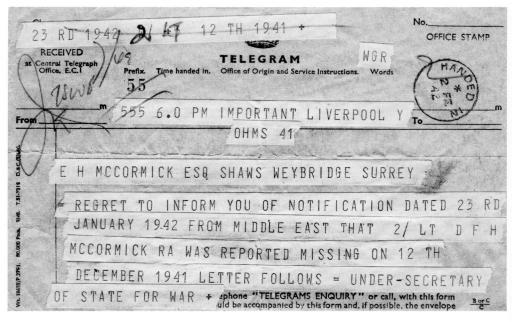

Telegram reporting David missing, February 1942.

Pamela in ATS uniform, 1942.

Pamela's portrait as Frontispiece in *The Field*, 1943.

Early censored letter from David to his parents, 1942.

DARLING MUMMY AND DAD,

......hope that you will have had lots of letters from me by now. In case not here is my list of urgent requirements :- Long pants, thick short sleeved vests thick pyjamas and socks and thin shirts. Easier to wash a knife and spoon and 2 pounds in any clothes parcel please. I believe, chocolate is all that you can send. Red Cross food parcels are wonderful but I have only had 1¾ in 3 months and none have come to this new camp yet though they are promised. I hear that an arrangement can be made with the makers to send separate cigarette parcels taxfree. If so could I be sent 500 Players a month please. If you can send a separate medical parcel I should like dark glasses, a badger shaving brush + vaseline or oil for my hair. Sorry to do nothing but talk about parcels. I am in the mountains now in a beautiful old monastery. For a few days we went back to winter and it was very miserable, but now we sunbathe all day and at night it is cold. More about this place next time. It must be a year since I saw you last. Longing to hear from you and hoping you are well 14/4/42

All my love.

David.

The filming of *Strawberry Roan* in 1944, with William Hartnell and Carol Raye.

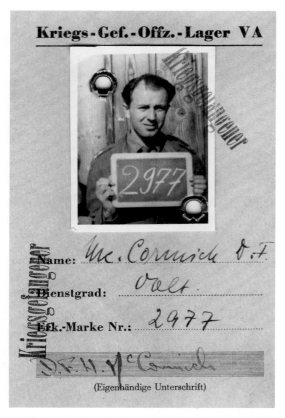

Kriegs-Gef.-Offz.-Lager VA

Name: Mc. Cornick D.F.

Dienstgrad: Olt.

Erk.-Marke Nr.: 2977

(Eigenhändige Unterschrift)

David's POW identity card, 1943.

Room 14, Oflag VA, Weinsberg; David middle row, second from left.

Oflag VA, Weinsberg, 1944.

David's Christmas greetings to his American godfather, 1943.

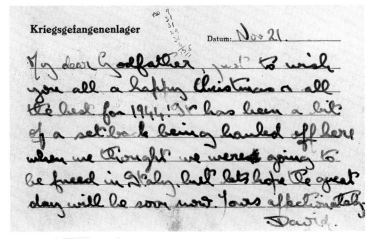

David and Bill (Quilly) Kerruish,
Stalag 383, Straubing, 1945.

Arthur and Vera Street, Phyllis and
Edward McCormick, 3 July 1945.

David and Pamela's wedding, 3 July 1945.

Pamela's portrait by
Philippe Halsman for
Pond's, 1946.

OUR ENGLISH cousins enjoying a day at Arlington. Mr. and Mrs. David McCormick of England found the Post and Paddock Club at Arlington Park a pleasant rendezvous for luncheon and the races during their visit in Chicago, where they have been guests of his cousins, Mr. and Mrs. Robert Hall McCormick III. The visitors returned to New York this week, en route to England.

'The Smart Set', *Herald American*,
25 July 1946.

David McCormick, the Managing Director of Massey Harris, Arthur Street at the Bath & West Show, 1949.

Street/McCormick
family, 1951.

In Spring the farmer sows his crops,
A busy man who never stops.

In Summer when the corn is fit
He has no time to eat or sit.

In Autumn when he's sold his grain,
He turns straight round to plough again.

But Christmas is the season when
The farmer acts like other men.

Pamela's Christmas card from the Manor Farm, Steeple Langford, 1951.

The first letter Pamela received directly from David and partially transcribed before forwarding to Phyllis McCormick, was dated 30 January 1942:

Ospedale Militari, Bari

I sent the first three to Mummy to be sure that she would know quickly that I was still in the land of the living, and am glad to be alive too! Though that is the only consolation in my present position. How long will it be for. I have certainly got myself into a fix this time but it might be worse. I have spent the last three weeks in this hospital with a dose of dysentry [*sic*] which has cleared up now and I am going out tomorrow I think. But there are some other officers here with horrible wounds. I am very sorry for them but there is not much I can do to help them. One there is who has lost an eye and an arm. He is very cheerful and never complains at his lot ... I lost all my kit except what I was wearing, so I consider myself fairly lucky. I have more than some.

Also transcribed in Pamela's handwriting is the following excerpt from a letter from David to his parents dated 28 February:

Campo 75, P.M. 3450, Italy

There is not much news here. The weather is a little warmer thank God and the almond blossoms are coming out. We had four falls of snow down here and without heating & living in a wooden hut I found it very cold. I have always an upset stomach and fleas and am pretty dirty as it is too cold to wash my shirt. I amuse myself by playing bridge, trying to learn various languages and reading ...

Phyllis McCormick's first letter to David, dated 5 March 1942, records his parents' relief at knowing that their son was still alive:

Darling David,

Just received your letter of Jan 10th. The first news we have had since you were reported 'missing'. Our anxiety has been fearful. We do hope you are now well again – We cannot send you anything until we get your full address – We are trying to do so through the Red Cross – The only way – Have informed Pamela, & everyone is delighted to have news of you at last ... We do hope you have been able to get the bare necessities. It makes us very anxious knowing you have no clothes or soap ...

Edward McCormick wrote David a very similar letter a couple of days later, ending with a practical suggestion for how he might occupy his time in captivity:

My dear David

We received your letter dated 10th Jan on the 3rd March. I can't tell you how delighted we were! … You were reported 'missing' on the 12th Dec, and we received no notification of this until 3rd Feb. Then followed a very bad time for me because Mum had been and was very ill with flu and a sort of pneumonia, and it was quite obvious to me that I could not possibly tell her about you …

We have been making all sorts of enquiries to try to get your final camp address. You see, we cannot send you any parcel until we know your address. We have had no official notification that you are a prisoner …

We shall do all we can to send you what little is allowed for your comfort and entertainment. I expect you will be given facilities for studying the Italian language. You will enjoy this and it will be useful knowledge …

Pamela's earliest surviving letter to David in captivity, dated 11 March 1942, is a somewhat chaotic outpouring of her relief at knowing that he was safe, with endless reassurances of her continuing affection for him and concern for his welfare:

Oh my darling – I don't know what to say – you're safe – it is so wonderful all I can do is thank God and ask Him to keep you safe and sound and one day bring you back to me – Darling I shall love you always – you do know don't you? Are you all right now from dysentry? I'll pray that you are. Your mother and father have been marvellous and sent me a telegram as soon as they got your letter – I hope this will find you but it is all the address we've got so far. Darling, thank you for having the horse-shoe and photograph. I hope it will always do its duty. Do you know it is a year this weekend since I first came down to see you – I can remember it all as clearly as anything – the hill in the sun and the iron gate – oh Darling if this is a silly letter please forgive – I am so happy I don't know what to put – but I do hope you're all right now and that soon I will get the letter your mother said you were writing. Do you know the news about you came the day after I was 21 – wasn't it odd? The funniest things seem to happen to us don't they? No one on earth could have had a more wonderful present. Darling I can write to you once a week and your parents the same – I will think of all the things I meant to say when this has gone but just for the moment God bless and keep you Darling, and remember I shall love you always.

Pamela

I'll think about you all the time – so when you think about me we shall be thinking about each other!

Once communications had been established and David's official camp address known, David and his parents got down to practicalities. Prisoners-of-war were allowed to receive, via the Red Cross based in Geneva, 'next-of-kin' parcels, 'medical comfort' parcels, and packs of cigarettes sent at the request of a prisoner's family or friends directly by the manufacturers (this being long before the dangers of smoking had been established). Cigarettes were useful not merely for consumption but as prison camp currency, being bartered for other goods. An early letter from David to his parents, and a letter from his mother crossing his, give examples of the kind of items that could be sent to prisoners via the Red Cross:

April 14th

I hope you will have had lots of letters from me by now. In case not, here is my list of urgent requirements: long pants, thick short sleeved vests, thick pyjamas and socks and thin shirts (easier to wash), a knife and spoon and 2 pounds of chocolate in any clothes parcel please. I believe chocolate is all you can send. Red Cross parcels are wonderful but I have only had 1¾ in 3 months and none have come to this new camp yet though they are promised. I hear that arrangements can be made with the makers to send separate cigarette parcels taxfree. If so could I be sent 500 Players a month please. If you can send a separate medical parcel I should like dark glasses, a Badger shaving brush, + Vaseline or oil for my hair. Sorry to do nothing but talk about parcels. I am in the mountains now in a beautiful old monastery.* For a few days we went back to winter and it was very miserable, but now we sunbathe all day and at night it is cold. More about this place next time ...

April 20th

Darling Dave,

We were so delighted to get your postcard dated March 3rd, & to hear that your tummy was better. I sent you a next-of-kin parcel as soon as we had your address, containing a shirt, vest, pants, socks, pyjamas, handkerchiefs, soap, towel, shorts, shoes etc, & some chocolate (the latter from Pamela). I do hope they arrive before many months have passed. I have also sent you a parcel of books & cigarettes. I am also trying to send you an air-mail parcel as you have been in such bad health, but I'm afraid I can't send the things you most need, owing to the many restrictions. So don't be disappointed when it arrives (if it ever does) ...

Phyllis McCormick then goes on in the same letter to describe in greater detail the relief and celebrations that followed the arrival of David's first letter home written from captivity. Clearly at some stage, despite Edward McCormick's attempts to protect his wife from hearing about it, she had become aware of the fateful telegram. Keenly aware of the inevitable inconsistencies of the postal service to and from

---

* This was the Certosa (charterhouse) di San Lorenzo in Padula, near Salerno, dating back to the beginning of the fourteenth century.

prisoner-of-war camps, David's ever practical father suggested early on a system for keeping track of the letters the McCormicks wrote to their son:

March 18th
    We shall try to number our letters to you, and keep copies. In this way you will be able to tell us if any are missing and we shall be able to fill up the gap in any news which you may have missed ...

He also clearly tried to put as positive a 'spin' as possible on his son's situation, offering him advice on how he might make best use of his time in captivity:

March 30th (no. 7)
    We are so glad to know that you are getting over your attack of dysentery. With the Spring coming on, in that beautiful Italian climate, you should soon be able to regain your strength, and may possibly become healthier than you have been for some time. I've no doubt you will find that things have been organised to help you keep busy, and that is most important. The busier you keep, both mentally and physically, the quicker the time will pass, and the better will you be equipped to meet the difficult times ahead of us ...

As previously explained, family and friends of all prisoners of war were anxious to avoid their letters being held up by censorship at either end, so at times it must have been hard to fill the pages with innocuous news from home that would escape the censor's black ink. This particular letter from David's father passed the test splendidly by continuing with an unintentionally humorous account of a current domestic problem the McCormicks were having with one of the members of staff back at Shaws:

We are having rather a tricky time here just now. Clar [Phyllis McCormick's family nanny, who had been staying at Shaw's to care for Phyllis during her illness] brought her young niece to us about a month ago to help in the house. She had had some kind of unsatisfactory love affair which had slightly unbalanced her and she had to be taken away from the works she was employed in. They thought the change of coming here would do her good, and for a time all worked well, and she was perfectly normal and worked like a beaver, but, some 10 days back she struck up a friendship with a married man, which was naturally unsatisfactory, and now she has gone crackers again and does the most peculiar things. Yesterday Paine found her trying to start up the Vauxhall. She had the starting handle in and had pulled everything in or out and had finally found the self-starter when Paine appeared.
    We had a soldier friend staying with us last night. This morning she found his belt and kept trying it on and looking at herself in the mirror.
    I am taking her off to see a lady doctor soon. It is all rather difficult ...

For her part, Pamela continued to write to David as often as the rationing of prisoner-of-war airmail forms permitted. Her second letter was very much in the same vein as her first, but also refers to the time she spent earlier in the year at his parents' home:

Your mother has given me all your love and messages in the 2 letters she's got – it has been so wonderful hearing & she has been marvellous about everything. Did you know I stayed with them in January? They were terribly kind and Rego* is quite the beautifullest dog I know. Judy [the Street family dog] is having puppies & I'm having one and calling it Rego too. Do you mind? It will be your only rival so you oughtn't to. I hope this doesn't sound silly but I know there isn't anyone like you anywhere and never will be and I shall love you always …

Like David's parents, Pamela never knew which of her letters would get through to him or in what order, so their contents were necessarily somewhat repetitive. For example on 31 March she wrote:

Darling, I got your first letter last week – it was so wonderful getting it – I've already replied to that at the time but in case you never get it please remember that even if you were at the North Pole and could only write once a year I would still love you just the same …

   Don't please feel useless <u>ever</u>. If you think about everything you have done you can't possibly and the war can't last for ever. Hasn't a lot happened to you and what a lot you've done in the last year … Darling I shall never stop asking you questions when I see you next except that as I said before I'll probably be quite tongue-tied!

As can be seen, Pamela's letters all served the same purpose: firstly to assure him of the constancy of her feelings towards him, and secondly to make every possible effort to raise his spirits. Judging from David's reply on receipt of Pamela's first letter to him, she more than fulfilled this aim. On 8 May he wrote:

Darling, I got your lovely letter last week & was terribly thrilled to hear from you after so long. Now I am just waiting for the next. I am afraid I can't write to you every week as I am only allowed one letter and a postcard per week. Darling, Mummy & Dad write that you stayed with them in January. They say they loved having you & they seemed to like you very much – I don't mean that that is surprising!! I hope you will go and stay with them again if you have any time to,

---

*   David spelt his dog's name 'Rigo'; Pamela, not realising, spelt it 'Rego', also the puppy
      to be named after him.

and cheer them up. Did you like Shaws & Rigo? I am very fond of him. Did he frighten you? He looks rather like the big bad wolf! I expect you saw all those awful photos of me when I was a horrid fat little boy! I wish I had been there too! Darling, I never liked girls in A.T. uniforms before, but now I have changed my mind.* I think you must look very sweet. Is your hair still nice & long? I think about you such a lot. What are you doing? Is it fun or awful? I hate to think of all your letters wandering around the desert looking for me, when they can never find me. All my love till next time I write. Your David.

Once Pamela received the news that David was safe, her life back at Wilton seemed to take on a different complexion. Despite the uncertainty about whether she would continue in the camouflage unit once her trial period was up, she appears to have enjoyed her work there more, even taking the occasional knock in her stride:

March 10th Started making a super house for a model. Large like a doll's house …

March 11th Capt Allan came and damned my house as too large so had to start all over again …

March 12th Started on suburban houses – at last they've got at what they want + scale …

March 13th Vera and I very peaceably made houses … and as Judith & the Major's away everything was wonderful …

After this brief period of tranquillity, a note of alarm creeps into Pamela's diary. On 18 March she wrote: 'Awful. They rang up and asked if I could go on a Clerks course for all the new girls in the Command, so Seago said yes & I think it is probably the end of me and camouflage …' The course in question began the very next day, and Pamela did not enjoy the experience: 'Started my course at the Town Hall. Simply terrific – lectures + lectures + lectures – awful. Wretched exam at the end. Oh dear oh lor.' After a further day or two of lectures Pamela sat another exam which, according to her diary, 'wasn't too bad'. This was just as well, because on 27 March the axe finally fell:

Have got the <u>sack</u> … It isn't surprising really – I felt it coming for ages. It's a pity but somehow I never fitted in – always felt awkward & I suppose my work is pretty rotten all told. Hope this doesn't mean my exit from Wilton. However

---

* ATS uniforms were generally acknowledged to be the least flattering of all the uniforms in the women's services during the Second World War.

– the world is what it is – quite a new experience for me – hope it isn't the first of many, though …

Pamela's rather untypically philosophical reaction to her dismissal may have been because another cheering event had recently taken place. On 14 March her parents gave her a belated birthday party, which according to her diary entry went extremely well:

Had the most wonderful 21st birthday fling. Sybil, Kay, Phil, Joan M … Mrs Sivewright + Sue Ramsay and 4 awfully nice men she brought … Major Dickson came + Philip Man & friend. It all went with a bang I think – it seems all wrong giving one but it was nice. Mummy provided marvellous eats …

Pamela would have been further cheered during this period by having received more news of David in the form of two letters from Phyllis McCormick, and on 25 March a letter from David himself:

Letter from David! Wonderful but he's so depressed – the hospital must have been awful – everyone there with wounds & things. I think the dysentry [sic] makes you feel like that but he talks of feeling perfectly useless and my having to forget him – oh this wretched war – if only I could do or get somewhere … What a pity you can't fly to Italy in disguise or something …

Despite 'getting the sack', Pamela was still obliged to work out the remainder of her trial period in camouflage. However, the atmosphere seems to have become more relaxed, with a marked change in Ted Seago's attitude towards her:

April 1st Major S … was v. sweet to me and I don't feel so bad about it …

April 4th Making some quite nice tanks for a change …

April 8th Seago has been simply sweet to me this week … admired my tanks & tractors no end – isn't it funny …

If Pamela's final days in the camouflage unit were relatively peaceful, the same could not be said about life back at Ditchampton Farm. The conflicting demands of his various wartime activities were taking their toll on Arthur Street. On 2 April Pamela reported in her diary: 'Pop's in an awful state of nerves.' Arthur Street's birthday was on 7 April, and the family were to have celebrated it with a lunch in Salisbury, but unfortunately events did not go according to plan: ' … had a blood test. Made me late for Pop at the Red Lion as we were to have had lunch

… He went home in a temp and Mummy was cross – 'cos he's very nervy now & anything upsets him.' Realising that he could no longer fulfil his many obligations, Arthur Street had no option but to let some lapse. On 13 April Pamela wrote: 'Pop seems a little better but has refused book & resigned Home Guard for 3 months … '

Arthur Street's mood would not have been helped by the current progress of the war. During the first part of 1942 there were several notable setbacks for the Allies. On 12 March Pamela wrote in her diary: 'The news is simply terrible. The Japs have got past Rangoon and seem to be <u>everywhere</u>.' A month later her diary contains a similar reference: '*April 13th* The news is pretty ghastly & this India business is the limit. No co-operation & Japan at the gates – enough to give anyone the pip …' Such diary entries would have echoed the feelings of all British civilians listening nervously to reports of military campaigns in the main theatres of war that spring, praying for more positive news.

Twelve

A Lighter Load, a Hampered Harvest and a Moment of Rejoicing (April–December 1942)

By late April 1942, the news may have been dire, with Axis forces gaining ground in all the main areas of the current conflict. For Pamela, however, everyday life had in many respects taken a turn for the better. David was now known to be safe for the immediate future, and finally she was about to start a wartime occupation that was well within her capabilities, whilst continuing to be billeted at home. Once she had left the camouflage unit, Pamela was able to enjoy a week off duty before starting her new job as a filing clerk in the Registry of Southern Command, situated in the cloisters of Wilton House – commonly referred to as 'the dungeons'. This time she had no qualms about going back to work after a period of leave:

April 23rd Went to see Pru [her commanding officer and friend, Prudence Perkins] & didn't mind going back at all like nursing – am starting in the command tomorrow …

April 24th G. Registry. Dear little man called the General looks after me – rather nicer than Cam because more people & not so cut off. I'm a terror – must have excitement …

April 27th Work as usual – it is quite fun & they are all very nice … much better than nursing.

Pamela's diaries give little clue as to the exact nature of her day-to-day duties. The 'Registry' in service institutions collected and collated documentation of all their operations and activities. It has been suggested that some of the material that Pamela handled may have been of a highly classified nature, but it is doubtful whether she would have realised this at the time. Clearly Pamela felt happier in her new occupation at the Registry, buzzing with people coming and going, whereas the camouflage unit hut in North Street had been a comparatively isolated environment in which to work, with tensions between work colleagues making things even more difficult.

Being less stressed at work, Pamela now had time to give consideration to another aspect of her life that was far from satisfactory. Regardless of the sincerity of her feelings for David, after such a long separation it was only natural that by now an attractive girl of her age would be missing male company. Pamela's diary entries over the past couple of years, with many envious references to friends becoming engaged or married, make it clear that she feared being 'left on the shelf'. In prison camp in Italy, David was also painfully aware of this, as a rather poignant excerpt from one of his letters later that year illustrates: 'It will soon be two years now. We will have to discover each other again, for we must have both changed. I hope you will not have changed too much. Is England still the same? Are all the young people still getting married?'

Pamela's diary entry for 15 April contains the following lament:

> Oh lor this war – can it ever end – I'm 21 now and I haven't done much with my life & somehow I seem to have missed things. If David were here perhaps it would be different but it's a year now since I was kissed & it's an awfully long time when you're 21 …

Such musings continue in her diary the following day: 'Sometimes I feel I shall go mad. It's terribly wrong really but this waiting I never was very good at it and I feel like a nun …' As already noted, Pamela's head had been temporarily turned by the dashing Tom Jago (now promoted to Lieutenant-Colonel) at the most recent New Year's Eve dance. Although she had not seen him since his departure from Wilton to take up a job in Whitehall, Pamela had not forgotten this fleeting infatuation. Before her week's leave between jobs she had taken the bull by the horns, leaving messages for him to say she would be coming to London that week with her father. This resulted in a rare treat, though the outcome proved a disappointment:

> *April 20th* Pop & I drove up. Tom did ring up after all my heart-searchings & we went to dinner at the Savoy & danced to Carol Gibbons* – he was very charming but looked rather over-worked. I think I must do things wrong somehow – he isn't nearly as keen as he used to be … He did everything perfectly even to a brotherly sort of kiss on the doorstep – but gosh I must have lost something or else I'm just the type of girl men don't want to kiss p'raps, except that he did at

---

*   One of the most famous band leaders during the Second World War.

Christmas & I wouldn't let him – why oh why do I miss my opportunities … it is awful to doubt about loving David but just right now I think I am very much in love with Tom, only that he isn't with me a bit I know. What shall I do? Is it that I want the moon too much – after all a Lieut Col & the Savoy & Carol Gibbons should be enough for any girl …

Back at Ditchampton Farm the next day Pamela continued musing along the same lines: 'Have that awful depressed feeling when lovely things that might have been lovelier are all over … I wish I had the more come hither look …' A week later this experience continued to bother her, though her disappointment now seems to have transmuted into anger. On 28 April she wrote:

Ought to get a letter from David soon. Gosh how I should like to be kissed properly. Really I am cross about Tom – don't know <u>what</u> was the matter with him & yet he was terribly nice – what did I do there – oh well …

There are no further mentions of Tom Jago in Pamela's diaries, but despite this experience, she was still on the lookout for male companions. Her entry for 28 April continues: 'Feel terribly old but am taken for 18 by all the men in the office – gosh I wish I was … What a pity one didn't think of no time like the present when one was younger – from henceforward it had better be my maxim.'

Pamela had plenty of opportunities to live up to this maxim during the next few weeks, during which she attended a number of dances, the first being a tea-dance at home at Ditchampton Farm for various young people from the forces stationed locally:

May 1st Our A.T. dance. Alan Billington, Sybil, Dinah, Henry, Gordon came … It went down well & we played planchette* afterwards & got thoroughly creepy … Alan is sweet. I do like him.

May 5th Went to Larkhill dance … Great fun – all went in a lorry … being gay for a change. Met Alan in Salisbury …

May 9th Went to Sukey dance with Peter Cash-Read, John Matthews, Sybil, Dinah … awfully good time – hit it up till 12.30.

May 30th Went to Lady L's & Mrs. Chamberlain's dance with Peter & Alan. Alan is sweet & I like him awfully. It was terribly good & I had a lovely time – all the girls I'd ever known were there …

---

*   A game in which the players attempt to communicate with the spirit world.

June 13th Di Schreiber's Sally Grey's & Babs' party ... Alan was there – he was very sweet – I do like him – he tells me he's fond of me but I don't quite know how much he's meaning – anyhow I told him about David ...

Early July saw the end of this more sociable period for Pamela, and the end of a potential romance with the aforementioned Alan Billington. On 4 July she went to one last dance organised by the redoubtable Jesse Sivewright; her diary entries for this and the following day read respectively:

Phil [Pamela's cousin] came ... Peter & John Matthews who are going, Alan who is going & Sybil who is going so it was a breaking up of the clans and I don't think I'll go to another for ages now because I'm sick of the whole lot and don't know <u>what</u> is the matter with me ...

July 5th Alan came to supper & I don't like him a bit & I'm glad he's going – how I ever could beats me – isn't life strange ...

★ ★ ★

Despite having temporarily relinquished his Home Guard duties, when it came to writing and broadcasting, Arthur Street certainly had no intention of lessening his load. Pamela's diary abounds with references to her father going to London or other parts of the country to report on the current state of British agriculture. Another frequent task was giving lectures to the troops.

During the early summer Pamela's diary records two visits to the army base at Larkhill on Salisbury Plain to hear her father perform, which she evidently much enjoyed. The first of these entries reads: '*May 17th* Went to Larkhill & met Major Hanscombe & friend who took me to Brains Trust to see Pop. He was quite good and it was fun.'

Entertainment was essential for the morale of Allied troops, both in training or awaiting deployment, or those already serving overseas. To this end the organisation ENSA (Entertainments National Service Association) was set up in 1939 with the express purpose of putting on shows of various kinds for the troops' recreation. Many high-profile artists took part, such as the singer Vera Lynn, who was quickly dubbed 'the forces' sweetheart'. Not all entertainments were of such quality, however, and in some quarters the acronym ENSA took on a new meaning: 'Every Night Something Awful'.

Hopefully this was not the case on the evenings when ENSA became the umbrella for a new panel discussion programme, *The Brains Trust*, the precursor to the long-running series *Any Questions?* The format was the same as today's, with a group of pundits led by a chairman taking topical questions from the audience, in this case made up of Allied troops on Salisbury Plain. By dint of his agricultural expertise,

Arthur Street became a regular *Brains Trust* panellist, and after the war would continue to perform on *Any Questions?* until shortly before his death. These subsequent broadcasts were mainly from the West Country, but back in 1942 he was in demand on ENSA *Brains Trust* panels not just on his home territory but in all parts of the British Isles, as Pamela's entry for 11 July makes clear: 'Pop went to London & then on to Scotland for the week's Ensa Brains Trust. Lucky thing – sounds wonderful. Very tiring I expect though.' This last comment proved prescient; Arthur Street was once again overdoing things, which would soon have serious consequences.

In the days before the introduction of combine harvesters, harvesting was a long, labour-intensive process. First, corn was cut and bound into sheaves by a reaper-binder, the resulting sheaves requiring manual stooking in order for the corn with its precious seed-heads to dry in the field before being threshed. Threshing was another labour-intensive business, with the sheaves being manually pitched into the threshing machine for the seed to be separated from the stalks and bagged into sacks to be carted back to the farm buildings to await sale, whilst the straw remaining in the field had to be baled. Finally, since a certain amount was inevitably lost on the ground during the harvesting process, fields needed to be raked to gather up the loose straw with corn-heads still attached. Only then could arable land be ploughed up and sown to seed for the whole process to begin again for the following year.

Although combine harvesters began to be introduced in the late 1930s and early 1940s, they were few and far between; the vast majority of arable crops in the British Isles were still being harvested by the reaper-binder/thresher method. In early 1942 Ditchampton Farm had acquired a new threshing drum which Arthur Street was keen to put to the test. This still meant, however, that Ditchampton Farm was heavily dependent on outside labour. At the beginning of August at Ditchampton Farm such labour seemed plentiful, and harvest progressed smoothly, or to use one of Arthur's favourite Wiltshire expressions, 'suently'. On 7 August he recorded on an upbeat note in *Hitler's Whistle*:

> This season harvest labour seems to be much easier to come by. All sorts of people volunteer, just as they did when Napoleon threatened invasion. In fact it seems that history is repeating itself, and that once again the harvest is not merely a farmer's harvest but a national one. I have a team of twelve good schoolboys, who already have done stooking, threshing, and flax pulling. In addition local policemen have lent a hand in their off-duty periods, and in the long evenings the local roadmen and soldiers take the place of the boys …

The employment of schoolchildren to help with the harvest was a current matter of controversy. Again in *Hitler's Whistle* Arthur wrote about a lively discussion he had had with an acquaintance who was against the practice, particularly during term-time, though Arthur Street clearly had no such qualms:

'I don't like it,' he said. 'It's all wrong to deny education to little children just to make profits for private individuals. It's a retrograde step, it's an attempt to put back the clock.'

'Listen', I said. 'The clock of history is being put back all right, but by Fascist dictators not by British farmers. And one small thing that will help to set the clock moving forward once again is the maximum production of food here in this island. Schoolchildren not only can but should help in that, in order that the clock may be set going forward again as quickly as possible. If the nation is beaten by starvation what will happen to those children?'

On that score I cannot see any valid objection to schoolchildren doing what they can to help food production this summer and for as long as the war lasts. Neither does there seem to be any objection by the educational authorities to their doing this during holidays. It is when farming wants their services during term-time that the difficulties arise. The educationalist argues that this upsets the school time-table. Agreed, but what time-table has not been upset by Hitler & Co? Goodness knows the British farmer's has been turned upside-down.

Today we tend to think of vandalism as a comparatively modern phenomenon, but it seems it has always existed. Whilst schoolchildren clearly could and did have their uses during the Second World War, they could also have a severely detrimental effect on the farming process, as Arthur Street laments elsewhere in *Hitler's Whistle*:

I want to mention something that is causing serious trouble in the countryside, and for which there seems no workable remedy. This is the great increase in trespassing damage by people of all ages, and a tremendous increase in wanton damage and mischief by children. And I don't mean town children or evacuees, but homebred village children.

This sort of thing. Hayrick left one evening nicely tucked and topped up ready for the thatcher. Unwisely the ladder was left there, so children climbed up and pitched off a lot of hay to the ground, and burrowed a large hole in the roof. A tractor in the field started up by boys and driven into fence, with considerable damage to both fence and machine. Paraffin tap of tractor turned on and tank emptied. Paths made through standing corn and so on …

Arthur Street goes on to make it abundantly clear who he considers is to blame, and suggests a remedy:

No one can control children out of school hours save their parents, and on them should fall the responsibility of damage done by children … If William Smith had to pay a fine of a pound for one of little Tommy Smith's escapades, he would see to it that little Tommy thought twice before transgressing again. And how!

Whilst the harvest at Ditchampton Farm started well, before long it was once again being hampered by bad, or to use another favourite expression of Arthur Street's, 'caddling' weather. Soon the farm's workforce was seriously behind schedule, and more outside help was required. Besides this, however, Arthur now found himself facing a challenge of an even greater kind. On top of his nervous illness in the spring – from which, judging from Pamela's diary entries, he had still not fully recovered – the effort of travelling continuously all over the country seemed to have taken its toll. Pamela's diary entry for 31 August is particularly grim:

> Pop is in bed with a bad leg. I should have made him go to the doc because I thought it was serious – flebitis [*sic*]. The weather is awful & the harvesting going on in fits & starts – the war continues – Russia hanging out but on the defensive of course. Egypt about the same but better in the Far East but oh the strain …

At the end of *Hitler's Whistle* Arthur elaborates on his illness and the frustrating consequences. He had recently returned from a trip to Scotland and had negotiated a month off from the BBC to see in the harvest of 1942, but the fates were to decree otherwise:

> Alas! Next day curious pains developed in my left thigh, but I put off seeing the doctor until three days ago. He then sent me to bed with orders not to put foot to ground. Apparently, phlebitis cannot be ignored, and rest is the only cure. The sentence is a month probable, and three months if I don't obey all prison rules. So that was that. I laid on my back, looked at the rain, and cursed my luck. Also I had bedroom conferences with my foreman …
>
> This is going to be the hardest harvest for me that I have ever known. Charlie, my foreman, will not have an easy time; for, after each long day of work and worry with all sorts of amateur harvesters, he will have to report to me, here in bed. He has my deepest sympathy.

Watching from his sickbed as the rain trickled down the window panes, and fretting over the lack of progress with the harvest, Arthur's thoughts began to turn to his own father, who towards the end of his life was bedridden with arthritis, yet still managed to remain in charge of Ditchampton Farm. Arthur began to wonder what, in his place, Henry Street might have done to expedite matters:

> Somehow I found myself with much more sympathy for that irascible Victorian than I had in days of my youth. What was it we used to call him in those days? Ah, the organiser. But experience had since taught me that he was always a good man to copy. All right! I would do some organising.

Somehow the stacking speed should be doubled. To do this would require not only more men, but also more vehicles, as all mine were in use. I grabbed the telephone by my bed and rang up the army. Were there any means whereby so many lorries, drivers and men could be hired to go harvesting on the morrow if the weather held fine? There were and in half-an-hour they would ring me back; and before I finished a cigarette the necessary information was forthcoming, and also a definite promise of a balanced team of men and vehicles for the next day … Father wasn't the only farm organiser from a bed. And how pleased with his son he would have been!

Pamela put in a request for compassionate leave, which was quickly granted, to help on the farm while her father was incapacitated.

She recorded that for the remainder of the harvest a new team from the army came each week to lend a vital hand:

September 9th Barley carting – Six ricks now – terrific. Quite a lot of volunteers from the Signals. All the M.D.O. men.

September 16th Threshing still up at Wishford Arch. Soldiers etc come every morning from 3 Command signals – good team this week.

Despite the army's presence, there were inevitably odd days when nothing seemed to go according to plan. Pamela described one such day, including a mention of the kind of damage done by children to which Arthur Street had earlier referred in *Hitler's Whistle*:

September 21st Day of days. Nearly a hundred sacks got wet and we had to shoot the lot – Gale kept saying 'terrible show, Miss' which was <u>infuriating</u>. Finally we got the lot off by 7 o'clock with a rescued truck from the station. Thank goodness that's over but to crown everything Milner's rick caught fire this evening due to children and they broke our scales yesterday too … the juvenile way of going on is truly awful but the parents are to blame …

For the most part relations between the disparate elements of Ditchampton Farm's harvest workforce were harmonious, but it seems that two regular hands were not seeing eye to eye: '*September 18th* Everyone works quite well really except Lodge and Gale have arguments, but Wilfred is sweet & the soldiers have been v. good this week…' The disagreement between the aforementioned 'Lodge' and 'Gale' to which Pamela referred must have been serious. This type of behaviour between farm staff was something that Arthur Street would not tolerate, and he would have made it his business to investigate the matter and assert his authority. It therefore comes as no great surprise to read in Pamela's diary for 25 September: 'He has given Gale the sack.' At least Arthur sensibly waited until the harvest was safely gathered in before wielding the axe.

A couple of days earlier, a relieved Pamela recorded that the harvest was finally all but over: '*September 23rd* We've moved the thresher to Milner's now. In the afternoon Lodge, Lawes, Tom, Keith, Gale and I to all intents & purposes finished harvest. I got stuck with the Fordson on the down, but pitched up the last sheaf myself.' Fittingly, the other members of the workforce evidently granted the young daughter of the house the symbolic gesture of pitching the last sheaf of the 1942 harvest.

Pamela's period of compassionate leave was now over, and on 28 September she found herself back at the Registry at Wilton House: 'Started A.T.S.ing again. Had a trade test in which I made an awful lot of bloomers. Everyone was v. nice including Pru. Seems v. strange to be back. We have 6 people on Registry now.'

As for Arthur Street, he evidently obeyed doctor's orders and by the end of September was on the mend: '*September 29th* Nice to have Pop downstairs. His bedroom is the dining-room! He has to go quite slowly for some time. Mummy is looking v. tired. I hope they can go away together afterwards.'

★ ★ ★

The British military may have scored a minor domestic victory in helping gather in the harvest at Ditchampton Farm, but it was about to win a battle overseas on an infinitely greater scale, and one that would turn the tide in the Allies' favour in the Mediterranean theatre of war.

The first battle of El Alamein in the summer of 1942 had ended inconclusively. Afterwards, a frustrated Churchill flew out in person to assess the situation in North Africa, a visit that resulted in a new chain of command and Lieutenant-General Bernard Montgomery appointed to the leadership of the Eighth Army, now dug firmly into the Egyptian side of the defensive El Alamein line. Throughout the autumn reinforcements were steadily brought in, including the new American M4 Sherman tanks, whilst Montgomery made meticulous plans for a decisive attack to drive back the Afrika Korps. At the same time, diplomatic and military plans were being made for Allied landings, code-named 'Operation Torch', in the Vichy French-held dominions of Algeria and Morocco, which, if successful, would enable the Allies to continue eastwards to wrest Tunis from Axis hands and cut off any further retreat westwards by the Afrika Korps.

Montgomery began his advance on the evening of 23 October, and several days of fierce fighting ensued. Rommel, who earlier in the autumn had been obliged to fly back to Europe on sick leave, was now compelled to return to take command again; however by 3 November he had no option but to order a retreat; the

Allies had won the second battle of El Alamein decisively. A few days later came the news of Allied landings at Casablanca, Oran and Algiers. After much wrangling behind the scenes with the Vichy French leaders of these dominions, 'Operation Torch' had begun, and the scene was set to remove Axis troops from North Africa once and for all.

Back home, after all the dispiriting setbacks of earlier in the year, the news of the breakthrough at El Alamein was received ecstatically. This was the much-needed fillip to the nation's morale that had been absent for so long. On 9 November Pamela wrote: 'Terrific news from North Africa. American landings & goodness knows what.'

The following Sunday, 15 November, the Wilton church held a special thanksgiving service: 'Church Parade & I was marker as usual. This was a celebration for our terrific victory in Libya & the church bells were rung for the first time!'

News from the Russian front was now equally encouraging. On 4 December Pamela wrote: 'The wonderful news from N. Africa & Russia still continuing.'

Just how much of these glad tidings reached prisoners of war is unclear from David's letters to Pamela. He had continued to write to her throughout the summer and autumn of 1942, his letters giving what details he was allowed to divulge about life in the prison camp and how he and his fellow POWs kept themselves occupied. It is clear from such letters and postcards that reached her, albeit at irregular intervals, that he relied on her constancy and greatly valued the letters she was writing to him in return. For a start, she unwittingly raised his kudos amongst fellow POWs, as a letter from him written on 5 June illustrates:

I have bought a frame for your photo now & you sit at the foot of my bed & I say good morning & good night to you every day, & everyone is amazed that I should have such a 'lovely' there and wonder how I did it!!

David goes on to look forward to their eventual reunion:

Darling, you must promise as soon as I get home to get away from those A.T.S. & come & stay at Shaws & help me celebrate my return. We will go up to London for an evening or two & you will have to stop me from getting drunk & eating myself silly! How I am longing to do all those things which we can't do here, but more than anything to see you again.

Both to avoid censorship and at the same time reassure his parents and Pamela, David clearly made as light as possible of his physical ailments and discomforts in his letters home. Although the attack of dysentery from which he suffered earlier in the year had cleared up, his stomach trouble still persisted. Many years after the war David recounted to his family how, during his period of captivity in Italy, the only foodstuff of which there was an abundant supply was onions, which formed a significant part of the prisoners' meagre daily rations. This could hardly have helped anyone suffering from a digestive disorder, and for the rest of his life David disliked onions in his food.

Another explanation for David's lifelong aversion to onions may have been that at the time they were thought to have another, potentially more positive, use. Whether as a result of stress, poor diet or simply for congenital reasons, during his late 20s David's hair began to recede. One of the theories of the day was that one antidote to baldness was for men to shave their heads and then rub their scalps with raw onions. David tried this remedy enthusiastically, though it had little effect, for by the time of his eventual release his temples and top of his head were quite bald.

By 22 May he evidently felt sufficiently recovered to write reassuringly to his parents: 'You mustn't worry about me. I am quite all right & my stomach is better than it has been for some time.' Similarly, on a postcard of the same date, he wrote to Pamela: 'I am quite well again & getting very brown in the sun, so there is no need to worry about me! As a matter of fact I am feeling much younger so don't get too old or you will overtake me!'

One contributory factor to the improvement in David's health would have been the fact that by the early summer of 1942 parcels, as well as letters, were beginning to reach him. Back in May, he had included in one of his letters to his parents the following request: 'Lots of officers get food parcels from America. Could you please get Uncle Leander or someone to fix that for me please?' It seems this request later bore fruit. Subsequently, David remained in touch with his influential American godfather throughout his period of captivity, as demonstrated by a rare surviving postcard he sent the latter from German prison camp with greetings for Christmas and the new year 1944.

David's letters home all begin with a grateful acknowledgement for parcels received; to Pamela in particular his concern was that she was being over generous. On 27 August he wrote to her:

I have had several parcels now. A clothing one, 2 invalids food parcels & some cigarettes including one from you, bless you for them. It is terribly sweet of you but I hate you spending your money on so unworthy an object … Thank you for the chocolate in the clothes parcel. It was wonderful.

Red Cross parcels and those from relatives continued to reach David well into the autumn, so that by 5 November he was able to write to Pamela:

I have had 2 more cigarette parcels from you. This means 3 altogether. It is very sweet of you, but please send them less often, as I don't like you wasting your pay on me. They are very much appreciated. I must repeat so you can pass it on to Mummy if she hasn't heard that I have now had 2 next of kin parcels, 4 invalid comforts & am consequently well-equipped for the winter & need no more clothes. Sorry to bore you with this. I am afraid my letters to you, few and short as they are, are all about parcels & letters & I have no room to say what I feel about you, but I know you know.

The books that family and friends were allowed to send to prisoners of war were almost as important as food, clothing and cigarette parcels. For the morale of young men cooped up together in such cramped and basic conditions for an indeterminate period of time, keeping their minds occupied was essential. This was recognised by the authorities, and bookshops were encouraged to make arrangements to dispatch books to prisoners of war on behalf of their customers. As early as 12 May Pamela recounts a rare visit she made to London with her parents, during which she had lunch with Phyllis McCormick and was able to introduce her future mother-in-law to her own mother. Afterwards she records going to Harrods to have books sent to David:

Went to London with Ma & Pa and met Mrs. McCormick at the Hyde Park Hotel for lunch – she was perfectly sweet. Never nicer ... We talked David solidly all through lunch & then Mummy came and it went very well ... Went to Harrods & sent D Peking Picnic, 3 Men in a Boat & Literary Lapses.

Having been informed of the contents of this parcel in advance, David again wrote to Pamela expressing his gratitude. Reading was clearly a major daily activity by this stage of his captivity:

I've never read '3 Men in a Boat', you will be surprised to hear. I never used to read anything, but now we have quite a good library & I read almost a book a day including all the old classics which I should have read years ago.

In another letter he told Pamela that he had read her father's second novel: 'I read "Strawberry Roan" the other day and enjoyed it very much.' Evidently other books by Arthur Street had made their way into the prison camp library by the summer of 1942 as well, for on 27 August David warned Pamela: 'Don't buy your Dad's books for me if you haven't already as I think I have probably read them all.' Arthur Street's books were particularly popular with British prisoners of war, because they evoked with such clarity the countryside to which their homesick readers yearned to return.

On hearing that Arthur Street had been going through a difficult period in the spring of 1942, David replied to Pamela with some well-meant advice: 'I am so sorry to hear your Dad was ill in April & expect & hope he is well again. I think he works too hard! A great mistake!'

On 1 October he wrote:

My Darling Pamela, I expect it will be quite cold when you get this, yet here we have had the 2nd hottest day of the year last week. I have had your letter of Aug 27. You had just had lunch with Mummy in town, & bought me a wonderful mug. I had quite forgotten that I had ever asked for one, but am very pleased as I am still drinking out of old tins and need one. Thank you very much for the chocolate you gave Mummy for me too. I have just heard that two more parcels have arrived for me too but don't know what they are yet. A big day for me! Life here is going surprisingly quickly now that we have Red X food parcels once a week & have plenty of clothes. I learn Italian & French all morning, sleep after lunch till about 4, then play poker or go to a French class till dinner & play bridge from then till midnight. Do you play bridge? Mine is getting revoltingly good.

Bridge was one thing; however it is surprising that David also mentioned playing poker, given its somewhat louche reputation. He was evidently a dab hand at both. Although it was contrary to military discipline to play cards for money, to get round this issue, and on the assumption that an officer's word was his bond, the prisoners played for IOUs to be redeemed after the war had ended and they had been demobilised. One family member even cynically suggested that in this way David amassed sufficient capital to fund some of his post-war enterprises.

On 5 November David replied to a letter he had just received from Pamela, urging her once again not to write to him if so doing was becoming a chore. He went on to explain his recent promotion from Second Lieutenant to full Lieutenant, which Pamela must have noticed and queried from the details on the outside of his airmail letters, on which the sender's name and rank had to be printed:

Are you finding it an awful duty to write to me so often? I do hope not, but don't write if you don't feel like it, darling. Yes, it is 2 years that we have known each other, & perhaps in all a week that we have been together! I must put you wise about this Lieut business – it was unavoidable & happens when you have been an officer 18 months – I believe it has changed to 6 months – it would be, wouldn't it!

By the beginning of December the POWs were already planning how to make the best of Christmas given their limited circumstances, and saving up rations for the big day. On 3 December David wrote to Pamela:

There is snow on the surrounding hills & it is pretty cold. I think we are going to have a good feed on Christmas Day as we are putting all sorts of things from our Red X parcels into the workhouse for the occasion. Unfortunately our issue is being cut to one a fortnight which makes a big difference … Well Darling I shall be thinking about you on Christmas Day & hoping you are having a good time. My love to you, David.

David described how the POWs' festive season was spent in a letter to Pamela written on 6 January 1943, mentioning *inter alia* an evidently well-received visit by a Papal envoy. He goes on to conjure up in his mind's eye a rather touching picture of how Pamela and her parents might have spent Christmas Day:

Darling, I have had two more letters from you since Christmas, Nov 6 & 16, both very sweet, and a sweet little photo of you in uniform. The hair is just right & I realise what I am missing. We really had a very good Christmas here considering, lots of food & sort of parties & everyone gave a Christmas present & then they were all drawn for so that everyone got one back. That's democracy! We also had lots of services, cards, a pantomime which was very funny & a visit from a wonderful papal delegate, who brought the Pope's Christmas message to us & a whole lot of papal medals & stamps which were drawn for. I thought about you more than ever on Christmas day and I imagined you having rather a quiet day at home resting & eating too much & sitting in front of a fire with Rigo, and oddly enough you were wearing the long red dress with the painted buttons which you thought I didn't like. I have always felt guilty about that dress because actually I thought you looked lovely in it. 1943 is in & I am sure we will be together before it is over.
With a huge kiss,
    Your David

During the run-up to Christmas, Pamela's diary records her going to various parties, some of which she enjoyed more than others, but David was correct in that Christmas Day itself for the Streets was indeed a quiet affair. Whether or not Pamela was wearing her red dress is not recorded, but quite possibly she wore it on the following day, for which the Streets were evidently keeping their powder dry. They were to hold what appears to have been a highly successful Boxing Day party, as Pamela described afterwards:

December 26th Our party. It was terrific. Cuban Pete came to help in the afternoon. Everyone came [there follows a long list of names], Americans & lots of friends of people, all my A.T.S. & Dinah's Fannies. It really went with a swing & quite the best we've had though I say it myself.

However, a few days later Pamela attended a New Year's dance which only served to make her more aware than ever of her single status, and left her in a very different mood:

> It was an awful flop. Jimmy had a cold & Major K G was sweet but old & Capt Evans was a sop & John Matthews a twirp & I wonder if it's me or if I'll ever find anyone nice to run round with. Gosh I feel ancient & unwanted & miserable … oh blow everything.

Pamela was not to know it at the time, but things would change dramatically for her in this respect the following year, though this in itself would present a new set of problems. Meanwhile the rest of the civilian population could take comfort from the turn of the tide in the Allies' fortunes that the battle of El Alamein and success so far of 'Operation Torch' signified. As Churchill famously said about this particular stage of the war, whilst it was not yet even the beginning of the end, it was 'the end of the beginning'.

Thirteen

American Impact, 'Operation Husky' and an Unwelcome Move (January–October 1943)

After the debacle at Pearl Harbor in December 1941 that brought the USA into the war, it was only a matter of time before American troops would come over to the UK to prepare for the Second Front. With its nearby army bases, Wilton had to accommodate a good many of these new arrivals, who proved something of an eye-opener for the locals. The differences between American servicemen and their British counterparts were legion. Though united by – almost – the same language, their cultural backgrounds were worlds apart. For a start, the hierarchy of the American army was essentially meritocratic, whereas in the British army, class differences still played an almost automatic part in the question of promotion. Then whilst the British took pride in their traditions, Americans celebrated everything modern. British citizens typically spoke in understatements, whilst Americans bragged of their exploits. A major cause of British servicemen's resentment towards their new allies was that the Americans were paid roughly five times as much as the British, and this inevitably led on to perhaps the most resented issue of all: the success American servicemen enjoyed with the British female population. This is how Pamela later described their arrival:

> Over came the yanks to the Old Country, tens of thousands of them, their influx so aptly described by that catch-phrase, however hackneyed: oversexed, overpaid and over here. With their chocolates, nylons and uninhibited sweet-talk or sweet-drawl, they woke up the English girls, none more so than myself.

For parents of girls of Pamela's generation it was a case of 'lock up your daughters'. Arthur Street could never sleep at night until all his 'womenfolk' were safely under his roof, and having so many Americans in the neighbourhood only served to fuel his paternal anxieties. Pamela later recalled in *My Father, A. G. Street* an incident at this stage of the war when she had been asked to a party and failed to arrive home when expected:

> In vain I pleaded that I hoped he might have been asleep and did not want to disturb him; in vain I said, quite truthfully, that the taxi which was to have brought me back failed to arrive; in vain I said I'd been offered a lift by some Americans who seemed to be on the point of leaving every minute for at least two hours. It was to no avail. According to my father I had neither the 'courtesy' nor the 'gumption' to telephone, and when he arrived at two a.m. on the doorstep of the house where the party was being held the wrath that I engendered on the way home was something I remember to this day.

Some of Pamela's diary entries for late 1942 suggest that these new visitors were becoming more accepted and indeed welcome:

December 9th Colonel Dickson brought an American, Colonel Joseph, to dinner.

December 20th The Americans came to tea & Robbie G & Jane B & Joy & Rosalie & Dinah. It was quite fun.

December 24th Went to New Year's dance with Colonel Joseph. Great fun & came back in a truck + darkies.*

It was not the aforementioned Colonel Joseph who, in Pamela's own words, 'woke her up'. Instead it would be a certain US army captain, Holden Bowler, who caught her eye.

In the absence of diary entries (Pamela later explained that from 1943 onwards she was 'too busy, too tired or too ill' to continue to keep a diary), it is unclear exactly when and how Pamela and Holden became acquainted, but in her autobiography Pamela made a remarkably frank admission about the effect he had on her:

> I can't remember where we met, only that there was an instant rapport. He was a singer, older than any of my other escorts and, for the first time in my life, I knew what it was like to want to go to bed with someone of the opposite sex.

---

*   This sounds somewhat irregular at that time, for black American soldiers were strictly segregated from their white colleagues, both in accommodation and leisure activities, during their period of service in the Second World War. Possibly the 'darkies' to whom Pamela referred were drivers.

Holden was indeed a talented musician, who having dropped out of Idaho University to pursue his dream of a musical career, ended up in the late 1930s as the lead singer aboard an American cruise ship, where he met and befriended J.D. Salinger, author of *Catcher in the Rye*. Salinger was working as a staff boy, a job which included dancing with unattached female passengers; perhaps, having had enough of such activities for a lifetime, this is one reason why, after the success of *Catcher in the Rye*, Salinger became more or less a permanent recluse. When on shore leave the two young men would explore their new surroundings together on rented bicycles. Salinger later borrowed the name Holden for the protagonist of *Catcher in the Rye*, Holden Caulfield.

Holden may or may not have been amongst the earliest American visitors to Ditchampton Farm, but by the spring of 1943 he appears to have been readily welcomed by the family for, being a country boy from Idaho, he was a keen fisherman, and later fondly recalled time spent fishing on the River Wylye with Arthur Street. In the run-up to D-Day, his wartime role was as a liaison officer supervising the reuniting of American servicemen with their equipment, which had arrived in different ships at different ports. He was billeted in West Street, Wilton, with a childless couple, Charles and Clara Elliot, who quickly took Holden under their wing. Holden's and Pamela's paths must have crossed frequently on their way to and from work at Southern Command headquarters, and their meetings would therefore have been easily witnessed by the Elliots. Judging from an extract from a letter Holden wrote to Pamela later that year after she left Wilton, Clara Elliot seems to have taken a particular interest in his moral welfare:

> Things in Wilton don't change … Clara still stands guard over all activity in and around W. St. – as you well know. Needless to say when I found yours [letter] it was high on a mantle – & knowing looks were in abundance – Dear old soul, she will live so much longer, given a bit of food for her active if misguided imagination.

Clara Elliot's imagination was not entirely misguided. From the spring of 1943 Pamela and Holden had entered into an increasingly serious relationship, if Pamela's later novel about the Second World War, *Many Waters*, is anything to go by. This is how she described her heroine Emily Mason's near affair with her American admirer, Vernon Keeler, during this period of the war:

> Both had known … that their love affair was rather more than *Just One of Those Things*, as the popular song of the moment put it. They had therefore met, secretly, whenever possible. The coming of lighter evenings … had given them more opportunity for cycling into the countryside together. Such assignations had often, Emily feared, been tempting fate. But their love-making, largely thanks to Vernon, had always stopped just short of what she supposed was the point of

no return ... Her whole being felt on fire as she went to meet him. She had not stopped to think where their relationship was leading. She only knew that she had to see him, that she lived to see him ...

As Pamela's feelings for Holden intensified, she soon found herself consumed by guilt, for all the while she was still writing to – and receiving letters from – David McCormick. David wrote to Pamela as often as his meagre ration of prisoner-of-war airmail forms permitted. In a letter dated 11 February 1943, thanking her for several Christmas gifts, he once again commented on how much Arthur Street's books were appreciated by him and his fellow prisoners of war: 'I have had a very fine Christmas present from you, 2 parcels of cigarettes & "Country Days" & "Hedgetrimmings", which I had not read and enjoyed very much. Everyone borrows them because they take one back to England for a while.' But was it coincidence, telepathy, or something in the tone of one of Pamela's more recent letters that caused David to end this letter with the admonition: 'Don't get snapped up by one of those Americans! It is one of my major anxieties!'

Another, more practical matter, was by now also bothering Pamela. At the time, the Streets were housing two billetee colonels who began to suggest that Pamela could use her talents to better effect than in her menial job at the Registry, and that she should apply for a commission in the ATS. No doubt their advice was intended to be encouraging and in a sense flattering, but Pamela took it as a swingeing criticism which evidently goaded her into action. An additional incentive may have been a desire to demonstrate both to David and to Holden Bowler that she was capable of more serious war work, even if deep down she knew it went against her natural inclinations:

'With your education,' they kept saying, fixing me with a stern officer stare, 'you should take a commission. You are not pulling your weight.'

Conscience makes cowards of us all. I gave in. The accusation about not pulling my weight was hurtful. So off I went to the War Office Selection Board – WOSBIE – in North London, was tested and deemed suitable to go on to OCTU.* But although I may have satisfied the examiners as to a few academic capabilities, knew how to organise a stretcher party so that it got a prostrate dummy body over a wall – I dare say my nursing experience came in useful here – and passed various other fairly ordinary tests of competence, they didn't reckon on my ball and chain. Even the lady psychiatrist didn't pick that up. I suppose they were looking for conscientiousness, but only up to a point. They didn't spot that they were dealing with someone who had it to such a degree that it was more a hindrance than a help.

---

*   Officer Cadet Training Unit.

Once David got wind of Pamela's intentions he was suitably encouraging. In a letter dated 13 May he wrote:

> I hear you stayed with the parents on your way to the city to be fleeced. They loved having you, but I hope you weren't over-shorn. But I hear it is in a good cause – to help towards getting a commission. Good luck with that, Darling. I don't know why they didn't give you one straight away.

By now news of the Allies' progress in North Africa during the spring of 1943 had reached David and his fellow captives. On 27 May David wrote Pamela a particularly upbeat letter:

> At present I am having a sort of 2nd childhood & am playing lots of games like football & basketball & on the whole am feeling pretty fit … Well, now that Tunisia is finished I suppose one can be optimistic about being home soon. It is a great step forward. I wonder where the cat will jump next?

★ ★ ★

Where the cat would jump next had, in fact, already been decided as a result of the Casablanca conference of January 1943 at which Churchill, Roosevelt and their respective military advisers planned Allied strategy once Axis forces had, as anticipated, been driven out of northern Africa. It had not been an easy meeting. The Americans were initially in favour of an immediate all-out assault in northern France pushing through to Germany. Churchill opposed such a plan, arguing that more time was needed; British forces were not yet ready for a second front; the Luftwaffe and German U-boats had to be effectively annihilated, and more landing craft needed to be manufactured. Churchill argued that in the meantime Axis forces, who were currently concentrated on the Eastern Front in the long drawn out, bitter battle for Stalingrad which they were on the point of losing, should be further stretched by being engaged on as many other fronts as possible, particularly in the Mediterranean. The obvious next move was the invasion of Sicily, followed by that of Italy, whose hopes of creating an African Empire had been dashed by the defeat of its North African colonies. Churchill managed, in large part, to get his way, though his idea that Italy would prove to be Germany's soft underbelly would prove wide of the mark.

Following the formal surrender of the Axis forces in North Africa on 13 May, the Allies needed a period of consolidation and planning before launching their invasion of Sicily (code-named 'Operation Husky'). The battle for North Africa had proved something of a learning curve for the novice American troops. British veterans of the Second World War invariably describe their new allies both in this and other fields of the conflict as very 'green'. Whilst better equipped than their British counterparts and commendably enthusiastic, they were inexperienced and liable to panic under pressure, resulting in poor discipline and consequent unnecessary casualties.

General Dwight Eisenhower was appointed Supreme Commander of the invasion of Sicily, with the British and American forces under the command, respectively, of Lieutenant-General Bernard Montgomery and Lieutenant-General George Patton. The operation was planned for the second week of July, when the position of the moon would be at its most favourable to guide the invaders. In the event the invasion, on the night of 10 July, was hampered by an unusually vicious summer storm, which led to many casualties during the landing process, particularly amongst the airborne troops. The upside of the storm was that the defending Axis forces were taken by surprise, little suspecting that the Allies would attempt to invade on such a night, and the landings themselves received scant opposition.

The plan was for Montgomery's forces to land in the south-east and Patton's in the south-west, both aiming northwards to reach Messina as quickly as possible to cut off any Axis retreat over the Straits to the Italian mainland. Although the American forces had farther to travel, Montgomery's men, progressing up the coast via Syracuse and Catania, were met with stiff opposition from the Germans, particularly in the foothills of Mount Etna; therefore when they finally entered Messina on 17 August they found themselves narrowly beaten to it by Patton's American troops. Meanwhile the Axis forces had managed to execute a surprisingly orderly retreat back to the mainland.

The Italians, having lost their North African colonies, were by now thoroughly demoralised and war weary. On 25 July Mussolini was stripped of his powers and succeeded as Commander-in-Chief by King Victor Emmanuel, who promptly imprisoned the former leader. Marshal Badoglio was appointed prime minister with the aim of getting Italy out of the war altogether; a difficult diplomatic game ensued with Badoglio on the one hand conducting secret negotiations with the Allies, whilst on the other hand assuring Hitler that the Italians would remain loyal. Badoglio feared the collateral damage to his country if Allied and German troops were to fight over it, fears which would prove well-founded later that autumn.

★ ★ ★

David's letters home during this period give little clue as to how much of these developments had filtered through to him and his fellow prisoners, but certainly their hopes must have been raised at the prospect of imminent release. Recent events had evidently interrupted mail deliveries, for on 24 June David wrote to Pamela saying that he had received no letters from England for a good two months, and he was eager for news from the Home Front. He went on to reminisce:

Well, it is just exactly 2 years since I arrived in Egypt – what a waste of time! It must be jolly nearly 3 since Mrs Thing's dance at the White Hart … When did we meet, Darling? Can you remember? I feel that this can't go on much longer now, don't you? How is your work going? Are they going to give you a pip? Is your Dad writing a book about the Home Guard?* There is no news, but I am always thinking of you and longing for our reunion.

A week or so later David finally received several letters all at once. On 8 July he wrote to Pamela: 'I have been very lucky & had 3 letters from you this week … What a wonderful typist you are now! … I am so glad you passed the O.C.T.U. board, though there could never have been any doubt about the result.'

A letter David wrote to his parents that same week paints possibly the clearest picture of the conditions in which he had been living since his capture:

Well, I have been in gaol for some 20 months now. Apart from half a dozen mass walks I have been enclosed in 5 acres or less all the time … I expect you think I am having a wonderful opportunity for studying, but I am afraid this is not really so. Application and concentration are both impractical as our bed-living-room is a rectangular cloister with some 300 beds arranged end to end in two rows, so that what with a few gramophones, people always hammering stoves out of old tins, doing a bit of one's cooking, and general conversation and flies, things aren't easy. We get the Italian newspapers, and occasionally home news from new arrivals. Perhaps the most important thing in our lives after the general news are our Red Cross food parcels. At present they have ceased.

This life was about to change, however. With southern Italy under threat of Allied invasion, David and his companions suddenly found themselves evacuated *en masse* from Padula and sent to other prison camps further north. On 6 August David wrote a brief postcard to Pamela with his new address, trying in typical fashion to make the best of his changed circumstances: 'Have not been able to write for a few weeks, but am now in a new camp. We have all been moved. In many ways it is an improvement, but I shall miss the view.' In a subsequent letter dated 14 August David was able to expand a little on his new surroundings:

This camp will not be too bad if we only have a short stay, but would become very monotonous after a bit. It is a modern affair of brick bungalows & barbed wire & vaguely reminds you of petrol filling stations. There is no view & very

---

* This was a reference to Arthur Street's *From Dusk till Dawn*, which was first published in 1943. A revised edition appeared in 1945.

poor space for games & nowhere for plays & things but the washing and messing facilities are an improvement on 35.

Prisoners were not permitted by the censors to reveal the localities of their prison camps, which were simply referred to by a number for address purposes, Padula being PG (*Prigione di Guerra*) 35; later records show that David's new camp, PG 19, was situated near Bologna, deep in northern Italy.

Censorship appeared to be tightening up at this critical stage of the war, for David ended his letter with the somewhat cryptic words: 'I am not allowed to make any comments on general news and feelings.' It is not hard to guess what such feelings might have been. Word would have reached the prisoners of the successful outcome of the Sicilian campaign; surely it would only be a matter of weeks before the Allies came on over to the Italian mainland and David and his companions would finally be freed.

★ ★ ★

The Allied landings did indeed go ahead as anticipated. On 3 September the Eighth Army crossed the Straits of Messina from Sicily, and on the same day an armistice with Italy was signed. Further Allied landings took place at Taranto and Salerno on 9 September. Although there was fierce fighting for a while at Salerno, the other landings met little resistance. However the German forces, retreating northward, fought with dogged determination, using the Italian terrain to thwart the Allies' progress wherever possible. Later in the autumn, after Naples had fallen into Allied hands, stalemate was reached at what became known as the Gustav Line, stretching from west to east across the country and incorporating the now notorious hilltop village of Monte Cassino, the scene of much heavy fighting to come. Despite the armistice, as the Italians feared, their country had effectively become two separate warring states, with the Axis forces in northern Italy – nominally headed by a rescued and reinstated Mussolini – keeping the Allies in the south at bay at every opportunity. This situation would continue well into 1944. Italy was not the Germans' soft under-belly that Churchill envisaged; rather it would prove to be its backbone.

Churchill was not the only one to be frustrated by the slow progress of the Italian campaign. David and his fellow prisoners, whose hopes of imminent release had run so high earlier in the summer, suddenly found themselves about to be taken in cattle trucks to a new prison camp deep inside Germany itself, a place later identified as Weinsberg.* To avoid being thus transported, David hid in the rafters

---

*   Its official war address for correspondence was '*Oflag VA*'. '*Oflag*' was short for *Offizierslage* – officer camp, as opposed to *Stalag*, short for *Stammlager*, permanent camp for other ranks.

of the Italian POW camp, but was discovered at the eleventh hour and forced to rejoin his fellow captives. Once again, the McCormick name may have saved him from being summarily executed, the fate of most prisoners attempting to escape.

In David's first letter to Pamela following this latest move, dated 22 October, he made his feelings clear, though in typical stoic fashion tried to remain philosophical about his new situation:

> Darling, This is the first letter I have been able to send you since I left Italy; as you will understand, I knew Mummy would be anxious and have written to her on every opportunity. To hear that an armistice had been signed & think one was free & then to wake up in Germany a week later was a shattering blow, but we have been marking time so long now that I suppose a bit longer won't hurt us. We were able to take all the kit we could carry – so we are not too badly off, though I had to jettison quite a lot of things, especially as I thought it wise to carry about 20lbs of Red X food. I am afraid all your letters are somewhere in Italy!

It was as well David did not know at the time that far from being just 'a bit longer', it would be a full year and a half until the war in Europe ended and he and his companions would at long last be liberated.

Fourteen

ATS Promotion and Worrying Events (October–December 1943)

Despite having passed her ATS officer suitability test in the spring of 1943, Pamela did not immediately leave for training. It appears that she had once again been laid low by one of her recurring maladies, but no doubt after the difficulties of the previous harvest, Pamela wanted to be on hand to help with that of 1943 if needed. Another factor may well have been her burgeoning relationship with Holden Bowler; for this reason alone she must have been reluctant to leave Wilton.

So it was not until the autumn that Pamela finally found herself at the ATS OCTU training headquarters at Guildford. It was an exhausting experience, as she later described:

So, off I went again, this time to Guildford, to be knocked into shape – officer shape. Besides lectures and a certain amount of desk work, we seemed to spend an inordinate number of hours square-bashing. There was a fierce male ginger-haired sergeant-major who used to shout, 'Left right, left right. Pick up yer feet, ladies. Pick 'em up. Halt! Abaaat Turn.' We were all so tired at night, it was all we could do not to get into our camp beds without undressing.

In her letters home, Pamela not only complained about the physical hardships of the life she now found herself leading, but in particular bemoaned the fact that she constantly felt foolish and inadequate. Arthur Street's robust reply, in a letter dated 6 October 1943, was a typical blend of compassion and down-to-earth common sense:

I don't think you need worry too much about being slow on the uptake. I was always so, and I can assure you that these frightfully bright people don't really cut much ice. The English tradition is to remain silent and unmoved no matter what injustice or misfortune occurs, and thus to disarm the alien into thinking one is a fool. Then, at the right moment, one traps him hopelessly.

Even so, I don't think you should devote all your energies into making your-self appear an even bigger fool than you are. You see, after a while that becomes boring to other people. The great thing is to hang on to one or two principles that one is certain are right, hang on like grim death in the face of superiors if need be, and for the rest deal with life as it comes, feeling firmly convinced that the others are bigger fools than yourself ...

Only too aware of his daughter's sheltered upbringing, Arthur Street goes on in the same letter to explain to Pamela, in farming metaphors, why she was finding her current life so tough:

Also I shouldn't worry too much about disliking the job you're at, or rather the one life and other people have rather pitchforked you into. The whole art of living is to learn how to do something that one loathes. This happens again and again until one dies. Begins at boarding school, next at work, then in love, next in marriage, next with children, next with business worries, then with illness and so on. Life is always uphill, with very occasional glorious downhill short bursts.

For instance, you don't like the job of the moment. Well, I cannot remember ever liking being a retail milkman. Your handicap is that you're a colt that wasn't broken to work young enough, and now you're collar shy. You know, as I've told you, bone lazy. Well, so am I, but one comes of it [sic] in due course ...

By now Pamela had moved from Guildford to the Imperial Services College at Windsor for the second phase of her training course, which she was evidently finding even more gruelling than the first, for Arthur's letter continues: 'I'm sorry Windsor seems to be getting you down more than did Guildford, which most people consider to be the hardest part ... Apparently the policy is to treat cadets as being the lowest form of life. Then they blossom like the rose.'

Arthur's letter gives no inkling of a far more serious matter that would have been very much on his mind at the time of writing. From a family point of view, Pamela's OCTU course could not have taken place at a more inopportune moment. Shortly after she left Wilton her father, who had secretly been suffer-ing from shortness of breath and chest pains all that summer, was diagnosed with a serious heart condition. Despite wartime rationing, he was now tipping the scales at over 17 stone, and a drastic diet was prescribed to ease the pressure on his system, otherwise he might only have six months to live. His doctors recom-mended that he should spend three months at Ruthin Castle in North Wales, a private hospital-cum-nursing-home which specialised in weight-loss treatments, and in mid October he duly went there, leaving Vera Street nominally in charge of Ditchampton Farm. Vera might well have appreciated her daughter's presence and help during this deeply stressful period, but she and Arthur decided to keep the severity of the latter's condition from their daughter whilst she was engaged in her new patriotic duties, and it was only much later that Pamela was made aware of the danger in which her father had been.

Forbidden to undertake work of any kind, including journalism, Arthur contented himself with putting his literary talents to use in humorous letters to Vera and Pamela, describing his daily regime at the castle and the treatments to which he was being subjected. For example, in a letter to Pamela dated simply 'Wednesday morning', he details his experience of a 'douche massage' as follows:

> A small rotund Welsh nurse convoyed me along the corridor to the lift – rather like a fussy little tugboat pulling along a somnolent but huge tramp steamer. Then down we went to the lower or bath regions, where she installed me in a heated chamber with orders to take off jamas and array myself in a huge bath towel … This done, a cadaverous individual named Meredith, clad solely in a towel girt round his loins, came in and invited me to follow him into a chamber that dripped with water everywhere.
>
> I then lay, stark and supine, upon a drippy couch, and over me was a long tube from which streams of warm water jetted out at intervals upon my helpless person. Note – it tickled.
>
> From that moment for ½ hour Meredith prodded, punched, kneaded, and slapped me all over from chin to big toe both sides. The finishing touch was a fierce hosing down as I stood in a corner.
>
> After a swift rub down to take off all the actual wet I was enveloped in a huge warm towel and sent back to the warm room. There the Welsh roly-poly told me to lie on a warm couch, and then she swathed me from head to foot in 6 warm blankets. She then left me like a helpless cocoon for a 15 minute sweat.
>
> This over she came at 5 minute intervals to take off one blanket so that I cooled gradually. Eventually, done to a turn, and rosy all over, I returned to my room for dinner in bed. My nurse said I looked lovely, just like a Glaxo* baby, and that I was to be allowed 2 plums for pudding as a reward for good conduct.

In another letter Arthur explained how all the patients at Ruthin Castle were put firmly in their place by the sympathetic yet formidable matron in charge. In particular he described what might typically take place during one of the main features of the day, afternoon tea:

---

* At the time, people would have been familiar with the Glaxo advertisements for their baby food, featuring well-fed, happy toddlers.

This is a nursery tea around a big table, presided over by Matron, who is ancient, white-haired, 1066 and all that, and verra verra Scottish. She is, however, very nice, although she calls every one of her huge tea party of 20 people, dear. And in a sugary voice. Presumably this is a Scottish custom that has stood the test of time, but it is amusing to watch the reaction of newcomers to it. You know, some fat old tycoon of a business man, much worse for wear than your Pop, the sort of bloke that has a whisky throat, a port wine nose, a belly like a porpoise, a wife somewhere and a blonde somewhere else … He may be a hell of a gun at home and in his office and his club, but you should see his face blench when first he hears Matron address him in front of the crowd, 'Ay now, dear, will ye no have a scone. They're nice, dear.' I tell you, after that he is wax in the hands of his nurse …

Very soon Arthur Street became known as 'Uncle Arthur of the South Wing', and a familiar sight in the neighbouring countryside:

I keep pretty cheerful, my billiards is improving, and I am fast becoming a feature of the surrounding roads and lanes and footpaths. You know – that old gentleman from the Castle who always carries a shooting stick. Ye gods – what a fall was there!

In between such descriptions of his life Arthur also commented on how remote life at the castle seemed from what was currently going on elsewhere in the world: 'Up here you wouldn't know there was a war on – we hardly ever see or hear an aeroplane, and a soldier is a rarity.' Arthur's letters to Pamela never failed to include a few words of praise and encouragement. At one point, comparing their current circumstances, he wrote: 'your O.C.T.U. sounds much more trying, and I do congratulate you on getting through thus far so nobly.'

One can well imagine how frightened, frustrated and impotent the workaholic Arthur Street must have felt during his stay at Ruthin, but his letters to Pamela betray none of these emotions. On the contrary, he made out that he was having the time of his life and enjoying his enforced idleness. His letters clearly reassured Pamela that her father was in fine spirits, making good progress, and not in any obvious danger. As her course progressed, her main concern was whether her work was up to the mark. In one letter home she describes the official reaction to her attempts at lecturing:

I got through my lecturette this morning. It might have been worse. The criticism from Miss Malden afterwards was that I had a very friendly manner. She almost thought we were sitting round a dinner table rather than me lecturing or something like that – but my voice was too small & I would have to louden it …

Eventually assessment time arrived, and Pamela's anxiety was at its peak, as can be seen from a letter she wrote to her mother whilst waiting for – and then receiving – her results:

Oh dear one girl has come out & been told she isn't confident enough & she's ten times more so than me – oh dear this is terrible waiting …

Well it is over. I think very fair on the whole. My Cy [Company] Commander said my work was good, she had every confidence I would deal very fairly & sympathetically with anyone under me but I must cultivate a firmer manner & have a bit more self-confidence. She said not to 'push' not that she thought I ever could but must be confident in myself so that others would have confidence in me …

Then at the very end of the course Pamela wrote to Vera Street:

We all saw our reports today! They were frightfully complimentary on the whole. I cannot remember for certain but I think it was:

'She has made good progress all round during the course. Has a methodical brain with attention to detail (Ha!). She is essentially loyal and should do well in a company.'

Well I could scream with laughter over the methodical bit – they should see me sometimes & look in my barrack box, but I was awfully pleased with the 'essentially loyal' bit.

Up in Ruthin Castle, having read about these reports, Arthur wrote to Vera Street: 'Your news of Pam is excellent, and I am so glad that she must now realize that she has some worthwhile qualities that are recognized by others.'

Despite all her misgivings, Pamela had succeeded, receiving congratulatory telegrams on 7 November both from her father in Ruthin and from her mother back at Ditchampton Farm; these read, respectively: 'CONGRATULATIONS AND GOOD LUCK = DADDY' and 'HEARTIEST CONGRATULATIONS ON YOUR PREFERMENT TO HIGHER ESTATE LOVE AND KISSES = HOMEGUARD'. The next step was the Passing Out Parade. It was customary for family members and friends to attend such an important symbolic ceremony, but obviously Arthur Street, to his chagrin, could not do so. He hoped and expected Vera Street would make the journey, and wrote to her encouraging her to do so. Shortly beforehand, however, the delicate Vera went down with a heavy flu-like cold, and her attendance became uncertain. Pamela, writing to her mother a few days in advance of the ceremony, was at her most solicitous and understanding. Having given Vera detailed suggestions as to how and when to get to Windsor and where her mother might eat and stay, she went on to insist:

Please don't come if you've still got a beastly cold & don't feel like it because it really wouldn't be worth it – so don't feel you've got to drag yourself here on my account will you? I shan't mind at all & would only be worried if you tried to make it under those circumstances.

In the event Vera Street did indeed feel too ill to make the journey, a considerable blow not just for Pamela but also for Arthur, who on 16 November wrote to his wife as follows: 'Darling, You are an unfortunate person. I know that you and Pam will be very disappointed that you can't go up to her P. out, but from all up here I can only say that you know best.' The letter ends with a postscript revealing once again Arthur Street's pride in his daughter's achievement: 'Please tell Pam how much I've appreciated her letters – one came yesterday – and also how proud and glad I am that she has done so well, for I realize that it did not come easy to her.'

From family correspondence it seems that one person who did eventually attend Pamela's passing out parade was a certain 'Mary B', Arthur's literary agent who had become a personal friend. The Streets evidently considered it politic to ask her to take their place by way of a thank you, for she had recently pulled off something of a coup in selling the film rights of Arthur's novel, *Strawberry Roan*, which was due to be filmed the following summer. Arthur had previously given his daughter the film rights of some of his books, including *Strawberry Roan*, and Pamela now found herself in possession of a sizeable cheque. She evidently asked her father how best to invest such a considerable – in her eyes – sum of money. Arthur's answer is revealing as to how he and his contemporaries viewed Britain's financial prospects once the war had ended:

I don't know what to tell you to invest your money in at the moment, but I'll dig into possibilities when I get home. If you want dull safety and a poor return Defence Bonds might suit; if you would gamble mildly you might try industrials. You see when the war is over I can't see a £100 Defence Bond that only brings in £3 per annum being worth much more than £60 although it will cost you £100 to buy today. On the other hand when goods become available won't everybody be buying clothes, and every woman curtains and linens. If so, surely shares in shops like Harrods, Pontings etc ought to go up as those businesses must flourish after the war. Again you might care to invest a hundred or two in motor shares for everybody'll want a car, or even in aircraft as many will want private planes, and passenger air travel must boom.

Once Pamela had received her 'pip' she came home on leave whilst her first posting was being decided. She had been expecting to be sent to Torquay, but at the last minute was sent to Hilsea College on the edge of Portsmouth. Her stay there was short-lived, for within a week the ATS section was evacuated to make way for American servicemen. Probably on account of her experience of doing the pay at Ditchampton Farm as well as her officer training, Pamela found herself immediately chosen from the new intake of junior officers to undertake what seemed to her an awesome responsibility. In a letter to her father at Ruthin Castle she described her first few days as an ATS officer as follows:

> Well I'm still alive but I'm not sure if I'm me or not. Pop, you can have <u>no</u> idea. Every so often I look at my pip & wonder if they knew what they were doing when they gave it to me. I arrived in Hilsea on Monday night – the officers (5) are all v. nice but didn't seem to do much so I wandered about vaguely & got used to being called Ma'am which gave me an awful jolt …
>
> At the moment you'll never guess where I am. I was sent this morning to Gosport to take Pay Parade for an isolated platoon here & am staying the night. Together with £50* I started off clutching my suitcase for dear life and hoping my guardian angels would look after me … I had to come by ferry and feared I would drop the £50 in the deep blue sea. When I arrived at 11.00 and counted my money etc the C.O. rang up and was on the phone ages to the Sergeant about some form or another which made us ¼ hr late starting Parade & then suddenly the sergeant began to faint but didn't quite but I had to fly round for water etc. She revived in time and said she was all right & we started off … This afternoon we finished pay and according to the Sergeant are 6d up – I am praying that's right as I have sent off the Acquittance Rolls & feel something is bound to be more wrong …

During her short stay at Gosport, Pamela evidently found fraternising with male officers rather than with her female colleagues altogether more congenial. In a letter to her mother she says:

> I messed with the men officers' mess & the colonel was all very jolly and what do you know sort of thing & we got on fine. How I wish I felt so at home in the A.T.S. officers' mess as I do in a man's. It is shocking, isn't it?

Following the evacuation of Hilsea College, Pamela and her fellow new officers were posted to nearby Cosham. Their accommodation was a somewhat spread out series of houses referred to by Pamela as 'villas'; certainly the term lacks today's more luxurious connotations, for she went on to describe them as 'rather sordid somehow'. Four of the five newly commissioned officers in Pamela's 'villa' were due to be posted elsewhere, and on account of her father's illness Pamela immediately put in for a compassionate posting in order to be within striking distance of

---

* The equivalent of a little under £2,000 in today's money.

Ditchampton Farm if needed. Winchester was her first choice, being on a direct rail line to Salisbury, and her hopes were raised by a visit from the adjutant at the ATS base there: 'Today the Adjutant came from Winchester & the C.O. asked me how compassionate my posting had to be so I told her I didn't want to go on the doorstep but should be within reach.' An even more pressing reason why Winchester was a more attractive prospect was that Holden Bowler was due to be posted there, as Pamela intimated in a letter to her mother, all the while trying to make the best of her current situation: 'One thing is the air is bracing I think because I always feel better in a bracing place & I really do think this is. I try and cheer myself up by saying Winchester is damp but it would have been more fun especially if Holden was there!' Unfortunately for Pamela, however, her new commanding officer procrastinated endlessly about her compassionate posting, and Winchester became more and more unlikely. Evidently impressed by her new junior officer's conscientiousness, she appeared to do everything in her power to persuade Pamela to stay put, heaping more and more responsibilities onto her, as she went on to complain in a letter to her mother:

> I do hope you aren't terribly disappointed about Winchester not coming off … As far as I can see now I'm a fixture … If only I'd been a bit more pushing I'd have got Winchester. I'm blessed if I know why I'm so accommodating & conscientious. Now I'm landed with Messing and Q [quartering] and an Admin platoon I think. Today I nearly broke my heart sorting laundry for all the A.T.S. that have been posted & I just couldn't get it done & tied up so I came away and left it & the Sergeant says she'll help tomorrow. I must say the N.C.O.s are wonderful & will do anything for you …

In Pamela's next letter home she once again reveals her resentment at her commanding officer's attitude:

> I realise she just wants to keep me & I don't think she has any right to, being up for a comp posting and she makes more use of me so that t'other officers say I'm not to be so willing or I'll get worn out … D'you know Mummy the whole army's a wangle it seems – all they talk about is where they are going etc & trying for different jobs so I'm blessed if I want to stay here & be the C.O.'s stooge which I'm fast becoming …
>
> I am struggling with messing & Q and how. I went through the whole store with the 50 yr old sergeant yesterday and <u>none</u> of her books tally & the C.O. says she is famous for hoarding & is going to take her off rations, so that is another little job for Pamela. Drat …
>
> The quarters for some of the girls are awful and make me so depressed & sorry for them. I went & paid a personal visit to a Lieut in the R.E.s [Royal Engineers]

to see if something could be done & he was very nice about it and said all he
wanted was the A.T.S. cooperation as usually they gave him none. However in
spite of my valiant efforts no workmen have arrived and the sergeant-major says
'they'll break their legs if something isn't done about those steps soon'.

Pamela goes on to describe how she and her fellow officers were being looked
after in their own quarters:

Oh Mummy you would laugh. We have 3 privates looking after our house (villa)
& cooking for 5 of us & about 4 sergeants & themselves & they <u>hate</u> the work and
they try & get out of cleaning our buttons and I've been lucky to get my shoes
done the last week. The other officers grumble like hell and say the food's awful
but I think it is wonderful compared to O.C.T.U. The cook however is very dumb
& hates the world so we are really all quite frightened of going in the kitchen.

Pamela's letter ends with a rather telling assumption that she and David would set
up house together after the war: 'Don't let me & David ever live in a villa. I want
a flat.'

It was almost inevitable that, given Pamela's increasingly demanding work-
load, she soon went down with a heavy cold, and found herself laid up in bed.
Fortunately she got on well with the company's medical officer – a sympathetic
Scot – who was summoned to examine her, as she later told her mother:

Capt. Rossiter (M.O.) came in at six and was perfectly sweet & I have quite
taken to him and he said, 'Well lass, why don't you get into bed like a Christian?'
So I did & he has given me some jollop & I am to stay here until he comes this
afternoon. The C.O. fussed round this morning & lent me her mittens & couldn't
do enough for her blue-eyed baby – the wretch …

It seems that Pamela's conscientious, considerate manner was appreciated not only
by her superiors but also by her subordinates, for her letter continues:

I have completely thawed out the kitchen staff & nothing is too much trouble
for them. They pop up every so often & say 'Would you like a hot drink ma'am?'
and light my fire and are kindness itself. Treat people like humans I say and they'll
do anything for you. One of them said yesterday (the fierce one who we are all
frightened of) 'I don't like to think anyone's in bed and no one doing little things
for them' …

One welcome piece of news to reach Pamela during this period was that Arthur
Street had made such good progress at Ruthin Castle that he was to be allowed home

in time for Christmas – far earlier than had originally been planned – with orders to stay on the Ruthin regime of no work and strict diet for a further six weeks. In a letter dated 7 December he confirmed the good news to Pamela as follows:

> As you will have heard I continue to shrink and am to be allowed home on Dec 16. There, provided I have a sensible wife (Doctor's remark not mine) I can easily take off another 2 stones by Feb 1, after which I should be fit for more toil. With regard to feeding her family I think you will agree that our beloved Mrs. Meeks* is far from sensible, her obvious aim being to fatten them to butchering point in the quickest possible time. However, as starving me will mean the saving of lots of money each week in fees up here, it may be that the miser will overcome the cook …

It was fortuitous that one of Vera Street's main contributions to the war effort had been growing and tending vegetables in Ditchampton Farmhouse's large garden, which she had successfully transformed into a market garden, selling her produce to other Wilton residents. Indeed in a letter to Pamela earlier in the autumn Arthur Street wrote: 'Mummy is making a fortune selling vegetables.' Obviously there would be a plentiful supply of the right kind of food once Arthur returned home, and in a letter to Vera from Ruthin Castle written after Pamela had been home on leave, he jokingly warned his wife that he would be putting her out of business:

> I was amused, too, to hear that Pamela couldn't stand your rich food. Neither shall I, so you and Vi will be out of a job. However, I shall expect greenhouse lettuce when I return in mid-January, for I have decided to eat up all your market-garden profits …

In those dark days of 'make do and mend', another of Vera's talents proved particularly useful. She and her other Foyle sisters were all accomplished needle-women; two of her unmarried sisters were making a living together as dressmakers, including amongst their clientele the Pembrokes of Wilton House. Pamela was having difficulties getting her unflattering ATS uniform to fit, but her mother was well qualified to deal with the challenge. On 25 November Arthur Street commented in a letter to his wife: 'I trust you have managed to solve her uniform problems – after all when it comes to clothes the Foyles do stand supreme.'

Arthur Street was proud not only of his wife's accomplishments, but also of her good looks. He clearly enjoyed, and was currently missing, the physical side of their marriage, as illustrated by various remarks he made in letters to her during

---

* A late nineteenth-century Australian cookery expert and great proponent of cookery lessons in schools for girls.

this period. For example, commenting on the evident success Vera had enjoyed at a party she had just attended, Arthur wrote:

> I'm so glad you had such a fine party with the Yanks and Bucky Tyler [the Streets' new American billetee] and especially that you sparkled not merely as mother of Pam, but as a woman considered bedworthy. And how! I'm thrilled that you put it over the local tarts so definitively ....

At this stage of the autumn Vera Street was dithering about whether to take on a second billetee, and evidently asked her husband's advice, which when it came was both forthright and flattering: 'I think you did the right thing about Bucky Tyler's room, but don't be daft and let another room. I don't want money but a room with a good bed and you in it.' Arthur Street was clearly worried that his illness and weakened state might have lessened his former sexual prowess. When he knew he would shortly be coming home he wrote to Vera:

> You will have to co-operate with me for I shall be unable to play the role of commando in bed, although I think I shall be a rather attractive co-belligerent ... I have no desire to work yet, but merely to come home and play with you. Incidentally there has been no sign of stiffness up here, so maybe I'm finished for good, but I'm banking on your magic touch ...

Holding the fort back at Ditchampton Farm, Vera Street found herself confronted by an additional troublesome situation, as Pamela later explained: 'By now we had two land girls living in the converted stables ... The prettier of these girls, the daughter of an eminent legal luminary, began having an affair with one of our farm staff.' The warning signs had already been in evidence earlier in the year. In a letter to Pamela during her OCTU training, Arthur Street described the early stages in typically humorous fashion:

> Joan and Jean have each been away for a long weekend. They are both good workers, both daft and both man crazy ... Jean still casts sheep's eyes at Chas [Charlie Noble, the foreman], and he back at her, the fathead. In fact the two girls should be called Sampson and Delilah. Howsoever, I have spoken formally to Delilah, and demanded reformation or departure. What it is to have arrived at the old buffer class!

With no Arthur on hand to crack the whip, the situation deteriorated further, as Vera Street reported to her husband, for on 2 December he wrote back to her: 'I cannot help worrying a bit about Jean – silly little ass. Keep your eyes and ears open, and I will sack her when I return. Then if Noble is foolish enough to go he can.'

Whilst the land girls were busy burning the candle at both ends, Pamela's consti-
tution allowed her no such indulgences. Her new duties left her far too exhausted
at the end of the day for any form of social life, and by 9 p.m. she could be found
sitting on her narrow camp bed, writing letters to her parents and friends, including
David, who was still constantly on her mind.

It was a long time after the signing of the Italian armistice before Pamela heard
from David, and at the beginning she held high hopes that he would immediately
be liberated, as can be seen in one of her letters home during her period of training:
'I do hope and pray they didn't move him after August 6th … I see the Telegraph
says they "presume" our prisoners will be released. I wish it was stronger than that.
However I suppose it's just wait and see now.' David's mother was the first to hear
he was now in Germany, though she quickly passed on the disappointing news to
Pamela, who in turn told her parents: 'Mrs. McCormick has had a p.c. from David
dated 1st Oct but no address. Poor thing. It sounds pretty grim but I don't think it'll
last much longer really, do you? Did you hear them going out last night though?
I hope David isn't near a town.' This last remark was a reference to the bombing
raids the RAF and US Army Air Force were now carrying out round the clock
on strategic targets in Germany, the Americans in their new long-range so-called
'flying fortresses'.

On receipt of the first letter David wrote to her from Germany, quoted at the
end of the last chapter, Pamela commented to her parents: 'David's letter was very
nice – he doesn't complain ever – it is almost too good – I would sooner know
what it is really like.' Pamela was to learn more when she received David's next
letter, written on 27 November, in which he went into greater detail about his
living conditions and state of mind:

> We have not had any mail since we have been in this country, but are hoping to
> get some any day now … I must admit that I am finding life rather dreary. We are
> in wooden huts divided into rooms of 14 and sleep in bunks of 3 tiers. I live in
> one in the middle. We have 3 roll-calls a day & are locked into our huts at 5.30 to
> 6 after the last roll-call. Otherwise we are left to ourselves. We are very short of
> books, but the Y.M.C.A. are sending us a whole lot, which will make life better. I
> believe we are going to get a weekly cinema showing education films too. It has
> snowed once or twice & it is pretty cold here …
>
> I wonder if you are an officer yet? Darling, don't be a Major when I get back!!
> I am longing to hear from you, Darling, don't forget me.

To add to the prisoners' woes, by this stage of their captivity an all too common
event was the arrival for one of their number of what became known as a 'Dear
John' letter, written by a sweetheart or even in some cases a wife, informing the
unlucky recipient that in his absence she had met someone else and that their

relationship was now over. David dreaded the arrival of such a letter from Pamela; however being a sensitive and conscientious young man he felt guilty about holding her to a semi-promise made so many years previously. Consequently shortly before Christmas he wrote her the following thoughtful letter:

Darling Pamela,

I have just completed 2 years in the bag and feel it is time to write you a rather serious letter about our relationship. Looking back, the two years have gone very quickly for me as there are so few outstanding events, but I feel that for you it must be very different. You must have had all kinds of experiences and met many new people and I have got an idea in my head that you may easily have forgotten or 'got over' me, and yet feel at the same time that it would be unkind or unwise to tell me at present. Darling, if you do feel like that I think it would be best for me if you were frank about it. I cannot tell how I shall feel when I get home but at present I believe my best chance of a happy life lies in persuading you to marry me, & I certainly cannot imagine marrying anyone else. But from your point of view I am hardly eligible; I am none too fit, have no job to go back to, no special training & I believe my parents have recently suffered a severe financial set-back and I shall almost certainly have to live entirely on my own earnings.* I may feel it would be unfair to ask you to marry me. Darling, I would prefer you not to commit yourself either way. I still love everything about the girl I parted from in Weston nearly 3 years ago – do you feel the same about the joke officer or are you being kind? I have just had my first letter from Mummy in Germany (Nov 24). Could you please tell her that I am writing next week. Congratulations on the commission. I am very proud of you.

David

Pamela did not receive this letter until well into the new year, but once she did – not surprisingly – it made a deep impression on her, and she immediately set about composing an equally thoughtful response. Fortunately a copy of her reply still survives:

Darling,

I have read and reread your letter of the 17th December and I think it is the most wonderful one a girl could ever have. I understand everything you have said. I realise that people change, but I want you to know that in all the time you have been gone I have never (and I can honestly say never) met anyone like the David I parted from nearly three years ago. So I am not being 'kind'. There have been

---

★ Before the war David would have been expecting, like his father, to live off income from the McCormick family trusts, which had been badly mismanaged of late.

times Darling when perhaps you have seemed far away but I think I have always known in my heart that my only real happiness could be in trying to make you happy too. I do not know if you will think I am the same girl you left behind or not. That will be for you to judge. But I have tried very hard to remain the Pamela whom I hoped you loved. I do realise Darling that you may not and I may not think you the same David but something tells me that the person who has written me this letter is the one I know & still love and therefore I am prepared to take that risk. Darling it has been a long time but that spring still stands out as something very precious which I shall never forget and I would like you to know that if we do both think the same then whether you are 'eligible' or not will not make the slightest difference to the fact that I would still want to marry you.
     Pamela

Although Pamela had kept her previous letters from David private, this time she could hardly wait to tell her mother what he had written. Her pride shows in the following extract from her next letter to Vera Street:

Thank you very much for sending David's letter on in a separate envelope. I think it was the most wonderful letter a girl could ever have … I will show it to you when I come home as although I have never showed you any of David's letters before I think perhaps you would like to see this and he would not mind. Time alone will show what is to happen to us but I am more convinced than ever that what I am waiting for is worth it a hundredfold …

     I don't want you to think Mummy that anything at all has been decided because neither of us can tell what we shall feel at the end of this wretched war and what may happen before its end – all I wanted you to know was that I was very proud to get a letter like that & hope and pray that this year [1944] will see the end of the war with Germany & that better times will come.

Being from such a close and – to use Pamela's own words – tender-hearted family, one of Pamela's chief concerns during her period of ATS service was how and when to get leave in order to see her parents again. This seemed even more imperative once she knew that Arthur Street was to be allowed home early from Ruthin Castle; on hearing the news she wrote to her mother: 'It was lovely talking to you & it's <u>wonderful</u> about Pop. I am so glad. I must come and see him through hell or high water.' Although permission for Pamela to visit her parents over Christmas was initially uncertain, she was finally granted a reasonable period of leave. On her return home, however, her first reaction on seeing her father since his stay in Ruthin was one of shock, as she later recounted in *My Father, A. G. Street*: 'When I walked into the drawing-room and saw him sitting on the sofa, I was scared. He seemed to have shrunk out of all recognition, but he was as cheerful as ever.'

Pamela's presence at Ditchampton Farm turned out to be fortuitous, as she goes on to relate, albeit in typically self-deprecating fashion:

My mother and Vivi had gone down with influenza, so I did what I could towards the usual household chores and tried to produce a few meals for us all. They were not very well cooked, and I can remember my father and myself sitting down to a rather poor supper together. When I apologized for it, he said, 'Never mind. As long as we see to the essentials and get the invalids fed, you and I can do without the frills.'

Arthur Street gradually regained his strength and went on to make a seemingly full recovery, despite once again topping 16 stone. Pamela wrote of his reaction when he learnt, many years later, that the heart specialist who had treated him during the war had died at a comparatively young age:

When he read about it in the newspapers, my father poured himself a large whisky and soda and shook his head. 'Doctors,' he remarked, 'they're all the same. They don't really know very much. That's why they're all *practising*, you see.'

Fifteen

The Build-up to D-Day and a Crisis of Conscience (January–June 1944)

The build-up to the Second Front was aptly code-named 'Operation Bolero', after Ravel's composition of the same name, with its insistent theme repeated by a variety of solo instruments, which gradually combine until the piece reaches its explosive climax. By the beginning of 1944, preparations for D-Day were approaching completion. The atmosphere of expectancy was palpable. All British citizens, military and civilian alike, knew that it would only be a matter of months if not weeks before the Allies would launch their strike on the other side of the English Channel, though only the very top brass knew exactly when, and just as crucially, where.

In a letter to her mother in early January 1944 Pamela wrote: 'We are just waiting for the news – there is some rumour of all leave being stopped soon – watch out for "South Coast" in the Field!' As an ATS officer posted on the outskirts of Portsmouth, Pamela was able to watch, at particularly close quarters, the military preparations for D-Day. During one of her periods of leave, she captured the feelings she shared with the rest of the British population in a poem that was published in *The Field* at the end of January 1944:

South Coast

There's a hush along the South Coast where
the shingle meets the sea,
Like the lull before a storm begins to break;
And shadows out of History Books pass by inquiringly,
Lord Nelson, Raleigh, Kitchener and Drake.

There's a murmur in the harbours all along
the South Coast towns
There's a humming in the ship-yards and the docks;
A wind sweeps seawards knowingly across the
Sussex Downs,
And whispers to the valleys and the rocks.

And as the darkness falls on this grey January day,
And in the sky there shines a crescent moon,
The waves beat out a lullaby in every South Coast Bay –
'Quite soon', they chant, and then again,
'Quite soon'.

By early 1944 Pamela's request for a compassionate posting had finally been granted, and she now found herself at a large military base in North Wiltshire. However in terms of her responsibilities, it proved a case of 'out of the frying-pan into the fire'. Many decades later she wrote about this period of her life as follows:

My new posting took me to Corsham in North Wiltshire where there was a large underground ammunition depot. An A.T.S. company of cooks, clerks and general dogsbodies catered for all the male personnel stationed there. My C.O., sensing, I suppose, that I was a so-called 'good' girl, told me she was putting me in charge of a platoon in which there was a disproportionate number of 'baddies': streetwise young women, mostly from urban areas, some of whom had married bigamists, knew all about abortion, pregnancies and had already been offenders in civilian life.

I found my new duties incredibly difficult. There were two peroxided teara-ways in whom she felt I might be able to instil some sense of morality. Petrified, I tried to do my best, but was convinced they fell about laughing once they got outside my office. To make matters worse, we officers had to take it in turns to escort lorry-loads of our charges to dances almost every night at various camps all over Wiltshire. It was this business of Paul Jones rearing his head again to entertain the troops, only a bit more basic. It was necessary to round up the correct number of girls for the journey home, practically having to detach them, physically, from their partners with whom they were in a firm clinch.

After a night such as this, I found it even harder to get up at some unearthly hour next morning, and walk through the dark country lanes to where the girls were breakfasting in a Mess half a mile away … In a hopefully formidable voice, I was instructed to say, 'Any complaints?' I can't remember anyone actually piping up that her porridge was burnt, but I should have been hard put to it to know how to deal with such an eventuality.

Although Pamela tried to soldier on as best she could, given the lack of sleep from which she clearly suffered, she became more and more exhausted. In a letter to her mother early on in her new posting she wrote: 'I've come to the conclusion that somehow or other it will soon be put to the test as to whether I can lead a normal life or not and if I can't I can't. I don't suppose I ever have really.'

Evidently Pamela's lack of stamina was understood by her commanding officers, who did their best to lighten her load, as a later letter to her mother reveals:

> They are very kind to me at the moment and not let me go to any of the duty social functions which happen every night but when my rest is over presumably I shall have to make up for lost time. I never have been able to work and play though so if I can't I can't – I feel so like a wet blanket as most of them are rung up every night & out somewhere and I toddle off to bed at 9 ...

Despite this special treatment, however, it was not long before Pamela succumbed to yet another flu-like illness, as she told her mother:

> I'm more certain than ever I wasn't made for work – this is the 2nd time I have lasted exactly a fortnight, smiled sweetly & retired to bed, and the C.O. has lent me her wireless. I'm a borrower of wirelesses, I am. I shall have spent so many days in bed at so many different houses that I shall soon only pack pyjamas & dressing jackets ...

Pamela never made a full recovery. Instead she was sent to the company's medical officer who, mystified by her case, sent her on in turn to a hospital in Bristol. Informing her mother of this latest development, Pamela wrote reassuringly:

> It is the Royal Naval & Military Hospital, Durham Downs, Bristol ... Now Mummy you aren't to worry – I may only be there 2 or 3 days as they want to take a blood test to see if I'm anaemic. As soon as they find out I'm not I'm afraid they will pack me straight away back as I know it's not that but just plain tiredness.

It is unclear how long Pamela remained at the hospital, but the upshot was that she was declared unfit for further military service, and received formal notice of her dismissal in a letter dated 5 May: 'The War Office takes this opportunity of thanking you for your services in the A.T.S. and expresses regret that ill-health has necessitated the termination of your employment.' What neither Pamela's parents nor her superiors realised during this period was that there was an additional psychological element to her illness that had nothing to do with her ATS work. What Arthur and Vera Street did pick up, however, was how unusually pre-occupied Pamela seemed during her last period of leave, so much so that she failed to notice that her puppy Rego – named after David's dog – was missing. It was only after she returned to Corsham that she realised, and wrote to her parents to enquire after his whereabouts. Arthur Street replied in typically compassionate but light-hearted manner, attempting to soften the blow, for Rego had indeed vanished:

> With regard to Rego – we all marvelled that you did not refer to his absence last weekend, but now you have inquired I must tell you that he strolled off the other week and has never returned. We have heard no news of his being run over, and are all convinced that he has been picked up by some troops. My own view is that he is now a popular figure in some American unit. You must admit that he had an American appearance, a decidedly American penchant for feminine society, and a rather swashbuckling appearance of transatlantic flavour. I feel convinced that by now he has learned to chew gum, to take flappers to the pictures, and that if any of we poor Wiltonians should meet him, he will say, 'Hiya babe, what's cooking' with a nasal twang in his bark. Seriously I think you can take it that he is alive and well, and being frightfully spoilt by somebody …

Arthur's reference to Americans was unwittingly not the most tactful at this point in his daughter's life. When Pamela returned home on leave over Christmas 1943, she not unnaturally resumed her relationship with Holden Bowler. This time, however, Pamela realised that things were getting seriously out of hand.

In her Second World War novel *Many Waters*, Pamela leant heavily on her own experiences, so it is reasonable to assume that what happened to the heroine of her novel, Emily Mason, and her American admirer Vernon Keeler on Boxing Day 1943, actually took place between Pamela and Holden. It would be their last encounter:

> She had happened to come home that afternoon surprised to find that Vernon was there and also appeared to have a few hours free. He had suggested going for a bicycle ride and they had gone up to Barbury [Pamela's fictitious name for Grovely], and then pushed their bicycles along the track until they reached the old keeper's cottage belonging to the Fairfaxes [Pamela's fictitious name for the Pembrokes]. It was semi-derelict, the only temporary occupants being members of the Home Guard who sometimes used it as a shelter at night. It had been a very clear cold day, the sky a pale icy blue, dotted about here and there with small white clouds like soap-suds. For a while, they leant against the porch looking down on the Willon Valley in silence. All at once, she had shivered and, without quite knowing how it had happened, she had allowed herself to be drawn inside. In a shaft of winter sunlight, filtering through one of the latticed windows, she had noticed an old primus stove, a kettle, a couple of tin mugs and a broken-down bunk.
>
> Vernon wasted no time. Leading her across the room, he pushed her gently down on the bunk and began kissing her firmly in a way she had not before experienced. When she made an attempt to stop him, he had put a finger to her

lips and said, with mock severity, 'Come now, Emily, you know perfectly well it's what you've been waiting for.' And, as he began kissing her again, she had known he was right …

It had been Vernon, not she, who had finally and abruptly broken off their dalliance. Pulling her almost roughly to her feet, he had said, 'Come on. We must go. Girls like you are too much of a good thing to be alone with in a place like this.'

She had known, without wanting to know, what he meant. She had known that she wanted to be alone with him, that she would have liked him to go on kissing her, that she would have liked …

As a result of this episode, Pamela realised that the time had come to choose between following the path that was expected of her, or casting all propriety to the wind and giving in to her instincts. She became more consumed by guilt than ever, as she later explained:

> But there was this other, younger man, a long-time prisoner of war, cold and hungry … to whom I was still writing regularly and receiving, along with his mother, letters full of cheerful stoicism.
>
> My conscience became unbearably active. Not only was I being mentally unfaithful, but if I went on seeing my American I was in danger of suffering the same fate as about three quarters of all the young girls in Wilton. I might become pregnant.

In this last statement, Pamela was almost certainly correct. Family planning was only available to the more sophisticated married couples, and the sheltered Pamela would have had no clue as to where to obtain such unmentionable devices. Although the Americans came over equipped with condoms, it would seem that few of them, in the heat of the moment, actually bothered to use them. For the dutiful Street daughter, terrified of bringing disgrace on her family, there was really no contest. In *Many Waters*, her heroine Emily follows the same course as did Pamela:

> At last, with infinite regret, she decided that the only thing to do would be to write to him, telling him that she had behaved wrongly on Boxing Day, that she would not be able to go out with him again and that their association must cease. It would be a difficult letter to word, but she would have to do it and the sooner the better …

Not surprisingly, Holden Bowler was mystified on receiving Pamela's letter, unable to fathom what crime he had committed to be shut out of Pamela's life so suddenly and comprehensively. It was perhaps as well that her letter coincided with orders for a new posting and that he would be leaving Wilton. His final note to Pamela reads:

Dear Pamela

Thank you so much for your note – please thank your Mum & Daddy for their good wishes.

Pam whatever I said or <u>didn't</u> say or did or <u>didn't</u> do, that sort of 'cooled' the family on me – I'm sorry. I couldn't mistake it of course – & God knows I can think of hundreds of things I've said that might have offended – but never <u>one</u> intentionally – am afraid that's just how I am. Would have confronted you with the question 'what have I done' the first time I met you in the street so at least you are spared that. I'm sincerely sorry, Pam, whatever it was. Forgive?

Trust David will be home soon & I can send you a congratulatory note.

Be happy, Pamela.

Ho

It was only once Pamela was back for good at Ditchampton Farm that Vera Street finally understood the full extent of her daughter's anguish. In *Many Waters* Pamela describes the relevant conversation between her heroine, Emily, and the latter's mother. What she wrote in her novel must surely reflect a similar conversation between Pamela and her own mother:

'You didn't actually …?'

'No, of course not, Mummy.' Impatiently, Emily cut her mother short.

'Thank God.'

Katy knew that her daughter would not lie to her. The worst had not happened. Emily had not been seduced. She was not pregnant. On the other hand, it was alarming to see her looking so wretched. Katy had long suspected that there was some trouble connected with Vernon Keeler, but she had never thought it was quite so serious …

'When did you realise you were … well, quite so attracted to him?' Katy could not bring herself to say 'in love'.

'Ages ago.'

'And Vernon?'

'I'm … not sure.'

'Has he said anything to you about marriage?'

'Yes. Soon after Christmas.'

'What exactly did he say?'

'That he probably had no right to ask, but if I wasn't sure about John, would I consider becoming his wife.'

'And what did you say?'

'What *could* I say?' Emily began to sob, uncontrollably.

So pitiful was Pamela's state, both psychological and physical, that Arthur and Vera Street decided that what she needed was a complete change of scene. Vera was also in poor health, and despite the fact that the Second Front might start at any minute, arrangements were made for the two invalids to spend a period of time in Tintagel in Cornwall, leaving Arthur to get on with his work in peace. After such a long period of enforced idleness due to his own illness, he had much catching up to do, which helps to explain a series of exasperated letters that he wrote to Vera during her stay. Once she and Pamela had arrived in Cornwall, Vera evidently had second thoughts about being so far away if or when D-Day happened, and felt they should return without delay. Arthur would have none of it, as his first letter shows:

> Dear V,
>
> Presume from your wire that you have decided to stay. Your rooms were booked for a fortnight, that is until next Saturday, and it was understood that you would try to get further accommodation for at least a second fortnight making a month in all. Knowing from bitter experience the way women's minds work it occurred to me that the real trouble is money, so I herewith enclose cheque for £50.
>
> The point is this. Neither of you are of any value at home, but both a nuisance and a worry to everybody here. I have to earn the money that enables you both to be useless nuisances. I can only earn it if I have a little peace from both of you. I have had eight days, got up with my work, caught a couple of trout, and but for your worrying over the telephone should have begun another book this week. If you come home I shall never write another, and this means you will starve. For God's sake have a little consideration for other people and stay away a full month. The hotel is comfortable, the food is good, the weather ideal, so what more can you want? Every other woman in Britain would envy you such a holiday during wartime. Daft as you must be please remember that to send the enclosed I have to work and earn nearly three times the amount, and I must have peace of mind in which to earn it.
>
> I go to London tomorrow, and shall not be back until Wednesday night, when I hope to hear some reasonable news of you.
>
> Yours disgustedly,
> Arthur

Arthur carries on in similar vein in a letter written in the evening of the same day:

> Dear V,
>
> Since posting my first letter I learn that Vi has been on the phone to you, and that apparently the only worry for coming home that you can think up or manufacture is that you feel so cut off should the second front start. That, you idiot, is

the whole idea, to get you both cut off and off my hands when it does start. If you can tell me one minute reason why you would be better here than at Tintagel when it starts, or of any use here, or that you would sleep better here, neither I nor anyone else can. But I and <u>everybody who knows you both</u> can find at least fifty good reasons why you would be an added worry to everybody here if you were here when it starts. So for Christ's sake stay put down there for at least a month, and thank your lucky stars that you have a husband who is willing to work to pay for your daftnesses, even if he has suffered from them for over a quarter century.

Now look, I mean this. Get some rooms for at least another fortnight, and stay in 'em. Otherwise if you come home, your train will cross mine taking me to Tintagel, for I'm damned if I'll live with you here until you've rested and got well, and I HAVE HAD A REST FROM YOU.

Yours,

Arthur

Vera was well used to her husband's tempers, and does not appear to have taken umbrage at this tirade, though she evidently considered it prudent to follow his advice. Arthur's next letter was far more conciliatory and even to an extent apologetic; it begins:

Dear V,

I'm so glad you managed to stay on, and hope that by now you're enjoying life minus drains and clocks and what have you. As you can imagine, I said, 'Of course, it would happen to them.' But, even if it did, I still stick to it that having made that long journey in your weak state it was best to stay on until you could benefit from the change. But it does seem a pity that you never take my advice from a logical reason, but only after an explosion on my part. For which I am sorry, but I was at the end of my tether ...

Arthur's tetchy mood was clearly aggravated by the fact that he, like the rest of the British population, would have been on tenterhooks waiting for the go-ahead for the Second Front, code-named 'Operation Overlord'. This was finally launched on 6 June 1944, a day later than planned owing to unseasonally stormy weather. The deception of the Allied troops' landing *en masse* on the Normandy beaches, instead of where the Germans expected them in the Pas-de-Calais area, proved ultimately successful. Although there was a great deal of fierce fighting and one or two notable setbacks still to come, the Streets – like the rest of the British population – followed the campaign with quiet optimism. This really was the beginning of the end.

Sixteen

D-Day, Dramatics and Winter Worries (July–December 1944)

The progress of the heavy fighting that ensued after the apparent success of 'Operation Overlord' was being anxiously followed, not only by the civilian population at home, but particularly by David and his fellow captives, who once again were hoping for imminent release. On 6 July he wrote to Pamela: 'Well, the war seems to be in its final phase now – let's hope things will move quickly, Darling. I hope these V1s aren't doing too much damage in England.' News had evidently swiftly reached the prisoners of the retaliation for the D-Day landings that the Nazis were wreaking on the population of south-eastern England in the form of their new V1 flying bombs, nicknamed 'doodlebugs'. These revenge weapons, fired from launching sites in north-eastern France, did indeed have a temporary but significant impact on British morale during the late summer and early autumn of 1944. This second 'Blitz' differed from the first, because the vastly increased speed of these new rockets gave the civilian population little notice of their approach, and no time to reach air-raid shelters. London, East Anglia, the South Coast and Home Counties found the advent of this type of bomb particularly nerve-racking. The 'doodlebug' would suddenly be heard approaching, then when it reached its target the engine would cut out and there would be an ominous silence before the sound of a massive explosion.

The situation improved once the Allied forces finally managed to overrun the launch sites in north-eastern France, but meanwhile by early September the Nazis unleashed their second version of the flying bomb, the V2 rocket, with a longer range, capable of being fired from a mobile launch trailer rather than a fixed site. The Germans would keep up their bombardment of south-eastern England by V2 rockets well into 1945.

Meanwhile the prisoners of war were doing their best to keep themselves occupied. One of the standard forms of entertainment all through David's captivity had been the production and performance of plays, and during the summer of 1944 it fell to David to take his turn on the stage, a prospect he viewed with some trepidation, as he informed Pamela in his letter of 6 July:

> You will be amused to hear that I am going on the stage in Sept. I have got a part of a rather irresponsible young dentist called Valentine in a Shaw play called 'You Never Can Tell'. I am a bit nervous about it as it is quite a leading part & I have never been on the boards before & the audience expects a very high standard by now – I will let you know how it goes.

This four-act play, written in 1897, is a comedy of errors and confused identities, described by one notable latter-day critic as one of Shaw's 'sunniest and funniest' plays, and therefore eminently suitable for raising the morale of David's fellow prisoners of war. It concerns a certain Mrs Clandon, who has returned to England with her three children having spent the past eighteen years in Madeira, and who has recently taken up temporary residence in an English seaside hotel. Unwittingly, the children, who have never met their father, invite him to a family luncheon. One of the leading characters is the old waiter, who dispenses kind and wise advice, such as his catchphrase 'You never can tell'. Another leading part is that of a suave young dentist, Valentine, who falls in love with Gloria, Mrs Clandon's eldest daughter. Gloria fancies herself as a modern woman, uninterested in such frivolities as love and marriage, which makes for a somewhat stormy courtship, though Valentine finally succeeds in winning her hand. The play ends happily all round, with Mrs Clandon becoming reconciled to her estranged husband. To play the part of Valentine was indeed something of a tall order for a young man who had never previously trodden the boards, so his anxiety was hardly surprising.

By the end of September the play had completed its short run, seemingly successfully, as a relieved David reported to Pamela on 23 September:

> I have been very busy with my acting all this week. It is all over now though. We had a dress rehearsal & four performances, & I think I managed to get through it without making too big an ass of myself! Once I got over my nerves, which were pretty bad at first, I thoroughly enjoyed it, and it has kept me busy for a long time.

At about this time, events of a thespian nature were also taking place back at Ditchampton Farm. By late summer the filming of *Strawberry Roan*, based on Arthur Street's second book, was well under way. The two main filming locations were the little village of Wishford, a few miles south-west of Wilton along the Wylye Valley, and Compton Chamberlayne in the neighbouring Chalke Valley. Pamela later wrote in *My Father, A. G. Street* about her role – or non-role – in the filming process, and how exotic the production team seemed to ordinary Wiltshire folk:

> I used to hang around, hoping they might need an extra, but, as a lanky untidy young girl did not appear to be on their list of requirements, I contented myself with remaining fascinated by all the queer types, especially the camera-men with beards, who pranced about and must have badly shocked the little villages of Wishford and Compton Chamberlayne ...

Many years later, Arthur described *Strawberry Roan* as 'the story of how you get your pint of milk, and all the animals and all the people who go towards its production'. The 'heroine' is a fine roan-coloured calf, whose life is followed from her birth until her maturity as a milk-producing cow. At different stages in her young life she is sold on to a succession of local farmers. Much of the book concerns one such, a well-to-do young bachelor called Chris Lowe. Much to the disappointment of the local mothers, Chris finally falls for and marries Molly, a spirited young dancing instructress, unlikely material for a typical farmer's wife. The first years of their married life are idyllically happy, but as the agricultural depression intensifies, Chris realises that he has spent far too much money on his adored new bride and ends up in severe financial hardship. To add to his woes Molly succumbs to a mysterious stomach complaint, and eventually dies following a complicated operation. Much of this draws on the early part of Arthur's own marriage, though happily Vera Street survived.

At the time Arthur Street's account of the physical side of Chris and Molly's early married life was considered by some readers to be somewhat racy, scandalous even, but despite this controversy Arthur remained well pleased with this, his first, 'proper' novel, as he admitted to Roy Plomley in his *Desert Island Discs* interview. He maintained that it was an author's second book that establishes him or her, for which reason 'I always had a sneaking regard for that one'.

The film was directed by Maurice Elvey, and starred Carol Raye as Molly, with Chris Lowe being played by William Hartnell, who went on to become television's first 'Doctor Who'. There was also a part for a new child actress, Petula Clark. The plot of the film varied from that of the book in a number of ways for dramatic effect. Molly was a chorus girl rather than a dancing instructress; Strawberry Roan was a calf given specifically to Molly to look after by her new husband, whereas in the book she was simply one of several calves being reared on Chris's farm; in the film it was Molly's discontent with country life and inability to settle down that caused her to spend all her husband's money, and her death was the result of a riding accident rather than an illness. The film was to hold its trade premiere in early 1945. Arthur Street travelled up to London to view it, and seemed well satisfied with the final result; in a letter to Vera afterwards, he said:

Well, I saw S. Roan next morning at the Rialto Cinema near Pic Circus. And it is ten times better than I expected. I don't mean it's a world-beating film, but the trade audience liked it, and it's good enough to show cinema people that my stuff's worth filming …

Back in prison camp in Germany, David McCormick was glad to read from Pamela's letters about the filming of *Strawberry Roan*. On 2 September he replied:

I am so pleased to hear about your Dad's book being filmed. I feel it will cheer him up a lot. I remember him telling me that he hoped 'Strawberry Roan' would be filmed. What company is doing it and who are the principal actors? I think you ought to be the young chap's wife!!

However in his next letter to Pamela, dated 23 September, perhaps guessing how the character of Molly might be portrayed, the ever-sensitive David wrote:

By the way it is a long time since I read 'Strawberry Roan' so that I have rather forgotten the story. When I said you ought to take the part of the young wife I thought she was rather sweet, but thinking it over I wonder if she didn't become rather silly, did she? Of course I didn't mean that …

All through his period of captivity David did his best to think up innocuous snippets of news to put in his letters home that would pass the beady eyes of the German censors. On Easter Monday 1944 he wrote of one welcome development, the reporting of which might even have pleased them:

We have been provided with a sportsfield about 2 miles away & once a week my turn comes to walk up there on parole & wander about in comparative freedom for a whole morning or afternoon. I have been out twice & how good it feels to be out of the camp after all this time & to be able to go & lie under the pine trees on the edge of the field & watch their tops blown about …

In letters to Pamela, David constantly requested a more recent photograph. Occasionally, in the latter stages of his captivity, David was able to send one of himself back in return, for now that the tide of the war had turned – probably for propaganda reasons to show that their prisoners were being well treated – his German captors were having group photographs taken. On 8 May David wrote to Pamela:

Darling, I think about you more than ever these days, perhaps it is because I feel I shall really be seeing you again soon now …

I am rapidly approaching 29 which seems rather middle-aged to me – and I am afraid I am getting very thin on top. I have 3 white hairs in my moustache, which is a bad sign ... Darling your hair must be beautiful now, & I should like to see you in your uniform. What about a photo? I think I may be able to send you a new one soon, if you would like it, as we have had some groups taken ...

Inevitably, cooped up together as they were after such a long period of captivity, prisoners could occasionally lose their tempers with one another. In a letter simply dated 'Midsummer', David described the consequences of one such falling out, though he quickly went on to comment on how remarkably few such episodes he had witnessed, and how well he and his fellow room-mates generally got on with each other:

Your photo got hit the other day by someone throwing something in a rage at another chap & the glass is smashed, so I have had to put it away. It is really extraordinary how few rows we have in our room. We all get on very well. I have my old friend Quilliam, a stockbroker of 12 years standing, 2 doctors (one Scotch & one half Norwegian), 2 regular army captains (one was at school with me), 2 people who are stage struck & go about in a flat spin, 2 playboys of a fairly intellectual variety & a very vague solicitor, who is the best pianist in the camp and took a first in Philosophy at Oxford. So you can imagine there is always plenty to talk about ...

In the same letter, David painted a rather touching picture of a recent arrival in his hut:

We have adopted a kitten in our room. It is about 3 weeks old, grey & white with the palest blue eyes, & its name is Poupon. When I am sitting back reading it climbs on my arm and goes to sleep under my chin. It is so small that I am afraid someone will tread on it ...

Sadly the hut's little four-legged room-mate was only destined to spend a short time there, for on 19 October David wrote:

I am afraid our kitten died within a few days of its adoption. It fell out of a window (some say it was helped out by a certain minority element in the room who disapprove of pets) & declined rapidly. We had one evening when it was very ill & we all talked in hushed tones, & next morning it was dead & a general feeling of depression prevailed ...

Not surprisingly, the factor that most influenced the prisoners' overall mood was the progress or otherwise of the Second Front. On 17 August David wrote to Pamela:

There seems to have been some hitch in the parcel mail ... I don't think we can expect much more now that the second landing has taken place. I should imagine that everyone is terribly excited about everything in England. We all feel very optimistic here ...

In a later letter to Pamela dated 3 November, however, David's positive outlook had changed:

I am very disappointed not to be home now. I'm afraid we were a bit over-optimistic at Arnhem & now the programme has been put back a few months. At present I don't feel as if there is much chance of being home before April, but perhaps this is because we are out of Red X parcels & rather cold. We get locked into our huts at 5 these days & I have started the winter 'bridge' round again. I feel we are rather like a 2 act play where it reads 'Same scene 4 years later' & you do not know what has happened meanwhile, & these letters are like a secret light shone from the castle tower to show the prisoner is still alive – that is all they can be ...

The aforementioned 'Arnhem' was part of 'Operation Market Garden', Montgomery's uncharacteristically bold plan for an Allied airborne assault of the bridges at Eindhoven, Nijmegen and Arnhem to establish a clear route for the passage of the British troops across Holland to the northern German plain to breach the top end of the 'Siegfried Line', the fortified German boundary with its western neighbours. The operation was ill-conceived, and the British airborne troops suffered heavy losses at Arnhem, dubbed in consequence 'a bridge too far'. Following this setback a stalemate ensued for some weeks, dashing any hopes that David and his fellow prisoners may have held of being home in time for Christmas.

The second significant setback, which was to delay the Allied advance by some six weeks, was the surprise Nazi counter-offensive launched shortly before Christmas 1944, which was to become known as the 'Battle of the Bulge'. It was a repetition of Hitler's 1940 strike through the Ardennes, this time with the aim of splitting the British and American forces, crossing the Meuse and re-taking Brussels and Antwerp. The German offensive was contained and eventually squeezed back, but the battle continued all over the Christmas period and well into January 1945.

Inevitably the festive season of 1944 was a disappointing one for the entire British population, particularly so for the Street family who, for a different reason, were unable to spend it together under the same roof. Vera's chronic stomach condition had taken a turn for the worse, and it was decided that at the beginning of December she should go for investigations and subsequent treatment to the Ruthin Castle clinic that had so successfully treated Arthur a year earlier. Arthur and Pamela would, if necessary, travel up to North Wales to spend Christmas with her.

Unfortunately this was not to be, at least in Pamela's case. For the past several months she had been in a permanent state of depression, suffering from rampant headaches. To make matters worse, in early December she went down with a bout of flu from which she did not sufficiently recover in time to accompany her father to Wales to spend Christmas with her mother; instead she was obliged to stay with Vivi at Ditchampton Farm. Despite her depressed state, shortly before Christmas she managed to write her mother a light-hearted letter of greetings:

> My dear Mummy,
>
> This is to wish you a very happy Christmas with Pop and I hope you will get well soon now. I'm sorry I haven't done you a card but hope you will forgive me this year …

Ever since her brief period at the Salisbury College of Art, Pamela had always drawn personal Christmas and birthday cards for her parents, a tradition she would continue in her later life. This year instead, at the bottom of her Christmas letter to Vera Street, she drew a rough map of England and Wales, with two little cartoon figures waving handkerchiefs from a big dot in south-west Wiltshire to another big dot in North Wales.

Arthur and Vera Street were also to receive Christmas greetings from Germany, in the form of a postcard dated 25 November:

> This is to wish all at Ditchampton a very happy Christmas. I do hope you and Mrs. Street are both feeling fitter. This will be my 4th Xmas in the bag, but I am not quite round the bend yet, & I am hoping to visit you very soon. I often think of the good times you gave me & some of the dinners. Love & best wishes, David.

Inevitably this card did not reach Ditchampton Farm until well into the new year, but on forwarding it to Vera Street, still at this stage at Ruthin Castle, Arthur commented:

> [Pamela] asked me to enclose this postcard that arrived from David this morning. Ha ha, you are already the Ma-in-law. But doesn't that boy write cheerfully after such a long time in prison. It makes me, and I think Pam, feel very humble.

Seventeen

The End of the War and an Awkward Reunion (1945)

With the British and American forces crossing the Rhine from the west, and the Russians now pressing into Germany from the east, David and his companions were moved to yet another prison camp, deep in the German stronghold of Bavaria. It seems that at this critical time for the Nazis, both officers and other ranks were herded together, for this was Stalag 383, Hohenfels, near Straubing. Before this, however, David wrote his last surviving letter to Pamela from captivity, dated 2 January, describing the prisoners' recent Christmas and the harsh winter conditions, but also looking ahead to how he would earn a living once the war was over:

> We were all terribly optimistic about being home for Christmas, & now I think that most of us feel we shall be content to be released any time before next Christmas. It is all very disappointing, & I am afraid many more lives must be lost to no purpose ...
>
> We have been having very cold weather here. Last night the barometer registered 19 below zero (centigrade) & there is snow on the ground. The days are mostly clear & sunny & everything looks beautiful, but there is not much warmth in the sun. We had a quiet Christmas here. We saved up & had a big meal & felt quite full for once ...
>
> Isn't it funny that I am approaching 30 & I still don't know what I am going to do after the war for a living. Sometimes I think the Stock Exchange is the best thing, sometimes I have an idea of trying to get into the Foreign Office, sometimes of colonising in Rhodesia. I am going to take the final of the Chartered Insurance Exams here ...

Despite the fact that from early on in the war great efforts had been made, particularly by the Educational Books Section of the British Red Cross POW Department, to provide prisoners with the means to study all manner of subjects, and in many cases to enable them to sit professional exams *in situ*, David and his fellow prisoners had hitherto found prison camp conditions hardly conducive to serious study. Clearly the fact that the war was drawing to a close was now concentrating their minds. David would indeed go on to use his knowledge of insurance shortly after the war ended.

David and his fellow prisoners were finally liberated by American troops on 29 April, a week before the official armistice. During their last few days of captivity there was much concern in the camp that their guards might wreak final revenge by executing them all, but mercifully at the eleventh hour they simply laid down their weapons and melted away into the neighbouring countryside. No written record survives of how David and his fellow prisoners were repatriated, but events evidently moved swiftly after the armistice was declared, because on 10 May Pamela received a telegram from David's father stating: 'DAVID IN ENGLAND EXPECTED HOME THIS AFTERNOON – ALL WELL – MCCORMICK'.

Pamela's reaction to this news, which should have been one of rejoicing, was in fact one of profound consternation. In her novel *Many Waters*, Pamela described how the book's heroine, Emily Mason, discovered that her erstwhile American suitor, Vernon Keeler, had become engaged to a new partner:

> It was not until the beginning of the New Year that she saw the news. She happened to pick up Monica's discarded copy of *The Times*, open at the Court Circular. Idly, Emily glanced down the Engagements column. When she first saw the names she looked away quickly, as someone unwilling, then unable, to witness something repugnant. Then, slowly, she turned back to stare at the words which seemed to bounce back at her, stark and hideously irrefutable:
>
> 'The engagement is announced between Elizabeth Brewer, youngest daughter of Mr. & Mrs. Donald Brewer of Broadstones, Nr. Westonbury, and Captain Vernon Keeler of the United States Army.'

It is more than likely that during the winter of 1944–45, Pamela's similar discovery that Holden Bowler had become engaged, caused her depression to descend into a full-blown nervous breakdown. She may well have been harbouring lingering, romantic notions that Holden might not have taken her abrupt dismissal of him at face value. Maybe he would seek her out once more, in which case she would willingly have let him back into her life, whatever the consequences. Now cold reality set in. Describing this period of her life in her later memoir, Pamela wrote: 'I felt a complete failure. I had made a total mess of the past five years and, during the final winter of the war, I broke down completely.'

The early months of 1945 were also an extraordinarily difficult time for Arthur Street. Not only was his wife Vera still away at the Ruthin Castle clinic, complaining that her stomach was no better, that the food did not suit her, and constantly begging him to come and fetch her home in the temperamental family car despite the treacherous road conditions (there had been widespread heavy snowfall that winter), but now he had to deal with the marked deterioration in his daughter's health. Initially, Arthur kept this news from Vera to avoid worrying her, explaining instead the practical difficulties preventing him travelling to North Wales to collect her and suggesting other means by which she could get herself home, and also pointing out the effects her demands were having on him:

Oh my dear, can't you understand? I know your troubles and ailments loom large to you, but do try to minimize them and conquer them a bit more for my sake. For I'm about whacked, mentally, physically, and financially. You see, my income doesn't come from a business, but out of me, from my personal efforts on paper. Please, you've never let me down yet, despite all your illnesses. Do try and help me now, for I need it.

You see, like you, I am now getting sorry for myself, which is always a mistake. So I won't indulge in it any more. Neither will you, unless you've forgotten the many good things in our life together during the last twenty odd years.

Cheer up, old thing, and plan to get home some way or other ...

It seems that despite her husband's pleading, Vera was still unwilling to take no for an answer, for in Arthur's next letter he finally felt obliged to explain what had been happening back at Ditchampton Farm:

Dear V,

I'm afraid you will be very disappointed on reading this letter, for I have to tell you quite definitely that I cannot come up to drive you home ... The real reason is that I cannot do it. I'm too done up, both physically and mentally ...

I have kept it from you all these weeks as you were ill yourself, but Pamela has been very ill during the last month. She had an utter collapse, gave up all hope of ever getting well, said that when David returned he would not want her, wept day and night, and could not sleep. Whether it is all due to a nervous breakdown or whether there is something wrong we don't know but Buttar [the Streets' GP] said we could do nothing until all the physical possibilities had been checked up.

So for weeks now Vi and I have taken it in turns to sleep with Pam, I have taken her for a walk just before she went to bed, but neither she nor the person with her has had more than two hours sleep each night ...

The local doctors were mystified, and in order to rule out any hitherto overlooked physical problem, it was decided that Pamela should go to a London hospital for a thorough examination; Arthur would stay at the Savage Club until her results came through. During their time in London Arthur spent much of each day at Pamela's bedside, and in the evenings wrote regular reports to Vera in Ruthin Castle. In one

such letter he gave his own assessment as to how Pamela's illness had developed,
and how only she, ultimately, could pull herself out of it:

> What happened was that when David went away, she shut up shop, and built a
> wall round herself against anything to do with men. This would not have mat-
> tered if either of two things had happened. Had the war finished eighteen months
> ago, say, and he had come back and married her, this breakdown would not have
> happened, and she would have carried the strain that long. Secondly, having
> decided to shut the door to that side of life she should have filled the gap with
> some other interest – ambition, pride, career – in fact vice or virtue, anything
> being better than nothing. As you know she did not do this, and hence this illness.
>
> Poor kid, the way she leans on me up here is pathetic. I ring her up each morn-
> ing at nine. I spend the visiting hours, 3 – 6, with her. Then when I get back here
> about 7, I ring her up to say goodnight …
>
> She will have a hard row to hoe her way back to health, for only she can do
> it. You and I must help all we can, but I'm hoping to get some definite direc-
> tions in writing from the doctors, and then she <u>must</u> obey them, in spite of tears,
> headaches, no sleep, everything …

This explanation of Pamela's illness misses one vital ingredient. There is no reference whatsoever to her infatuation with Holden Bowler and her ensuing confused
emotions. Possibly both she and her mother managed to conceal these elements
from Arthur Street, fearful of his probable reactions.

The decision to send Pamela to the hospital had not been taken lightly, for
staying in London was a risky business; in early 1945 German V2 rockets were still
regularly bombarding the capital, as Arthur explained in another letter to Vera once
he and Pamela were safely back at Ditchampton Farm:

> That, of course, was my main worry last week. I had to take the decision to send
> Pam up to the Northern Hospital, knowing all the time that there was a certain
> amount of risk from bombing. Result was I didn't get any sleep, for I would hear
> a bump somewhere, and then of course, wonder where. One morning at six I
> was awakened by a big bump, and it dropped quite close enough to the hospital
> to shake the glass out of the bedroom windows of the room above and the one
> below Pam's. Which is near enough, believe me, too near to be funny. And of
> course, each day when a rocket dropped, some silly ass at the Savage would be
> sure to say I reckon that's about four miles north of here, which is where Pam
> was, and I used to feel awful …

The specialists at the Northern Hospital found nothing physically wrong with
Pamela, so she and Arthur returned home, as his letter to Vera continues:

However, all's well that ends well, and we now have her home with all her fears explained away, but are still up against this sleeplessness. Vi and I are doing our best with walks and baths just before bed, whilst we are waiting a vacancy at a place where they give sleep treatment in such cases. If she can break this sleeplessness before it arrives, there may be no need for her to go, but it's a wearing business meanwhile. I'm firmly convinced that once she settles down to natural sleep she will soon be quite fit again …

The arctic conditions persisted, so collecting Vera from Ruthin was still out of the question. Instead Arthur wrote to her with regular updates from Ditchampton Farm:

Dear V,

This weather is a proper B----- Like you we are snowed up and it's cold as hell. Well, we've had a week like a year. Pam was better at first on her return from London, but by last Monday the sleeplessness had got on her nerves, almost an obsession, and she was begging to go to the Staines Place for some sleep treatment …

As a last resort, it was decided that Pamela should go to an experimental clinic suggested by the London specialists. Many years later Pamela set down her recollections of what proved to be an extremely unpleasant experience:

My own sleeplessness came to such a pitch that a pioneer doctor in a nursing home at Staines tried to render me more or less insensate for three weeks. He said he had used such treatment to rest many overstressed members of the Services – mostly male, I think – with great success. But three weeks is a long time to be put out for the count. In my case it didn't work. I was horribly sick.

One of the conditions of the treatment was that there should be no initial communication with family and friends, and having managed to get Pamela to Staines despite the icy conditions, it was a good three weeks before Arthur Street was able to see his daughter again. When he was finally allowed half an hour with her, he was so overcome with fatherly concern that afterwards he felt he had left many important things unsaid, as he explained in a letter written to her immediately following this visit:

Look, here is one thing I meant to say, and didn't. Get all the benefit you can from the treatment while you are at Staines, and realize without any question that when you are well enough to leave – say in a fortnight or so from now – you can come home for a long rest to get quite strong before you even think of anything else. The great thing to do is to get well – then everything will be easy, and I shall feel so happy and proud. I'm afraid all this sounds selfish of me, but until you are well and happy again I somehow shan't be much good for anything myself.

The only positive effect of Pamela's illness was that it brought father and daughter closer together than ever before, as Arthur commented in one of his updates to Vera at about this time: 'One good thing has come out of it all – that is that Pam and I are great friends, and she trusts me implicitly, even though all these doctors have, I'm afraid, proved me right and her wrong …'

Another duty that fell to Arthur Street as a result of his daughter's illness was to compose a letter to David McCormick, explaining why Pamela had been unable to write to him during the past few weeks. In a letter to Pamela at the Staines clinic dated 24 February Arthur told his daughter:

I have written to David today, and told him why there was a gap in your letters to him, and that now you are on the road back to health all right, and will shortly be writing to him yourself. I complimented him on the boasted improvement in his Bridge, and also on the cheeriness of his letters to you, at any rate the bits of them that you have told me. Also that I am looking forward to sitting down with him as a partner, when we would challenge all comers. Also that no one in England would be more glad to see him back home than myself. I told him the catkins were on the hazel, that Mummy was better (she is definitely), that Violet was a tower of strength, Judy a ball of wool, and that I had a whiter poll than the one he remembered. I trust this fits the bill …

The pioneer doctor at Staines probably helped Pamela more than she gave him credit for in her later memoir, as she clearly came home in an improved state, even though her return to full health was a long, gradual affair. Whilst the rest of the British population was following the unfolding events in Germany with quiet rejoicing, Pamela's reaction was more muted:

Once back at Ditchampton Farm I remained in limbo. Having sent my American packing, I now awaited the return of my English 'intended' but, I am ashamed to say, with trepidation. For there was no question now that we were winning the war. The British and American forces under Montgomery and Eisenhower were racing each other to Berlin. The Russians were closing in from the east. Apart from the unbelievably shocking discoveries of the Nazi death camps which did not really penetrate the national consciousness until later on at the Nuremberg trials, it seemed as if, daily, good news came in like that from Ghent to Aix. Hitler committed suicide in his bunker and when German High Command surrendered to Monty at Luneberg on May 5th and the armistice came two days later, I happened to be staying with my cousin in Romsey …

My father drove down to collect me, knowing that the young man I hadn't seen for five long years would soon be home. But, to my chagrin, I still felt wretched and confused …

Having been reunited with his parents, David arranged to visit Pamela the very next day. Uppermost in both their minds would have been the all-important question: now that they were actually to meet again, how would they feel about one another? During those five long years of separation, had they merely been holding on to a dream? Both had their own reasons for wanting to get married. David, after his wartime adventures and privations, wanted nothing more than to settle down gratefully to a peaceful life with the young woman who had waited for him. For her part Pamela, at the ripe old age of 24, feared being left on the shelf, the pool of potential suitors having been so tragically depleted as a result of the war's innumerable casualties. She clearly hoped to be able to rekindle her love for David, and forget her earlier infatuation with her American captain. However when they were finally reunited, David must have appeared a shadow of the handsome, newly commissioned officer to whom she had bidden farewell some five years previously. This is how, decades later, she described this crucial meeting:

He was very thin, very pale and had the most enormous bump on his forehead. I was meeting the London train on Salisbury station a few days after V.E. Day. I wore a blue dress with white spots and bows on it, for which I had given several clothing coupons. I can't remember if we kissed. I don't think so, not until a little later on when we stopped on the way back to Ditchampton. We were both very nervous.

He apologised for the lump on his forehead, explaining that on his first night of freedom some Belgians had entertained a whole bunch of prisoners of war rather too enthusiastically and afterwards he had met up with an anti-tank trap. He talked a great deal, not just to me, my parents and Vivi, but everyone he met. He so desperately wanted to get four years 'in the bag', as he called it, off his chest as quickly as he could …

It was not merely David's appearance and speech patterns that had changed. Pamela found certain aspects of his behaviour curious in the extreme:

There were other after-effects from his incarceration, some understandable, others more unexpected. He scavenged. That is to say, whenever we went for a walk up to Grovely or down through Wilton, his eyes would be on the ground looking out for anything that might come in useful: a piece of wood, an old tin can, things like that. As for food, he couldn't bear to see anyone leave anything on their plate. When my mother failed to eat her last few strawberries, he finished them off for her, although prisoners of war had been warned not to eat or drink too much too soon …

During one of their first conversations, the ultra-conscientious Pamela had immediately owned up to her relationship with Holden Bowler: 'I had, of course, told him about my American boyfriend almost as soon as we met, and he had said, in a shocked voice, "You didn't *sleep* with him, did you?" When I assured him I had not, he looked infinitely relieved and the matter was closed.'

Clearly David and Pamela needed time and opportunity to get to know one another again. As Pamela went on to explain in her memoir: 'I don't think either of us realised that we were two very different people from the ones who had had such a circumspect juvenile romance five years before; nor – which was even more important – that we had really known very little about each other even then.' To accelerate the process, following his visit to Ditchampton Farm David took Pamela back with him to his parents' home in Weybridge for a prolonged stay. How their relationship progressed was closely watched by David's parents, and on 20 May Edward McCormick reported to Arthur Street:

Dear Street,

I have delayed writing to you for a few days as I wanted to have the two young people under observation for a while before doing so.

They appear to be blissfully happy together.

Unfortunately, they are, neither of them, in perfect health. It is possible that matrimony will prove the best doctor.

It would be well, I think, if you and I could meet before long to talk things over. Will you have lunch with me in London some day next week. Any day and any place will suit me.

My wife and I are already very fond of Pamela. She is a sweet and charming girl. We both feel so sorry for her and for you and your wife that Pamela has had this long period of ill health.

We are taking good care of her. She has been sleeping fairly well and I think she looks a little better already than when she arrived here.

I enclose a suggested draft 'engagement' announcement for the children.

Phyl joins in best wishes to you both.

Yours very sincerely,

Edward McCormick

Although the final version of Arthur Street's reply no longer exists, a draft copy with many crossings-out reads as follows:

My dear McCormick,

Thank you so much for your charming letter. I agree with you that the children are very much in love with each other, and am thankful that the long period of waiting in uncertainty for both of them has at last come to an end.

When David asked us if he could become engaged to Pamela, my wife and I told him that there was no young man to whom we should be more pleased to give her, but suggested that on the grounds of health it would be best not to rush things too quickly. David wanted to be married very soon. However, I managed to convince him that things had to be done with a certain amount of decorum; that before any announcement was made or anything definite settled he must first go home and talk it over with his mother and father; and that we should do nothing until we had heard from Mrs McCormick and yourself. We were glad that he took Pamela back with him, so that she would get a much-needed change from the setting in which she had been so ill and so worried with wondering about David's safety, and also that you would be able to meet her again.

The announcement you enclosed seems admirable, save that my wife wanted to delete the word Street after Pamela. I mentioned this to Mrs McCormick over the telephone this morning, and she agreed, and suggested that we should send it off. However, I have just talked with Pamela, and she wants to wait until Thursday after she and David have seen her doctor. So I shall wait for his report before I send it off.

When it came to the question of marriage, as can be seen from the above correspondence, Pamela found that the matter had already been taken out of her hands and that she was being swept along by events. In her later memoir she explained, rather wistfully, how this somewhat unromantic state of affairs had come to pass:

Having let my diary-keeping lapse during the last half of the war, I have no record of being formally proposed to. It just seemed to be taken for granted that we would marry and a date was fixed – July 3rd – which happened to be my fiancé's thirtieth birthday and my mother and father's wedding day back in 1918.

David and Pamela were officially engaged for some six weeks. David's return to normality after his long period of captivity inevitably proved a protracted affair. Now safely back in England, he was finally able to reveal to his shocked family and friends, in a way that had not been possible in his heavily censored letters home, just how severe his ordeal had been. For example, he told Pamela that during the last months of the war, when Red Cross parcels had dried up, he and his fellow prisoners had come so close to starvation that at one point he had swapped a dead mouse for some orange peel by way of a scrap to eat. He also recounted how at the end of the war, when their guards laid down their arms and left the camp, the prisoners had become so institutionalised that during their first few days of freedom they continued to conduct twice-daily roll-calls. It would be many months before David was able to shake off what had become instinctive prisoner-of-war habits, and the scars of warfare and captivity, both physical and psychological, would remain with him for a long time to come.

Meanwhile wedding plans were progressing, with Pamela's doting seamstress aunts finally able to go ahead with the wedding dress that they had been longing to make. Pamela's best friend Sybil Edmunds was to be her bridesmaid, also wearing an outfit made by the aunts, and David's great friend and fellow prisoner of war, Bill (Quilly) Kerruish, his best man. The marriage ceremony would take place in Wilton's architecturally incongruous church of St Mary and St Nicholas, rebuilt from medieval ruins in the mid-nineteenth century by the Pembroke family in the style of an Italian basilica, complete with tall campanile.

At one stage during their engagement, David took Pamela to meet his grandfather at Breckenbrough Hall. Pamela later wrote of this experience:

> I think my visit to Yorkshire must have taken place during a cold snap. In spite of the time of year there were open fires in the vast downstairs rooms, while a tweeny maid came to light one in my bedroom every morning, reappearing later on with a brass can of hot water so that I could perform my ablutions at the old-fashioned washstand. The eldest and unmarried daughter of the house was a somewhat fearsome and eccentric chatelaine, going round muttering to herself and jangling a bunch of keys. The atmosphere was remote, vaguely *Wuthering Heights* stuff, but most romantic, or so I felt. I fancied I was in love, or did I make myself fancy this?

Shortly before her wedding, Pamela began keeping another small pocket diary. On 21 June she recorded an event which could have led to the postponement of the impending nuptials: '*June 21st* Daddy's fallen down & had a bad heart attack. He is very ill. Sybby got Dr. B over <u>at once</u>. It is very serious.' Whether or not Arthur Street's heart was to blame for the fall proved uncertain. In *My Father, A. G. Street* Pamela describes this incident in greater detail – and her father's reaction to it:

> Just a few days before our wedding, my father fell down in the haymaking field and hurt his shoulder. It was thought that possibly his fall might have had something to do with his heart, and the doctor raised doubts as to whether the wedding ought to be postponed.
>
> However, my father would have none of that. With his arm in a sling we walked up the aisle of Wilton church together on the appointed day. I do not know what his heart was doing just then, but I know my own was bouncing around in the most extraordinary manner …

The wedding very nearly got cancelled at the last minute for an entirely different reason, which Pamela later explained:

A few days before our wedding, my fiancé did something which seemed to me *really* eccentric. It was so extraordinary that I could hardly believe what he was saying on the telephone from Weybridge to Wilton. He told me that he had asked his mother's other sister and her Brigadier husband – both of them artists – to come on our honeymoon with us … Apparently, he had been feeling terribly guilty because he and his brother had both returned safely from the war and his aunt and uncle's only son – a commando – had been killed just before the end of it. They needed a break, he said …

Pamela and David had earlier decided that it would be suitably romantic to spend their honeymoon at Weston-super-Mare, where they had said goodbye to each other in 1941. Despite the fact that in the summer of 1945 hotel rooms were full to bursting with American and Colonial servicemen waiting to sail home, they had managed to acquire a room at the Grosvenor Hotel, whose manageress Arthur and Vera Street happened to know. Pamela's memoir continues:

My fiancé had evidently cashed in on this and, without consulting me, had telephoned her and managed to get another room for his aunt and uncle, who would be arriving three days after our wedding. I was devastated and, after ringing off, burst into tears. I don't know why I didn't make more fuss. Yet it seemed so mean, when I thought about losing their son.

There was an additional reason for David's curious action, which only came to light many years later, and which is yet another indication of how unstable both young people were feeling at this landmark moment in their lives:

Once … when I talked to my husband about this, he admitted that he hadn't been exactly honest or fair about it all. I suppose he was having pre-wedding nerves, as I was. He felt it would be nice to have others around him whom he knew, rather than to be alone with me for ten days. He always liked a party.

The entries in Pamela's pocket diary give little indication as to whether or not the marriage was consummated during the honeymoon, although they do mention long periods spent in bed simply recovering from the stress of the wedding. One clue can be found in her entry for 8 July, the fifth day; Pamela, who at the time barely touched alcohol, recorded drinking two double vodka and ginger ales that evening, presumably to help her relax. It is doubtful whether this 'medicine' had the desired effect, for in her later memoir Pamela wrote, somewhat cryptically: 'It was not surprising that our honeymoon was not a success.'

Like countless other newly-weds at the end of the Second World War, David and Pamela had no home of their own or jobs to which to return. It was by no means unusual for such young couples to start their married lives living with their parents or in-laws, and David and Pamela were no exception. After their honeymoon they returned from Weston-super-Mare to the McCormick family home in Weybridge, breaking their journey for the night at the conveniently situated Ditchampton Farm. Pamela begged her mother to be allowed to stay on alone for a few days to recover, but the astute Vera Street – sensing that things had not gone exactly according to plan at Weston-super-Mare, but keen that her daughter should make a go of her marriage – forbade this, telling her daughter, 'You are a married woman now. You should go with your husband.'

This proved sound advice. Although Pamela never completely forgave David for asking his aunt and uncle to share their honeymoon, she appears to have put the matter behind her fairly swiftly. Her diary entries for the remainder of the year record her settling down to her new duties as wife and daughter-in-law comparatively happily. Her artistic talents were almost immediately put to use in arranging the household flowers, and she willingly did her and David's washing and ironing, and from time to time a little cooking. She clearly enjoyed walking David's dog Rigo, and did her best to fit into the busy St George's Hill social life. Nevertheless, for a Wiltshire farmer's daughter, this whole new environment continued to feel very alien.

There are no mentions in Pamela's diary during the summer months of 1945 of the continuing war in the Far East, although on 15 and 16 August there are two little notes against each date, 'VJ Day' and 'VJ2' respectively. Whether or not the cataclysmic dropping of the two atomic bombs on Hiroshima and Nagasaki – which finally ended the Second World War – truly sank into the British national consciousness at the time is debatable. Many years later, however, in the closing pages of her novel *Many Waters*, in which she wound up the lives of her main characters, Pamela included the following moving account of how she imagined the fall of Japan might have felt like to its ordinary citizens:

> On the other side of the world, in a land where the sun had already risen heralding a new day, a little Japanese boy called Taro Suzaki looked up from where he was playing by a stream. Suddenly, in the distance, he saw a strange dark mountain rising in the sky, its top spreading out like a mushroom and growing larger and larger. Panic-stricken, he ran indoors screaming, 'Okaa-san, Okaa-san,' and his mother came at once and held him close, while she, too, stared at the terrifying sight – then quickly turned the other way.
>
> What had been the city of Hiroshima at eight-fifteen a.m. on Monday, August 6th, 1945, had now gone up in a cloud of dust-filled smoke. The Second World War was over.

Although for Pamela tiredness continued to be a problem, it was her new husband's health rather than her own that now became her chief cause for concern. David's long period of incarceration and inadequate diet had left him severely debilitated and unable to resist any prevalent infections. Shortly after the young couple returned from honeymoon, a cocktail party was arranged at Shaws to celebrate their marriage. The day before, however, David went down with a severe cold and high temperature and was obliged to remain in bed. Pamela wrote of the party afterwards: 'It was a great success but shame about D.'

More such diary entries crop up throughout the remainder of the year. On 23 July Pamela wrote: 'Doing my nursing act'; at the beginning of August she commented: 'David isn't at all fit.' In mid August he was again in bed with a high temperature, and the family doctor insisted on a blood test. The main cause of David's ill health was finally diagnosed; like so many soldiers who had served in the Middle East he had unknowingly contracted malaria, and would suffer repeated bouts for some time to come. Later that winter, one such proved so severe that it required hospitalisation. David was still technically in the army, and at the time had been seconded to the Army Educational Corps in North London. David and Pamela had temporarily acquired a room at one of George Cross's hotels in the Cromwell Road; no sooner had they settled in, however, than David developed a high fever. Pamela later described what happened next:

> When the ambulance came to take him to hospital, having no idea how far away this might be, we traipsed through the lounge carrying hot water bottles and blankets, much to the consternation of some aged residents, only to find he was going to St. George's, half a mile along the road at Hyde Park Corner ...

David had the misfortune to be put in a bed next to a patient who kept him awake by striking matches and looking at his fingers, saying, 'See these hands? They were once man's hands. Now I am turning into a woman.' After a few days of this, David could stand no more, and took matters into his own hands. Pamela's memoir continues:

> One morning my husband simply discharged himslef, with various members of the nursing staff running after him down the corridor. But he merely pressed on, hailed a taxi and arrived unexpectedly at the hotel.

The upshot of this incident was that after many months of waiting to be demobilised, David was now formally discharged from further military service. At last he was free to embark on the next stage of his and Pamela's life together.

Despite the inauspicious start to her marriage, 1945 ended for Pamela on an infinitely happier note than on the previous year. During the autumn, whilst getting used to her new life, she was still able occasionally to indulge in her favourite pastime, writing poetry. The following poem was accepted by *The Field* and published shortly after Christmas. In it, Pamela captures what would have been the prevailing sentiments of most British citizens at the time. She compares wartime Christmases with the one just past; she intimates her relief that the Second World War is finally over, and dares to look ahead to a better future.

Christmas

I walked abroad on Christmas day,
The ground was hard and dry,
The clouds rolled westwards, large and grey,
Across the wintry sky,
And as I walked up Ibsbury way
The leaves went whistling by.

I trod the old green downland track
And thought of other years,
And memory brought strangely back
Those hopes that turned to fears,
When Christmastide was grim and black
And joys gave place to tears.

But when at dusk now homeward bent,
I paused by Ibsbury wood,
It seemed the light before me meant
That life might still be good,
For Christmas day this year was spent
In peace, as Christmas should.

Eighteen

Post-War Life: America, London and 'Operation Farming' (1946–49)

After the war, with the benefit of hindsight, Pamela wrote that it would have been far better had she remained helping out on Ditchampton Farm, rather than attempting other types of war work for which she was plainly unsuited. Arguably she might have been spared her ultimate breakdown and the intense anxiety it caused her family, particularly her father. What she perhaps failed to appreciate, however, was that her training as a VAD nurse and as both clerk and officer in the ATS equipped her – along with so many other young women of her generation – with life skills which would prove invaluable in years to come. In particular her nursing experience was almost immediately put to use in caring for David during his frequent bouts of ill health as he recovered from his prison camp ordeal.

The first few years following the end of hostilities were a deeply worrying time for all servicemen returning to 'civvy street'. Concerns about how to support himself and his new wife, and where they might live, certainly would not have helped David's physical recovery. Early in 1946, however, shortly after he was demobilised, an unexpected and exciting opportunity arose. A family friend, a partner in an insurance firm with American branches, suggested that since Edward McCormick was an American domiciled in the UK, this might enable David to acquire dual nationality, enabling him to travel to Chicago to see whether he could drum up some insurance business from the wealthy McCormick relatives. Negotiations with the American Embassy in London were ultimately successful and he was granted a visa, and eventually Pamela also obtained permission to accompany him as a GI bride.

Accordingly, in June 1946 the young couple set sail on the SS *Argentina*. The ship had not yet been converted back to peacetime use, so the sexes were segregated, David sharing a cabin with several other men and Pamela with a number of other GI brides and a middle-aged American woman. A seasoned traveller, she took a shine to Pamela and gave her many valuable tips on life in the USA, such as never wearing white after 2 September or 'Labor Day'.

On arrival, first in New York and then in Chicago, the young McCormicks found themselves immediately fêted by David's relatives and their friends. Pamela later described their welcome as follows:

> We were hailed as the poor dear heroic British who had *been through the war*. Everyone wanted to hear all about it. I think many of them, especially the men who had not been involved, felt guilty at having had so much while others across the water had had to get by with so little. Their wives could hardly credit stories about rationing, particularly clothes' rationing. They showered me with presents: nylons, shoes, dresses, swimsuits. Their spontaneous generosity was endearing. They even offered us free use of their homes.

As things turned out, Pamela was the first to earn any serious money on the other side of the Atlantic. Almost immediately, one of David's aunts pulled off something of a coup on Pamela's behalf by arranging for her to be photographed for the cosmetic firm, Pond's, by the leading portrait photographer Philippe Halsman. Pamela later wrote of this experience:

> Suddenly I found myself all dolled up with an unrecognisable hair-do, wearing a hired evening dress and fake jewellery, and described as *the lovely British bride of the famous Chicago family* etc, seemingly unable to live without a face cream I had hardly ever used. But it was fun, fun for which I received five hundred dollars* and an enormous supply of cosmetics, which I posted back home to my mother and Vivi.

Pamela had initially regarded the trip to America as something of a late, extended honeymoon, and had not seriously contemplated the prospect of living permanently across the Atlantic. Despite the kindness and generosity of her new friends and relatives, she found their way of living so alien to her previous life in England that she soon began to feel intensely homesick, sentiments she did little to conceal in letters home to her parents. Although Arthur and Vera Street missed and sympathised with their daughter, they did their best to encourage her to give life in America a go. In a letter dated 6 August 1946, Arthur Street – using typical horticultural metaphors – wrote to Pamela:

> Naturally we would have preferred that you made your home in England, but we both realise that at your age you are right at any rate to give this American thing a fair trial ... Please don't imagine from this that I don't see your side of it, Pam, because I do. You have roots in England; you haven't been away from home

---

* A little under £4,000 in today's money.

much before; and the American way of life from what you have seen to date, doesn't attract. It doesn't attract me … But in spite of your deep roots, you are young and therefore more easily transplantable …

In the event, the insurance world in Chicago proved something of a closed shop. David briefly took up a job on Wall Street with an investment banking firm with a semi-promise of being seconded to their London office; however the offer of a London job failed to materialise, and in the autumn the young McCormicks decided to cut their losses and return to England. Getting a passage home was by no means easy, owing to a prolonged dock-workers' strike; however David and Pamela managed, by the skin of their teeth, to acquire two berths on the *Queen Elizabeth* with the help of what Pamela later called 'a rather shifty type in a travel agency who told us that "the boys in the back room are kinda thirsty"'. Pamela's joy on reaching England could not have been greater. Her parents and her cousin Vivi were all on the dock to greet the young couple, and her diary entry for the day in question contains, amongst other ecstatic remarks: 'Dear Old England, no police with guns.' She had finally made it home. Many decades later, reflecting on this period of her life, Pamela asked herself: 'What on earth would I have done if I'd married my American?'

On returning to England, David and Pamela found themselves back to square one, once again heavily dependent on their parents. In her unpublished autobiography Pamela wrote of the immediate post-war years:

Reading my diaries for those years just after the war makes me amazed how much we relied on and took for granted from the older generation: the practical help in the form of cash handouts, lending of cars, the constant providing of accommodation and food; for rationing was still severe, although my own parents, living on a farm, seemed to be forever coming up with produce of one sort or another. Indeed, even during the war, my future mother-in-law used to say she didn't know what she would have done without the little parcels – perhaps not strictly legal – of butter made by Vivi, which arrived from time to time. There was one occasion when my well-meaning mother posted her some home-bottled blackcurrants, which exploded in the Weybridge post office and caused a considerable amount of alarm and damage. They had so little in common, the two sets of parents, yet the four of them pulled together nobly on our behalf.

In early 1947 David at last managed to land a job in a stock-broking firm for which one of his prisoner-of-war friends worked, and shortly afterwards he and Pamela acquired a small flat off Hyde Park Square. This was not, in those days, a particularly fashionable part of London – indeed prostitutes walked the nearby streets; but Pamela revelled in finally having a home of her own, and threw herself whole-heartedly into its furnishing and decoration. Another of Pamela's artistic talents, painting furniture, was once again put to good use, and she took pride and pleasure in tending the little flat's window boxes – her first 'garden'. Oxford Street, with its cheaper, tempting versions of Dior's 'New Look' fashions, was within easy reach, as were many of David and Pamela's newly married young friends, with whom they socialised.

But however much Pamela enjoyed living in London, the same could not be said for David, who frequently arrived home at the end of a working day completely exhausted, often needing to be given supper in bed. The term 'post-traumatic stress disorder' had not yet been coined, but this was almost certainly still afflicting him at the time. After his lengthy wartime incarceration, commuting to and from a cramped City office seemed to David too akin to being cooped up in prison camp, and he yearned to be his own master in a wide-open space. Finding City life increasingly intolerable, he consulted his father-in-law, initially without Pamela's knowledge, about the possibility of a layman such as himself taking up farming. In *My Father, A. G. Street*, Pamela reflected on how her father rose to the challenge:

> I suppose my father's feelings about the matter must have been very mixed. He knew that my husband did not know wheat from barley or an Ayrshire cow from a Friesian. He knew that he did not have very much capital to invest, and the risk was obviously very great. On the other hand, he was always willing to help anyone 'have a go'. He reckoned that young people were like unbroken colts. One could never do anything with the ones who dug their heels in and refused to 'go', but one could do anything with the ones who would.

Accordingly, Arthur Street set about finding a suitable farm within easy reach of Ditchampton Farm, from where he could dispense advice and loan men and machinery as required. In early 1948 he negotiated, on David's behalf, and with the help of a large agricultural mortgage, the purchase of some 600 acres of farmland in Steeple Langford, some 6 miles west of Wilton down the Wylye Valley. This came with a small, redbrick modern house in the orchard (which Pamela later described as resembling a police station) rather than the original old farmhouse, which was still occupied by the late farmer's widow; for this reason the farm was being sold relatively cheaply. Even so, the responsibility for such a purchase did not come lightly to Arthur Street, as Pamela recounted:

> After my father had bought the Manor Farm, Steeple Langford, on our behalf, I understand he went home feeling sick. He never liked dealing in large sums of money, and now he had pledged somebody else's. The enormity of the undertaking must have hit him so that even his enthusiastic optimism was open to doubts.

Arthur Street need not have worried. David proved a keen and apt pupil. He still suffered from tiredness, but as Pamela later wrote: 'It seemed to be a much more natural tiredness than the devastating kind which had afflicted him in London.'

David and Pamela stayed at Ditchampton Farm until they were able to move into their new home; meanwhile the Street parents gave them every help and encouragement, as exemplified in a further extract from *My Father, A. G. Street*:

> One night, when some new heifers arrived for us at the station, I remember sitting in the car with my father, whilst, in semi-darkness, my husband chivvied the last reluctant animal through thick mud at the entrance to one of our fields. It seemed to me to be a far cry from Threadneedle Street, and my father must have been thinking much on the same lines. 'Bless my soul,' he remarked, 'I never thought to see that young man doing anything like this. Isn't it wonderful?'

Certainly 'Operation Farming', as David and Pamela called it between themselves, got off to a good start. This is how she later explained her father's role:

> My father promised to oversee the venture for a year, teach my husband all he could and, because of his many friends and acquaintances in the farming world, make sure his son-in-law got every conceivable advantage – from engaging the right staff and seeing he got the right discount from seed merchants to never letting him be ripped off by cattle dealers, who negotiated the buying and transportation of our dairy herd. In fact, such was my father's reputation that we got preferential treatment all round and, what is more, from one quite unexpected quarter: the glorious summer of 1949 which produced a bumper harvest. 'I will look after you for twelve months,' my father said, 'but after that I will never visit or give advice unless requested.' And he was as good as his word.

David was well aware of the enormous debt he owed his father-in-law towards the end of his first year of farming. With harvest safely gathered in, he went to spend a few days with his parents in Weybridge, during which he wrote Arthur Street a long, thoughtful letter expressing his gratitude for the countless ways the latter had helped him during the preceding year. It is something of a master-class in the art of the 'thank you letter', and as such deserves to be quoted almost in its entirety. Dated 25 August 1949, it reads:

> To The Best Unpaid Foreman in Wilts, Ditchampton Farm, Wilton
> Dear Father-in-Law,
> Although my first year's farming will not be completed until October 11th, and your stewardship will not therefore be officially over until that date, it would seem that with the harvest behind us the yearly farming cycle is completed and

the results of our endeavours approximately known. I feel therefore that it is opportune to try to express to you my appreciation and gratitude to you for all that you have done to make my entry into farming the success which it has undoubtedly been.

Looking back I don't quite know how it all came to pass. I remember that in a fit of ill health and depression over City life I asked you if you thought it would be possible for a person like myself with no knowledge of farming or country life to take a farm, and start farming under the guidance of an expert such as yourself, and if you would be prepared to give me that necessary guidance. You immediately said you did and you would. I don't think at the time I fully realised quite how much I was asking of you, and I rather doubt that you quite realised to how much time and worry you were committing yourself. Though perhaps you did. At any rate shortly afterwards you telephoned, knowing that I had some £15,000 at my disposal, to ask for my sanction to offer up to £33,000 for a farm, which must have been a great responsibility to take upon yourself. Next I heard you had bought the Manor Farm on my behalf for £27,000. It is for this, for putting your experience as a dealer to my great advantage and buying the farm at an unquestionably bargain price, that I must first thank you …

Next I should like once again to thank you and Mrs. Street for putting us up at Wilton for a long period while moving and starting farming, and for all the help you both gave us in preparing our house and furniture, and in moving from London to our new home.

Then I must thank you for the actual farming. Not only for the general principles, the way the farm should be run, the policy, the labour and implements necessary, the crops to be grown and the livestock to be purchased, but also for putting all your own men and implements at my disposal, for producing combines, balers, drills, etc., at Steeple Langford just when they were required, and for even planning your own farming to fit in with mine so that this could be done to my greatest advantage. Then I must thank you apart from farming policy for all the detailed work and time you have spent during the year to ensure that the year was a success, for all the trips to Steeple Langford that you have made to start us off on jobs and to see that they were being carried out correctly, to solve any problems immediately they arose, and for the sheer drudgery of filling up another's countless forms as well as all your own ones. Next for introducing me to all the local experts, and seeing that I met everyone in the district who might be of assistance to me in the business of farming, and for helping me through your personal contacts and friendships in such ways as obtaining credit facilities and instruments on test etc.

Then I must thank you for your friendly counsel in assisting me towards appreciation and correct valuation of country life and sport, and finally for your valiant attempts to teach me something about the rudiments of farming. And here I must thank you for your wonderful tolerance and patience. Many a time when a fairly important decision was needed, I know you have quietly explained the pros and cons and left the actual decision to me accordingly, when you must have been very tempted to just say 'Do this', or 'Do that'. And many a time you have painstakingly explained farming procedure to me to pass on to my men, when it would have been far easier for you to drive down to Steeple Langford and tell the men what to do yourself.

What do I owe you for all you have done? In terms of money I have said, I know, that the farm owes me a good £500 for my services. If so, what does it not owe you for yours? In terms of gratitude, which is, I know, all that I am allowed to offer – well, it can't be expressed in a letter …

You have enabled me to fit myself into a job that seems worthwhile, and into a way of life that seems clean and honest, and it is my great hope and wish that time will prove that you have found a suitable tenant for the Manor Farm.

Thank you.

David

It seems appropriate that this family memoir, which began with farming, has come a full circle and now ends with farming. In terms of his love of the land, whilst Arthur Street might have felt justifiably proud of his contribution to the war effort, he would surely have derived almost equal satisfaction on receipt of his son-in-law's thank you letter, in particular its closing paragraph.

Epilogue: 'Lest We Forget'

It is a curious perception, shared as children by many 'baby-boomers' such as myself (so called because we were part of the population explosion that occurred in the two decades immediately following the end of the Second World War) that the cataclysmic events of only a few years before our birth might as well have taken place almost a century earlier. For us, they were history – though not the kind we learnt at school. Our parents rarely referred to 'the war' in our presence, anxious to shield us from hearing about the hardships and atrocities they had experienced and witnessed. They wanted to create a new world of peace and prosperity for the next generation. When I look back at my childhood in the 1950s – possibly influenced by memories of grainy images of early black and white television – I see myself living in a kind of grey cocoon. For me, these so-called 'austerity years' did indeed feel very safe, though this might have been partly a result of my mother's over-protectiveness. We lived simply and frugally. Christmas and birthdays may have been the highlights of the year, but there were no expensive presents. Fortunately my mother's artistic talents came in handy here. As a small child I collected miniature teddy bears, and one of my best presents was homemade: my mother concocted a magnificent bed for my little bears out of an old shoebox and scraps of upholstery fabric. My father also did his bit. Post-war rationing continued well into the 1950s, and in a gesture that would horrify today's childcare experts, I understand that when I was a baby he gave up most of his weekly sugar ration for use in my milk-bottle.

Born a few days after the Manor Farm's first harvest, I grew up blissfully unaware of such sacrifices, happy enough in an only child's world of the imagination. Little did I realise how very difficult both my parents were finding this period of their lives. It is clear from my mother's diary entries for early 1949 that finding herself pregnant filled her with dread. As the preceding pages make at times painfully clear, my poor mother was terrified of responsibility, of which she regarded parenthood as the ultimate. She would have far preferred to create in other ways, principally writing. Conscientious as always, however, she put the family first, though occasionally still managed to compose articles and poems which were accepted in certain magazines of the day, notably two poems in *Punch* in the early 1950s. One was a humorous reflection on the differences between modern-day farming, with its reliance on new machinery that was constantly breaking down, and the traditional, well-tried methods of the past. It was illustrated by no less an artist than E.H. Shepard.*

In the mid 1950s my father was diagnosed with severe angina. A complete rest was prescribed, and having made suitable arrangements with a neighbouring farmer regarding the running of the Manor Farm, my parents set sail for a lengthy stay in South Africa. Presumably my father wanted to revisit, in peacetime, the country that had so appealed to him when his troop ship called there *en route* to Egypt over a decade earlier.

I was packed off to stay with my Street grandparents, who had now taken over the tenancy of the Mill Farm, South Newton, since Ditchampton Farm's land had been required for new post-war housing. I revelled in the comparative freedom I was allowed in which to roam their extensive gardens, and became particularly close to my grandfather Street during this period. We had pet names for each other; having heard one of the farm staff refer to me as a 'chip off the old block', my grandfather dubbed me 'Chip', insisting that I call him 'Chap' in return. I became the inspiration for one of his later novels, *Bobby Bocker*, about a small child left under similar circumstances with a crusty old widowed grandfather. He introduced me to all kinds of activities which fascinated me, such as dog training, fishing for minnows with a jam-jar in a shallow stretch of the River Wylye, and flying a box kite on the end of a fishing rod and line on the top of the Wiltshire Downs. How he found time for this I cannot imagine, for he was still pursuing his three careers of farming, writing and broadcasting as prodigiously as ever. He would continue to be a regular panellist on *Any Questions?* and write his weekly article for *Farmer's Weekly* till his final illness over a decade later.

The spell in South Africa evidently did my father good, and on their return my parents might have expected their fortunes to improve. In a material sense, they did. The farm prospered, to the extent that in the early 1960s my father had built up sufficient collateral to make what proved to be a shrewd investment in a run-down block of flats in London's West End, which he refurbished and sold on at a considerable profit. This, in turn, enabled him to purchase, a few years later, half the adjoining farm in the Wylye Valley and the Elizabethan farmhouse that went with it. Our days in the 'police station' were over.

Ill health, however, continued to dog our little family. Neither of my parents had fully recovered from the trauma, both physical and psychological, of the

---

* Illustrator of, *inter alia*, A.A. Milne's *Winnie-the-Pooh* series and Kenneth Grahame's *The Wind in the Willows*.

war years. Nor did it help that in my early years I suffered from a succession of severe bronchial colds; for my mother, nursing me through these became something of an obsession.

I have often wondered whether, with their differences in upbringing and aspirations, my parents should ever have married, though chance meetings during the war years led to many unlikely bedfellows and my parents were no exception.

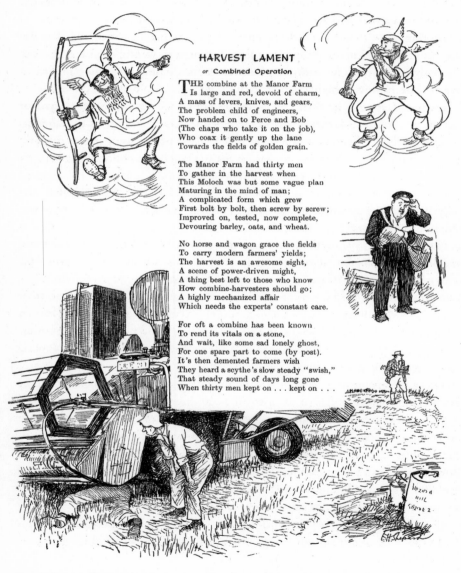

HARVEST LAMENT

or Combined Operation

THE combine at the Manor Farm
Is large and red, devoid of charm,
A mass of levers, knives, and gears,
The problem child of engineers,
Now handed on to Perce and Bob
(The chaps who take it on the job),
Who coax it gently up the lane
Towards the fields of golden grain.

The Manor Farm had thirty men
To gather in the harvest when
This Moloch was but some vague plan
Maturing in the mind of man;
A complicated form which grew
First bolt by bolt, then screw by screw;
Improved on, tested, now complete,
Devouring barley, oats, and wheat.

No horse and wagon grace the fields
To carry modern farmers' yields;
The harvest is an awesome sight,
A scene of power-driven might,
A thing best left to those who know
How combine-harvesters should go;
A highly mechanized affair
Which needs the experts' constant care.

For oft a combine has been known
To rend its vitals on a stone,
And wait, like some sad lonely ghost,
For one spare part to come (by post).
It's then demented farmers wish
They heard a scythe's slow steady "swish,"
That steady sound of days long gone
When thirty men kept on . . . kept on . . .

Pamela's poem 'Harvest Lament or Combined Operation' in *Punch*, 1952, illustrated by E.H. Shepard.

Despite their lengthy correspondence (carried out under strict censorship), when they were reunited at the end of the war they still knew relatively little about one another; both were trying to present themselves to each other in the best possible light. My mother was, obviously, a virgin on her wedding day, probably no longer physically attracted to my father; many decades later she intimated that she married him more out of pity than passion. Sadly events ultimately conspired to put these two decent, well-meaning people at odds with one another, and my parents parted company shortly after their twenty-fifth wedding anniversary.

On their separation, my mother went to stay in the little London top-floor flat that my father had managed to retain from his property venture a decade earlier. She fully intended to return to her beloved Wiltshire once the dust had settled. Meanwhile, however, she made contact with her father's old friend, the historian Sir Arthur Bryant,* who took her under his wing and persuaded her to remain in London. A long association ensued, which gave her the entrée in the London literary world she had always secretly craved. She went on to become a prolific author; by the end of her life she had three works of non-fiction and nineteen novels to her credit – no mean feat.

Further details leading up to my parents' divorce and the course of their subsequent lives are beyond the scope of this volume. One small episode is, however, relevant to this story.

In the late 1980s my mother, once again alone in her little flat, received a surprise visit from her American wartime boyfriend, Holden Bowler. He and his wife Ann (also a Wiltshire girl whom he met and married during the latter months of the war) had family domiciled in England, and on one of their trips to see their relatives in what he described as 'the Old Country', Holden managed to track down my mother via her publishers. From then on, Holden and Ann visited my mother whenever they came to London, and continued to correspond – swapping photographs of their grandchildren – for the rest of their lives. Ann was particularly tactful in disappearing on shopping expeditions in order to give my mother and Holden the opportunity, à deux, to 'chew the cud'. His reappearance in my mother's life was the inspiration for one of her later novels, Hindsight. There is a particularly poignant passage in Hindsight, clearly based on a conversation that must have taken place between Holden and my mother during one of these visits. The protagonists, now in their latter years, reminisce about their wartime romance. The fictional Holden, 'Rex', asks the fictional Pamela, 'Anna', why she cast him out of her life so abruptly towards the end of the war. This is how she replies:

'I realise I acted monstrously and I often wondered if I could ever be forgiven, but … you see, I was afraid of you.'

---

*   Arthur Bryant wrote the Foreword to My Father, A. G. Street.

'*Afraid?*'

'Yes. Well, more afraid of myself, perhaps. I suppose it sounds incomprehensible now. I mean when one thinks of today's youth.'

When he did not answer, she went on, quietly, 'You see, I wanted you to make love to me.'

'Was that so very terrible?'

'Fifty years ago and in the way I was brought up, yes.'

It is clear that the stigma of becoming pregnant out of wedlock and the disgrace this would heap upon the family was drummed into my mother at a tender age; Arthur Street would have been at great pains to prevent his daughter committing the same misdemeanour as he himself had committed in his youth. And indeed, the circumstances of her birth were subsequently a source of great unhappiness for his other, 'unofficial', daughter, who he never felt able to acknowledge.

★ ★ ★

Whatever twists and turns my parents' and grandparents' post-war lives – and those of their contemporaries – eventually took, it was their contribution to the Second World War effort that we should remember forever with deep gratitude. Their wartime sacrifices enabled my generation, and hopefully many British generations to come, to live in peace and freedom. The compilation of this volume has been my own way of thanking them.

Bibliography

Beaton, Cecil, *The Years Between: Diaries 1939–44*, Weidenfeld & Nicolson, 1965

Beevor, Antony, *The Second World War*, Weidenfeld & Nicolson, 2012

Brittain, Vera, *Testament of Youth*, Victor Gollancz, 1933

Dady, Margaret, *A Woman's War: Life in the ATS*, The Book Guild, 1986

Daily Telegraph, The, *World War II: Eyewitness Experience*, Eaglemoss Publications, 2010

De Courcy, Anne, *Debs at War*, Weidenfeld & Nicolson, 2005

Dimbleby, Jonathan, *Destiny in the Desert: The Road to El Alamein*, Profile Books, 2012

Farmer, Alan, *The Second World War*, Hodder Education, 2004

Gilbert, Adrian, *POW: Allied Prisoners in Europe 1939–1945*, John Murray, 2006

Gillies, Midge, *The Barbed-Wire University: The Real Lives of Prisoners of War in the Second World War*, Aurum Press, 2011

Ginn, Peter, Goodman, Ruth, Langlands, Alex, *Wartime Farm*, Mitchell Beazley, 2012

Goodenough, Simon, *War Maps*, Macdonald & Co., 1982

Goodman, Jean, *Seago: A Wider Canvas: The Life of Edward Seago*, The Erskine Press, 2002

Hastings, Max, *All Hell Let Loose: The World at War 1939–1945*, Harper Press, 2011

Hastings, Max, *Finest Years: Churchill as Warlord 1940–45*, Harper Press, 2009

Last, Nella, *Nella Last's War: The Second World War Diaries of Housewife, 49*, Falling Wall Press, 1981

McCormick-Goodhart, Henrietta L., *Hands Across the Sea: Reminiscences of an Anglo-American Marriage*, copyright H.L. McCormick-Goodhart 1921, privately printed; Second Printing 2004, copyright 2004 The Family of H.L. McCormick-Goodhart, McClain Printing Company, Parsons, West Virginia

Middleboe, Penelope, *Edith Oliver: from her Journals 1924–48*, Weidenfield & Nicholson, 1989

Milburn, Clara, *Mrs Milburn's Diaries: An Englishwoman's Day to Day Reflections, 1939–45*, ed. Peter Donnelly, Harrap, 1979

Nicholson, Virginia, *Millions Like Us: Women's Lives in War & Peace, 1939–1949*, Penguin/Viking, 2011

Smith, Daniel, *The Spade as Mighty as the Sword: The Story of the Dig for Victory Campaign*, Aurum Press, 2011

Somerville, Donald, *The Complete Illustrated History of World War II*, Lorenz Books, 2008

Street, A.G., *Farmer's Glory*, Faber & Faber, 1932

Street, A.G., *Strawberry Roan*, Faber & Faber, 1932

Street, A.G., *Wessex Wins*, Faber & Faber, 1941

Street, A.G., *Hitler's Whistle*, Eyre & Spottiswoode, 1943

Street, A.G., *From Dusk till Dawn*, Blandford Press, 1943, revised 1945

Street, A.G., *Holdfast*, Faber & Faber, 1946

Street, Pamela, *My Father, A.G. Street*, Robert Hale, 1969

Street, Pamela, *Many Waters*, Robert Hale, 1985

Street, Pamela, *Hindsight*, Robert Hale, 1993

Street, Pamela, *Poems by Pamela Street*, Delian Bower Publishing, 2000

Thomasson, Anna, *A Curious Friendship: The Story of a Bluestocking and a Bright Young Thing*, Macmillan, 2015

Wall Street Journal, the editors of the, *American Dynasties Today: Astor – Cabot – DuPont – Ford – Guggenheim – McCormick – Mellon – Sears*, Dow Jones-Irwin, Inc., 1980

Acknowledgements

I am grateful to the Wiltshire and Swindon History Centre, Chippenham, for access to the A.G. Street literary archive; to the Royal Artillery Museum, Woolwich, for access to David McCormick's regimental diaries for 1941, and to the Museum of English Rural Life, Reading University, for supplying the photograph of Pamela Street in ATS uniform from *The Field* magazine, 22 May 1943.

The excerpt from the Foreword to Vera Brittain's *Testament of Youth* is reproduced by kind permission of Mark Bostridge and T.J. Brittain-Catlin, Literary Executors for the Estate of Vera Brittain 1970.

My mother's poem 'Harvest Lament or Combined Operation', with illustrations by E.H. Shepard, first published in Punch in 1952, is reproduced by kind permission of Punch Ltd, www.punch.co.uk.

My mother's poems 'Gone Away', 'South Coast' and 'Christmas', published in *The Field* in January 1941, January 1944 and January 1945 respectively, are reproduced with the permission and (in their own much appreciated words) 'blessing' of *The Field*.

I am deeply grateful to Sir Max Hastings both for his earlier advice, and for his *Foreword*, which undoubtedly lent credibility to my typescript at the time when I was approaching potential publishers.

I am also particularly grateful to Jonathan Dimbleby for his generous endorsement of this memoir on the back cover.

I am similarly indebted to Michele Brown (Brandreth), Michael Dobbs and John Martin (Professor of Agrarian History, De Montfort University, Leicester) not only for their endorsements, but also for their advice on areas of concern to me during the compilation of this volume. In particular, Professor Martin's expert knowledge of agricultural practice during the Second World War has proved invaluable.

I would also like to acknowledge two inspirational teachers, who took a personal interest in my studies at different stages of my education: firstly, Dr Simone Scott, my French teacher at Heathfield School, Ascot, and secondly Dr Christina Roaf, my Tutor in Italian at Somerville College, Oxford. Although their subjects were not directly connected with the content of this volume they, in particular, equipped me with the learning tools required to undertake a project of this kind. Whilst revising my typescript, I received the sad news that Christina Roaf had left Oxford – and indeed this world – forever, so this book is now also in her memory.

I am grateful to my relatives Sargeant Collier, Penelope Dodd, Catherine Mant, Leander Paul McCormick-Goodhart, April Mesquita, Clare Sanders Hewett and Diane Want, for supplying the missing pieces in the jigsaw as the typescript progressed.

I am equally grateful to the following for their help and support in a wide variety of ways throughout the compilation of this volume: Sarah Adlam, Robin Baird-Smith, James Burge, Randolph Churchill, Isla Dawes, Michael Parr, Rupert Pengelley, Nick Strachan, Joe and Frances Summers, Charles Ward, Brian Wiltshire, Nicolas Wright, and many other friends and acquaintances, some of whom have asked to remain anonymous.

I owe additional thanks to Charles Ward who, in the course of his own research for a forthcoming biography of A.G. Street, had already catalogued much of the AGS literary archive at the Wiltshire and Swindon History Centre, this making my task very much easier.

Of all my family and friends, very special thanks are due to my son Rupert Davies and my dear friend Judy Umfreville, both of whom sat through countless readings aloud as this volume progressed, never failing to offer both constructive criticism and constant encouragement.

I am most grateful to my friend and fellow chorister Jacqueline Jackson for her professional help in the preparation of my typescript for final acceptance by the publishers.

This leads me to pay tribute to the 'the team' at The History Press: Shaun Barrington, Jo de Vries, Phoebe Coates, Helen Bradbury and in particular my most recent editor, Lauren Newby. I am well aware that at times I have tested their patience to the limit!

My greatest thanks of all are reserved for my friend Heather Holden-Brown. This volume would almost certainly never have seen print, had it not been for the guidance she gave me, whenever I most needed it, from the goodness of her heart rather than any professional relationship. To her I shall remain forever indebted.

Index